PRAISE I
WOMEN A.

"Alison has done a remarkable job of curating a wealth
tips and tools, along with valuable insights from a diverse array
of dynamic leaders in the business world. By bringing together
these concepts, she empowers women to confidently take control
of their financial futures. This book serves as both a guide and an
inspiring call to action, illustrating that financial literacy is essential
for personal and professional growth. It will resonate with many
women looking to achieve their financial goals."

Jessica Alba
Actress and founder of The Honest Company

"Alison Kosik's brilliant *What's Up With Women and Money?* gets
the conversation going about personal finance with a no-nonsense,
fresh take. Alison shares practical, easy tips that empower the
reader to take charge of her financial life."

Barbara Corcoran
Businesswoman, investor, and *Shark Tank* Shark

"To be financially strong and independent, women need to play an
active role in their finances. Alison Kosik's new book, *What's Up
With Women and Money?*, shows every woman how to change that
status quo and take charge of her financial future."

Sheryl Sandberg
Founder and author, *Lean In*

WHAT'S UP WITH WOMEN AND MONEY?

WHAT'S UP WITH WOMEN AND MONEY?

How to do all the financial stuff you've been avoiding

ALISON KOSIK

HARRIMAN HOUSE LTD
3 Viceroy Court
Bedford Road
Petersfield
Hampshire
GU32 3LJ
GREAT BRITAIN
Tel: +44 (0)1730 233870

Email: enquiries@harriman-house.com
Website: harriman.house

First published in 2025.

Paperback ISBN: 978-1-80409-053-4
eBook ISBN: 978-1-80409-054-1

British Library Cataloguing in Publication Data
A CIP catalogue record for this book can be obtained from the British Library.

For Sydney and Ethan—my inspiration
For Tony—thank you for encouraging me to keep going
and believing in me every step of the way

CONTENTS

FOREWORD
EMMA GREDE

AS A CHILD, I watched my mother sit at our kitchen table on a weekly basis. Pen in hand, she would painstakingly plan our family finances. She would research interest rates and read aloud from the newspapers about what was happening with inflation. My three sisters and I were marched into fruitless meetings at the bank—apparently bad news is better in person—and taught in no uncertain terms to never live or borrow beyond our means.

At the time, I thought our mother did this because my father was no longer living with us, because we were broke and because she needed to plan every penny in and penny out meticulously. While all this was true, what I didn't realize is that I was receiving a masterclass in financial management—a capability I would take into my teens and onwards as a mother of four and the serial founder and entrepreneur that I am today.

I learned early that my financial circumstances were mine to manage. That I couldn't hide from that which I had a hard time understanding, and that nobody was coming to save me. My finances—no matter how little I had—were mine to manage, and manage I would.

Today, the conversation about money is more important than ever, and it's one that women need to be at the forefront of. Yet, for many women, money has often been a topic shrouded in mystery, misunderstanding, and oftentimes fear. It's a reality that has deep roots in history, culture, and societal norms—forces that have long kept women on the sidelines of financial decision-making, both in their personal lives and in the broader economic landscape. The book you hold in your hands, *What's Up With Women and Money*, is more than just a guide to financial literacy; it's a call to arms, a manifesto for female empowerment, and a roadmap for women to take control of their financial futures.

For centuries, money has been a source of power, freedom, and opportunity—yet women have often been denied full access to these benefits. Historically, financial systems were designed by men and for men, leaving women with limited access to education, resources, and opportunities. Even today, despite significant strides toward gender equality, women still face unique financial challenges that their male counterparts do not. The gender pay gap, which remains stubbornly persistent, means that women often have to work harder and longer to achieve the same financial goals. Furthermore, women are more likely to take time out of the workforce for caregiving responsibilities, which can negatively impact their long-term earning potential and retirement savings.

But the issue goes beyond mere statistics. There's a cultural aspect to women's relationship with money that is equally important to address. Many women have been socialized to think of money as something that's not their domain, as something complex or intimidating. This cultural conditioning can lead to a lack of confidence when it comes to managing finances, making investment decisions, or negotiating salaries. However, financial literacy is not just about understanding numbers—it's about understanding the power dynamics that money represents and how those dynamics can be shifted to empower women.

This is where the true value of *What's Up With Women and Money* lies. This book is not just about teaching you the mechanics of budgeting, saving, and investing—though it does that exceptionally well. It's about fundamentally changing the way women think about money and, by extension, about their own power and potential.

Financial literacy, at its core, is about freedom. It's the freedom to make choices that align with your values, to take risks when the reward is worth it, and to say no to situations that don't serve your best interests. It's about the freedom to leave a job that's unfulfilling, to start a business, to support a cause you believe in, or to simply live life on your own terms. But this kind of freedom doesn't come without knowledge and preparation. It requires a deep understanding of how money works, how to make it work for you, and how to protect and grow it over time. This book provides that understanding, laying out a clear, step-by-step path to financial mastery.

However, the journey to financial empowerment is not just an individual one; it's collective. When women become financially empowered, the benefits ripple out to families, communities, and society as a whole. Women are more likely to invest in their children's education, to give back to their communities, and to support causes that uplift others. By achieving financial independence, women are better equipped to challenge the status quo, to push for policies that promote equality, and to create a more just and equitable world.

Yet, despite the clear benefits, many women still struggle with financial literacy. They may feel overwhelmed by the sheer volume of information available, unsure of where to start, or anxious about making mistakes. This is where *What's Up With Women and Money* shines. It demystifies complex financial concepts, breaking them down into manageable, actionable steps that any woman can take, regardless of her starting point. Whether you're just beginning your financial journey or you're looking to take your skills to the next level, this book meets you where you are and guides you toward where you want to be.

In the pages that follow, you'll find a wealth of practical advice, from how to create a budget that works for you, to how to start investing with confidence, to how to plan for the future you want. But beyond the tips and tools, you'll find something even more valuable: a sense of possibility. You'll come to understand that financial literacy isn't just about dollars and cents; it's about taking control of your life, your future, and your destiny.

As you embark on this journey through *What's Up With Women and Money*, I encourage you to approach it not just as a book, but as a catalyst for change. Allow it to challenge your assumptions, to inspire your ambitions, and to empower you to take bold action. Remember that financial literacy is not just a skill—it's a form of power. And when women harness that power, there's no limit to what we can achieve.

This book is your guide, your companion, and your cheerleader as you step into your financial power. Embrace it, own it, and let it propel you toward the life you deserve. The world needs more financially empowered women—women who are confident, informed, and unafraid to claim their place at the table. With the knowledge and tools provided in these pages, you'll be well on your way to becoming one of them.

Let the journey begin.

Emma Grede
Founder and serial entrepreneur

PREFACE

WHAT'S YOUR EXCUSE?

You know, your excuse for not taking the reins of your financial life? I'm not judging here. I get it, I really do. It's why I wrote this book. Alright, I'll go first.

My excuse for giving up control of my financial life was that I was too busy, and I felt overwhelmed, and I lacked confidence in my abilities. After a long day at work, where all I did was use my brain to write, report, and talk on TV, the thought of diving into a potentially stressful topic like money and finance to learn its many finer details made me cringe. As for having to make decisions and take action on things I felt I didn't know enough about? Forget it! I didn't want to deal with that.

Whether your excuse is similar or completely different, this book will help you take control of your financial life. It's a one-stop shop for all things personal finance, things I will help you learn without feeling judged or intimidated. This book takes complex personal finance topics and simplifies them into easy-to-follow steps and practical tidbits that will help you feel confident about tackling the financial stuff you've been avoiding. avoiding.

If you want to know why you have a complicated relationship with money, check out Chapter 1. You'll quickly realize you're not the only woman who feels this way.

If you're living paycheck to paycheck, barely making your bills on time, in Chapters 2 through 4 I walk you through—step by step—

how to change your situation and get a handle on your spending without feeling completely deprived.

Need to get that debt off your back and improve your credit score? There are lots of practical hints and tips in Chapter 5.

If you've got a more stable financial situation, you might find the most value in the chapters on purchasing a house (Chapter 6) and a car (Chapter 7). Though it might not be the most glamorous topic, you could also benefit from my advice on insurance in Chapter 8.

You may be surprised to find there *is* room in your budget to invest, so I guide you through an actual investment in Chapter 9. By the time you finish the chapter, you will *actually be* an invested girlie!

Planning on looking for a new job or expecting a raise where you work now? I've got you. There are scenarios and advice on how to manage those conversations in Chapter 10.

You may also be surprised to find that even if you only have $100 in your bank account at the moment, you still need an estate plan (Chapter 11).

I made this book intensely practical, so you can really use it to help yourself. I've also included lots of stories and advice throughout—check out the 'in her own words' sections in each chapter. Many of these inspirational stories come from names you may recognize, like actress Jessica Alba, fashion designer Rebecca Minkoff, Leanin. org's Sheryl Sandberg, *Shark Tank*'s Barbara Corcoran, and Sallie Krawcheck, the CEO and co-founder of the trading platform for women Ellevest—all of whom were kind enough to sit for interviews with me for this book. I hope you find their money stories helpful, relatable, and inspirational.

I also interviewed dozens of other women for this book whose names you may not recognize. Some have asked to remain anonymous because they were ashamed about their situations and didn't want to be viewed a certain way by their peers. These women courageously told me their stories to help prevent other women from making the same mistakes. These cautionary tales will seem grim, and they may scare and even shock you. But maybe that's what's needed to get us motivated to spend the time and the energy to focus on this subject.

This book is for every woman—whether you're having a financial crisis or not.

It's important and necessary for you to be informed about your personal finances—and realize that taking control of them is not a *choice*. It's a *must*. You shouldn't wait until it becomes necessary to take control—by then, it's often too late.

Through my research for this book and the dozens of interviews I conducted with women, I've found there's a real urgency here—among women across the socio-economic and age spectrums—to make the effort to become financially literate and engaged *now*.

So let's get started.

WHY I WROTE THIS BOOK

H OW COULD I, of all people, CNN's Business Correspondent
on Wall Street, be in this position—trapped in a failing
marriage because I didn't have the confidence to make important
financial decisions that would also impact my young children?
Despite spending my working hours on TV explaining financial
and business concepts on the daily, I allowed my husband to take
charge of all our big money decisions—from buying and financing
our house to managing our investments and retirement savings. I
had no clue how to do any of it on my own. I felt like a hypocrite.

Only after what felt like were endless nights of crying because I
was so unhappy and couldn't stand feeling 'stuck' did I put on my
big girl pants and told my then husband, "I want a divorce."

I had been unhappy for years, but in that moment I felt the rush
of adrenaline.

Yes!! Finally!! I CAN do this!!

Who the fuck was I kidding? I didn't have a clue. I had known
sadly this is the road I was going down. So, this moment was not
spontaneous. But I didn't plan for it. I didn't up my financial
knowledge. Because I didn't know *how* or *where* to start. It seemed
too overwhelming.

Sure, I'd go on TV almost every day—often from the New York
Stock Exchange, the biggest stock exchange in the world—and you
welcomed me into your homes to talk about the world of finance.

But in my private life? I was not on my financial game. I gladly delegated everything to my husband. Why? Because it was easy. I was afraid of making mistakes. Yes, I did the day-to-day stuff. But the long-term planning was all him. The car buying. Insurance. Investments. Home repairs. Heck, he even plunged the toilet. Yes, when we divorced, I didn't even know how to do that.

Part of the reason I didn't end my marriage sooner was because I didn't have confidence in myself to handle financial stuff. I didn't think I had the knowledge and good judgment that comes from experience of 'doing the financial stuff.' I was embarrassed and ashamed.

Then I realized it wasn't just me. I began opening up about what I was going through and asking other women if they could relate. I discovered they too were reluctant to admit they didn't take a leading role in the financial arena. And they were just as embarrassed about it as I was. The thing is, it's not that we're incapable or incompetent. We're just not *confident* because we're not actively involved in financial aspects of our lives.

Why does a lack of confidence hold us back? It's an important question and is at the root of how and why we handle money the way we do. I've learned we can't heal what we don't understand. And every woman has a money story. Once she unpacks that story, she can start to see some of the root causes of why she's where she is now.

Often, it's how we were raised. When I was a kid growing up near Miami, my dad tormented my sister and me. He told me I'd never amount to anything. He called me fat. Said I was stupid. And after a while I believed him.

Not sure if that was him or the drugs talking.

As far back as I can remember, my dad did drugs. Pot smoke seemed to always permeate the room where I watched TV. By age eight, I knew how to roll a joint, because I watched my dad at the table as I ate my morning breakfast cereal. He abused more than marijuana—there were quaaludes, there was cocaine, and those were just the drugs I knew about. I felt like I was living in chaos. My dad would yell and scream—he was unpredictable because he was often in various states of high, plus he was angry. My fears played out in a real confidence-crushing way: I wet the bed until I was 12 years old. He would yell at me for that. It was a vicious cycle that chipped away at my confidence.

Financial psychologist Brad Klontz told me he thinks I was cut off at the knees around confidence. That being emotionally abused in this capacity could make anybody wonder about their competence in probably every area.

I transformed my pain into purpose. I always wanted to be a journalist and I succeeded. The adversity made me a fighter. But as an adult, I still lacked confidence in my ability to make the right decisions because that confidence had been eroded by years of anxiety and mental abuse.

I felt I didn't know how to make the best choices for my family's financial future.

I felt, like many women feel, that we need to be experts and know all the answers before we roll our sleeves up and get in there. Gaining the knowledge can seem like a ginormous mountain to climb, so we overestimate what's required to scale it and instead do nothing. We procrastinate. We delay. We pawn it off to our husbands.

Well, no more. As you flip through the pages of this book, you'll realize you don't have to be a financial genius to take control of your relationship with money. To become a successful investor, it's more important to *be* in the market than to have it 100% figured out. You'll see that with a little foreknowledge you *can* combat the inherent sexism at the car dealership and in the housing market. That getting rid of your debt *will* get you closer to financial independence.

You'll read stories of inspiration and cautionary tales of why abdicating all the financial stuff over to someone else can be devastating.

When I set out to write this book, I wanted to give women the 'where to start' and the 'how to start' on the financial stuff that may seem overwhelming. I wanted to lay out a 'how to' of all the financial things I struggled with, but was too embarrassed to reveal. As with most things that are intimidating, I hope you discover, as I did, that these things aren't as complicated as you first thought. In fact, once I began tackling these transactions, each little victory made me gain a little more confidence. And over time, I wondered what I had been afraid of in the first place. And why I waited so long to improve my situation.

CHAPTER 1: HOW DID WE GET HERE?

"A comfort zone is a beautiful place, but nothing ever grows there."

Unknown

A S WOMEN WE want equal pay with men, but expect him to pick up the check on date night. We want our independence, but get antsy by our mid-30s if we're not married and having kids. *He* buys us an engagement ring, not the other way around. Yet we still want to be self-sufficient, kickass bitches (in the best sense of the word) who break glass ceilings and gender stereotypes. We're better educated than earlier generations and we're carving out careers, running companies, and theoretically decreasing our dependence on men. Yet many of us don't actively budget or spend time to learn how to invest the money that *we* are earning. Too often, we cling to traditional gender roles, and some of us still carry a Cinderella complex—a subconscious fear of independence—whether we're married or single. Once married, many of us cede control to men, who are much more likely to run the household finances than women.

How can that be? It wasn't that long ago that Supreme Court Justice Ruth Bader Ginsburg paved the way for financial independence for women—in 1974 she was instrumental in getting the Equal Credit Opportunity Act passed. The act allowed women to open bank accounts, take out credit cards in their own names, and get mortgages without having a male co-sign for the first time.

Look, I realize plenty of women are managing money very well, so I'm not trying to make generalities here. But many other women are taking these hard-won freedoms for granted and falling back into old patterns. Or they're just flat-out avoiding what they know they should be doing around money.

I decided to dig into the why. Why do so many women defer money decisions that have a long-term impact to their spouses, or avoid or neglect to prioritize learning money skills? More specifically, financial skills including personal financial management, budgeting, and investing? Turns out there are reasons. Lots of reasons. The good news? There are ways to flip the switch and change.

LOTS OF WOMEN LET HIM TAKE THE LEAD

If your arrangement with your spouse or partner is one where you handle the day-to-day bills and he handles all or most of the long-term financial stuff, you're not alone. Half of married women let their male partner take the lead in making long-term financial decisions, primarily because they feel he knows more.[1]

Breaking it down by age, 88% of millennial women plan to share long-term financial decisions equally before getting married; but after marriage, a full 51% let their husbands handle *all* the money stuff—more than any other generation.[2]

And two-thirds of women who defer say they just want to be taken care of.[3]

Even when women are the breadwinners—meaning they earn more money than the men in the relationship—only half of those women are very engaged in short- and long-term financial decisions.[4]

We're earning it but we're hesitant to handle it! Clearly our lagging financial confidence isn't because there's a lack of competence. So why are we relinquishing our power over the financial decision-making? Some reasons are:

- traditional gender roles
- women feel less knowledgeable and confident about investing and financial planning, assuming 'he knows more'
- women spend more time on household responsibilities
- women have no interest in getting involved in money decisions
- they have no idea where to begin.

A real head scratcher—younger women aged 20–34 are perpetuating the status quo. They're even more willing than older women to leave investing and financial planning decisions to their spouses. Nearly 60% of women under 50 defer to their spouses, compared to 55% of women over the age of 50. Younger women are most likely to say they have more urgent responsibilities than investing and financial planning. They are also most likely to believe their spouses know more about long-term finances than they do.

But it's such a bad idea to just sit on the sidelines and be uninvolved. What if he suddenly dies? Or you get a divorce? Things may be sweet and nice now in your blissfully happy marriage, but life can get messy, and things in a relationship can turn on a dime.

Forever isn't guaranteed.

Try this thought experiment. What if your husband got hit by a car and was in a coma. How would you pay next month's mortgage? What does his life insurance policy say? Does he have disability insurance? Do you know how much debt your family is carrying? What are the passwords to your family's brokerage account?

You need to have a proverbial plan B, right?

Or what if you're a bystander to your financial stuff, with no idea what he's invested in, and he simply screws everything up because he thinks he's the king of Wall Street and puts all your capital into a single stock that catastrophically tanks?

What are your checks and balances in that situation?

These are real possibilities. They're also realities for many women.

Whether you earn more than him or you earn less, don't just hand over the reins. You still need visibility over what's happening with every angle of the household finances.

There can be huge consequences of letting him handle the money. And women may not realize it until after a divorce or death of a spouse. One study showed many widows and divorcees were disappointed to discover hidden debt and inadequate savings that compromised their lifestyle. Seventy-four percent discovered negative financial surprises. With the wisdom of hindsight, 76% of widows and divorcees wish they had been more involved in long-term financial decisions while they were married. Nearly eight in ten of those women (77%) urge other women to take a more active role.

It's not just married women of all ages lacking confidence in the money stuff and outsourcing their finances.

Single women report feeling less confident than single men in making financial decisions. Single millennial women are the least engaged, yet 59% of them say they *know* they should be doing more with their finances. But they aren't.[5]

So, what are the reasons for this common denominator of a lack of confidence among women and finances? Let's get into the psychology behind why your relationship with money is the way it is.

CULTURE, TRADITION, AND SOCIAL NORMS

Socialization is a huge part of the problem. In the United States we socialize girls and boys differently around all sorts of things, from sports to STEM classes and money management. When girls are being brought up, they're not necessarily being told that they shouldn't care about money, but they have very different expectations around it. For example, studies have found that boys tend to be introduced to family finances earlier and are given the expectation that they have to become financially independent earlier. Boys are expected to have a job and be supportive even through high school. Whether overtly or covertly, many parents encourage only their boys to worry about money.

Girls who are less involved from an early age can grow to become women who avoid money issues. And avoidance can be compounding. The more you avoid something, the more fearful you become of it. What might start as a lack of interest can, over the course of time, become a lack of information, which can become a lack of confidence that you can tackle this thing. The more you don't pay attention to it, the bigger and more challenging that thing can become.

Not helping all this, according to Sallie Krawcheck, the CEO and co-founder of the trading platform for women Ellevest, is that women are told a series of money lies that are internalized over the course of our lives. The biggies are that we are not good with money, that we are risk averse, and that dealing with money is unattractive and unfeminine. When we internalize that it is masculine and unattractive, we hold back from it. Krawcheck quotes Gloria Steinem, who says this is an effective trick the patriarchy has played on us: Because money is power, if we believe we're not good with money then we don't ask for, make, or invest as much of it, which leaves us with less power.

SHERYL SANDBERG, FOUNDER, LEANIN.ORG

In her own words

It's the culture, it's always the culture. Why do we think women are not leaders? Why do we call girls bossy? Why do we accept leadership from men and not from women? The culture runs deep, and it runs deep in all of us—not just people who are old-fashioned. I—until I studied this deeply—would perceive strong women as bossy or aggressive.

Our culture states that men are strong, men are decisive. Men make decisions. Men are leaders. Men handle the finances. Women are supposed to be soft and make everyone feel good, not handle the finances. And it's all the same problem. It's the cultural expectation. But how do we shift it?

We identify, we acknowledge the problem. We give people the motivation to change. We educate on both sides. My book *Lean In* was trying to say we need to accept and embrace female leaders. And in order to do that, we need equality in our homes.

How do you change it? I was working with a friend of mine, while in our 20s, helping her with an essay. The question on her essay was "what causes change in human behavior?" And I thought I would ask the question at dinner with a group of therapists, and we'd have a robust debate. No debate. All of them were like, "Pain, pain, pain. You experience pain." And then they went back to their salads. The reason you change is because you have to. Until we are financially strong and independent, we are dependent. And just like we won't accept dependence in other ways, we shouldn't accept it with our finances.

IMPOSTER SYNDROME

Imposter syndrome, that nagging self-doubt in our intellectual abilities, often causes women to avoid financial responsibility and prevents us from staying on top of what we need to do to control our finances.[6]

A recent study shows that 92% of women want to learn more about financial planning, but a whopping 80% admit they have difficulty talking about money.[7] One reason: They assume they don't know enough about the subject. Fourteen percent of the women in the study worry that talking about money would be a waste of time and 10% feel as though they do not understand finance well enough to talk intelligently about it. The confidence gap can feel like a Catch-22: You feel foolish for not knowing things, but asking questions feels too intimidating. So you continue worrying in silence and assuming you don't know enough to talk intelligently.[8]

The irony? Fidelity's analysis of more than 12 million investors shows that women actually demonstrated stronger saving rates than their male counterparts and enjoyed better long-term investment performance when they did engage. Unfortunately, too many women still hesitate to take control of their finances.

JESSICA ALBA, ACTRESS AND FOUNDER OF THE HONEST COMPANY

In her own words

I believe imposter syndrome is something that happens when we do something for the first time without necessarily having the background, experience, or the wisdom you feel you need to see the full picture of your circumstance. It has made me feel tremendously vulnerable and exposed. Reflecting on it, it usually happens when I don't know something and there is often shame attached to my ignorance. On the flip slide... pushing through that 'ick' and focusing on the light or goal has helped give me the push I've needed to move forward. It's the 'fake it till you make it' mentality and focusing on the ideal outcome. In a way, you have to start behaving as if it's already happening. Then you eventually believe that it will manifest, it will happen. I think imposter syndrome is actually a necessary part of that process. It's just whether you look at it as a negative or positive. For me, it's a double-edged sword but I've found a way to make it work for me.

DEEPICA MUTYALA, FOUNDER AND CEO OF LIVE TINTED

In her own words

For the most part, I haven't had imposter syndrome. I've always had this delusional level of confidence that I was meant to be exactly where I am. I fully believe in the 'fake it till you make it' mindset. I've been in so many rooms that— as an Indian girl growing up in Sugar Land, Texas—it made no sense for me to be in, but I created my own opportunities, and that's because I genuinely believe that I am meant to be there. I am no less capable than the next person, and I refuse to let my background be the reason I don't reach my goals. The way I see it is you have two choices—you can wake up every day saying, 'My life isn't designed for me to win,' or you can say, 'I am going to create a new life for myself and generations to come.'

I remember telling people I would build my own beauty brand as a teenager and most people just laughed—I never cared because the reality is that I know it's hard for people to see things they haven't seen. I hope my success makes it just a bit easier for the next girl to say her dreams loud and proud.

GLOBALLY, WOMEN ARE SHUT OUT

Women elsewhere in the world face different challenges, especially when it comes to access and control over money. The World Bank's Global Findex shows there is progress being made in giving women access to money, but roughly 742 million women in developing countries are still excluded for what the World Bank calls "absolutely no good reason."

The Bill and Melinda Gates Foundation conducted a study of 400 people in rural Bangladesh, India, Northern Kenya, Nigeria, Pakistan, and Tanzania. Across all those locations, society does not see it as women's right or role to make financial decisions. Money is ultimately the domain of men.[9]

Though most women defer to their spouses on long-term financial decisions, there are significant differences across different nations. For example, women in Singapore, Hong Kong, and Switzerland are the most likely to defer. Women in the UK and Germany do so to a lesser degree. Just over half of women in Italy (52%) and the US (54%) defer. Notably, women in Mexico and Brazil are the least likely to hand over financial control to their spouses. More than half of these women either make long-term financial decisions jointly or take the lead themselves, the highest among all the markets surveyed.[10]

I talked with Nandini Harihareswara about the issue of financial inclusion for women. Harihareswara is a consultant who spent years with both the U.S. Agency for International Development and the United Nations. She told me that cultural and social norms underly everything. These norms are often unspoken, but are passed down through generations. This is the silent reason why women are in the dark about the money stuff. You see this especially play out in Turkey and the broader Middle East and North Africa (MENA) region, where the gender gap is large—about 30% of women don't have access to formal financial services and are even worse off in terms of savings for retirement.[11]

A study by MetLife showed that social norms may be working against women and their financial health—preventing them from holding assets in their name or opening independent savings accounts. These obstacles not only keep women from being financially independent but also impact economies. Every country wants to grow its economy and inclusive economic growth benefits the world as a whole, but when I talked with the executive director of the Georgetown Institute for Women, Peace and Security and the former U.S. Ambassador for Global Women's Issues, Melanne Verveer, she told me that in a good portion of the world, poor women don't have the benefits of being able to participate and to work to make money. This is the case even though when women *do* have resources, the impacts on the larger community are positive, especially in business, education, and health. So how can we encourage inclusivity? Verveer says it takes advocacy and enlightened people to help overcome these problematic norms.

But those norms are tough to shake. Why? The biggest reason is that money quite often equals power. And the power construct is that men control financial decisions. Also, cultural and social norms and traditions have been passed down through generations and reinforced over time. Although every culture isn't the same, it essentially comes down to power dynamics. And it's hard to change a power dynamic and a power structure. People often don't want to let go of power—it's human nature.

DEEPICA MUTYALA, FOUNDER AND CEO OF LIVE TINTED
In her own words

My relationship with money is complicated. It's always been a source of tension in my life. The biggest arguments I've witnessed, not just in my family, but within friends and just life in general, were about money. In my life, witnessing the hardships that people go through as an immigrant going from India to America and building a brand-new life for themselves in this country, it's not easy, and there aren't many doors open for you. If anything, they're shut on you.

That is why I crave a life where money is not an issue. I just want to be financially independent. I think my generation is at this interesting turning point—we had the girl boss era where us women felt the need to over exert our masculine and get our much deserved seat at the table. Now, I feel a bit of a shift. We are exhausted. Not only do we run businesses, but we are expected to still do all the things women do in the household as well. I find myself watching the women in my life and I'm constantly in a state of awe. The way they are able to captivate a board meeting and within the same day go home and take care of their kids—they make it look easy. I'm not there yet, but I'm certain when I do have children I'll operate similarly.

I'm in a new era of my life where I'm honestly trying to discover my feminine side. I never want to depend on a man for money, but it would be nice to find my equal because the truth is in my dating life, I've mainly come across men who have been intimidated by my success. I've now made it a hard constraint that if there are any flags that this person won't support me to reach my goals, to just end things right then. I refuse to downgrade my goals to make a man feel more adequate.

LAWS

Laws are driven by cultural and social norms and laws are still a barrier keeping women from having access to financial services. The World Bank says 178 countries have laws in place to keep women from fully participating in economies. That means 2.4 billion women of working age do not have the same opportunities as men. Believe it or not, progress is happening in some countries, though pretty darn slowly.[12]

WOMEN CONTINUE TO GET SHAFTED IN INHERITANCES

No wonder some of us still have a complex that he handles the money better than she does. My mother told me that her father left her brother (my uncle) the majority of my grandparents' inheritance because "he's the boy." And why is that a good reason? Well, that's a good question.

A recent study found that women are less likely than men to get intergenerational wealth transfers of inheritances and gifts during their lifetime.[13]

In countries other than the United States, cultural and legal factors and family dynamics and expectations favor male heirs in the distribution of inheritances. Patriarchal family structures prioritize men over women and expectations in society about women's roles as caregivers or the assumption that they will be 'taken care of' by a spouse may influence the inheritance pattern.

RELIGION

It's not just cultural norms that impact what we believe around money. Religion plays a role. In many faiths, there's nothing wrong with having money, but wealth has to be used wisely.[14] But in others there's a lot of negativity around money. Look at specific teachings in Christianity, for example. One of the most misquoted verses in the Bible is commonly understood to be "Money is the root of all evil." The verse *really* says, "The love of money is the root of all evil." Listen to that every Sunday and I'm not surprised that you would think it's bad for you to have money! Or consider another Old Testament classic: "It's easier for a camel to go through the eye of a needle than for a rich man to enter into the kingdom of God." That doesn't sound very supportive of a good income and substantial net worth. The New Testament maintains a fairly negative view about money: "One cannot serve both God and money," while Islamic law prohibits Muslims from earning or paying interest.

Financial psychologist Brad Klontz says the religious part of this can really condition us around our beliefs about money. He says it's often subconscious for people, but maybe there's part of them deep inside that believes that it would be wrong for them to have financial success.

For Racheal Ede the struggle between God and money has been real. She grew up in a middle-class family, raised by staunch Catholic parents. From a young age she saw money as an evil associated with unbelievers. Her religion stood in the way of her gaining wealth for a variety of reasons including guilt. When she started to earn three times more than she had as a freelance writer, guilt overwhelmed her. She undervalued her worth by overworking and undercharging clients. Uncomfortable talking about money, she was uninterested in being financially literate and had zero knowledge of managing money including budgeting, saving, and investing. Her low financial literacy led to poor financial decisions and she grew used to living paycheck to paycheck. Getting past these challenges was a painful process, but learning about money from experts and examining the messages she grew up with helped her move past her guilt.[15]

YES, YOU CAN BLAME YOUR PARENTS!

It's easy to blame our parents for everything, and when it comes to our attitudes toward money, it is likely their fault. Yes, you heard me right.

And here's where the psychology part of finance really comes in.

Klontz says your financial situation right now can be entirely predicted by your beliefs around money. And where did your beliefs come from? Your parents or the culture at large. We've inherited our parents' beliefs around money and they're so ingrained that they're now part of our subconscious. This is the key point that challenges the notion that our financial problems are the result of us being lazy, crazy, or stupid.

Women already *know* what they should be doing around money. They're just not *doing* it, in part because they fear they won't do it well. They lack confidence that is built by experience. It's rare that children enter adulthood being confident around money because they have very little experience around money. I mean, how much time do kids spend engaging in money activities? Money is one of those taboo topics you don't raise with your parents. They may not have given you the experience of managing money. As a child they gave you an allowance and you blew it and then they bemoaned the fact you didn't save any. And what were the consequences of that? Not much. So there was no lesson learned. I'm a parent and I'm just as guilty as any other.

And then we wonder why we're bad with money! Well, did you watch your parents save any money? Probably not. But did you ever go to the store with your parents when they bought a new TV? So what's the lesson? Did they show you how they saved up for three months to buy that TV? Did they show you how they shopped around? Doubtful.

This doesn't mean your parents are bad parents. It just means they were probably so busy trying to keep things going that they never got around to teaching you some of these life lessons.

THE PSYCHOLOGY OF HOW TO FIX YOUR FINANCES

Change is difficult. We'd rather not do it. We have a bias towards the status quo. It's a real thing! It's conveniently called the status quo bias. To break free of it we need to meet three conditions.

First, we have to feel like it's really important to make this change. Second, we need the confidence that this is a change we can make—that we have the ability, knowledge, and skills to make change happen. And finally, we have to be ready to do it.

How do you gain these three things to turn the ship around?

First, make a huge mental shift to release yourself from blame. That can be profoundly freeing. Here's Brad Klontz's suggestion of how to talk it through in your own head:

My financial problems are not the result of me being lazy, crazy, or stupid. The reason we become stuck is that we're ashamed of our financial situation. I ran up this credit card debt. What an idiot. I didn't pay attention to the card's interest rate. And so we feel really bad about ourselves. We feel stupid. We feel ashamed. Nobody likes that emotional experience. Our natural human tendency is to avoid having a terrible emotional experience and so we don't want to think about it. We avoid it.

Instead of going into avoidance mode, we need to pull ourselves out of that emotional glue trap. If you stay stuck there, the shame you may feel tells you there's something wrong with you. And when you believe you are defective you may think there's no point in trying to change.

But realize that your financial problems make perfect sense based on the beliefs you have about money—beliefs that you did not develop in a vacuum. These beliefs were taught directly to you. You developed them based on what your parents said or didn't say. Those beliefs lead to absolutely predictable results. So think about your financial problems, whatever they are. If you want to change those outcomes, you have to go back and figure out where you got your beliefs around money. You need to change those beliefs if you want to change your outcomes and break the cycle.

It's not enough simply to remember that your parents charged everything on their credit cards and to assume that's why you now do the same thing. You have to dig deeper. That was only their *behavior*. What was their *belief* behind the behavior?

I know what you're thinking: How does just thinking about this stuff actually enact change?

Don't brush over the incredibly powerful impact of identifying how you've been operating—the script you've been using to interact with money your entire life. Some ways you can do that include asking yourself:

- What are your earliest memories and experiences around money?

- What three things did your mother teach you about money?

- What three things did your father teach you about money?

- How much did money matter in the household?

- Was there a belief there will never be enough money, so why bother trying?

- Was there a belief there would always be enough money?

- What are your most joyful, painful, or fearful memories about money?

- How did your parents operate around money?

From your answers, ask yourself, what are the life lessons from these? What was the truth you learned about how money works based on their behavior? Your answers will tell you why you interact with money the way you do. By going back and figuring out where you got those beliefs around money, you can start to change. And while it's your parents' fault you had the beliefs you had, now that you know this, everything that follows is your responsibility.

BACK TO THE THREE CONDITIONS

Let's revisit the three conditions to make change happen: importance, confidence, and readiness.

By focusing and looking deep, you've probably cleared the importance hurdle. You've essentially gotten yourself psychologically organized so that you are prioritizing your financial health.

Confidence is the biggest hurdle, but you can gain confidence as you learn about where your beliefs come from and let go of the shame from your mistakes. And give yourself some grace, since you're in this situation because you're a human being and you weren't taught what you needed to be taught. Maybe say to yourself, 'It makes sense that I did this, but I don't want to do this anymore.' Accepting that gives an instant confidence booster. Want another one? How about the realization that women are wired to be better investors than men?

Women do it better

The irony of all this? While you think you're terrible at it, studies show women are actually better than men at investing. That's not a theory. It's a research-proven fact. And guess why. Women are more competent because they have less confidence. Their lack of confidence is a strength! Female investors get stronger rates of return than men. According to Fidelity's 2021 Women and Investing Study, women outperform men in returns by 40 basis points, or 0.4% on average. That may not sound like much, but this positive margin can translate into tens of thousands of dollars over time.[16]

How do women come out ahead? They trade less often than men. It's actually one of the more effective and simplistic strategies: Buy great companies and hold them for the long term. Men, on the other hand, have more ego and confidence and trade more frequently on average. This may be an attempt to time the market: Selling before the market drops or buying before the market increases. The problem is that timing the stock market consistently over time is virtually impossible. You're essentially gambling.[17]

Also helpful to women in their investing skills? Estimates suggest investing is 80% psychological and 20% math. And women have a leg up on their emotional attunement— their ability to understand themselves.[18] Unlike men, female investors do not generally jump on the shiny object bandwagon. They explore investment opportunities and stay in their investments longer. Women have more curiosity. They're more engaged in learning about the hows and whys of investing. So women have the psychological part down pat, and the math part of it is easier than you think.

Now comes the readiness. This is the part where you actually make changes. You don't have enough money to pay off your debt or invest in your future? You've got three choices:

1. Reduce your spending

2. Increase your income

3. Do both

So it's about downsizing or getting a side hustle or finding additional ways to make more money. Now you're like, Alison, got another choice? I know, this is the hardest part. Most of us don't want to do any of these. Then maybe you have to hit rock bottom before making changes.

Or visualization can help.

Picture yourself in a life where you have financial control. Are you on a beach? Can you feel the sun on your face and the sand under your feet? What does it smell like? What's another thing you want? A house? Where is it? What town, what neighborhood? In your mind, drive by, take a look at it. What's the square footage? Now let's visualize how much money you need to get that house and what you need to set aside every month to achieve it.

Don't laugh!

I did, because when I first tried this exercise I thought it was BS. How is it possible that just visualizing all this can make you actually move toward that goal?

Brad Klontz has conducted a study on this exact topic. After a one-hour session of visualization, he got people with little to no financial education to increase their savings rates by 73% within three weeks. Boom. He used the same technique on a group of people who had financial education and still saw a 22% increase in savings rates with them.[19] This shows that if you get emotionally engaged or emotionally connected to what you're saving for, you have a better chance of success.

Visualization can light a fire under your ass. Ask yourself: What are my financial goals? Get really excited about those. Maybe your first one is that you want to be able to retire. What does that mean? And when? Where will that retirement take place—on a beach, or at home?

So how does visualization work? Our brains are wired to focus on the present. They have hunter-gatherer instincts. For your brain, your situation ten years from now doesn't matter to your survival.

So for you to delay gratification today for something that might help you 10, 20, 30 years from now goes against everything that your biology is set up for. The only way to override this wiring is to take the future and bring it into the here and now, get super excited about it, get passionate and emotional about it. Until you can feel it. Until you can smell it.

Once you identify your goals, visualization brings them into the here and now. But the thing is, how do you keep that day-to-day passion? You can't. I mean you could try, but if you rely on yourself to write a check once a month to achieve those savings goals, chances are you're going to blow it. That's why you have to automate moving your money from your checking account into savings and investments. Automation is the ultimate wealth hack. This is a key component because you got super excited about it, next you just need to set it and forget it. That's how people in Klontz's study increased their savings rates. And so can you.

CHELY WRIGHT, SINGER, SONGWRITER, AUTHOR, ADVOCATE, BUSINESS EXECUTIVE

In her own words

Money was definitely part of the conversation when growing up in my small-town Kansas household. But the topic was almost always stressful. Yes, money was discussed—in that we didn't have much of it.

That's part of why, as a kid, I wanted to learn how to make my own money and, perhaps more importantly, learn how to save it too. My parents were extraordinarily hard workers and my focus on making my own money was sort of an act of love and respect for them because I wanted to lessen some of their hardship. I was pretty entrepreneurial, and I felt proud to buy my own lunch ticket for school and my sneakers for sports.

But I think a deeper part of my anxieties around money were rooted in fear, unfortunately. I was sincerely afraid of becoming an adult who'd be unable to feed or house herself. It seemed possible, even likely, that I could face the same financial stressors my parents had. I had no reason to believe I wouldn't. That stress was made worse when, at the tender age of nine, I realized I was gay. Of course, I didn't confide in my family, my pastor, or anyone for that matter because I knew if I did, I'd be kicked out of the house, excommunicated from my church, and shunned in my community. I would *truly* be on my own and that magnified an already-installed fear of being brought up in a home without enough resources. Being a closeted kid turbo-boosted my nervousness around money.

I moved to Nashville, Tennessee when I was 18 and by that time, although I no longer believed I was in spiritual jeopardy for being gay, I knew for sure that I was in cultural jeopardy and certainly in career jeopardy. No one in country music had ever acknowledged being gay. When I signed my first record contract and my first publishing deal as a songwriter in my early 20s, I was deep in the closet. And I knew my money-making opportunities in the business were fleeting as it was—given how few people actually 'make it' in Nashville, but that they were also intrinsically tied to keeping my secret. If I was outed, my earning money in the country music industry would be over in the blink of an eye.

One day, post 9/11, I was in my business manager's office near Music Row going over my financials when he said, "Hey, I want you to spend some of your money." I replied, "What? Why? What do you mean?"

He explained, "I've worked with you for years and I've never seen you take a vacation." I pushed back and cited the cool places I'd recently been. He said, "No, no, no, that was just tacking a day onto your tour—that doesn't count as a vacation. You don't spend anything."

He told me he was concerned about my relationship with money. "You're gonna burn out. You've got to enjoy it a little bit." A few months after our conversation, I did end up taking a vacation... and it was really hard for me. Every day of that trip to Europe, my inner monologue played on repeat. 'This is just money out the door. There's no return on investment here.'

To this day, I struggle to spend money for enjoyment because of the complex trauma I experienced being poor and around the fragility of the career I loved while being a closeted queer person. That stuff's deep. It gets into the marrow of your bones.

I *will* say there was an upside to my hypervigilance around money. Had I not achieved a certain level of financial security, I wouldn't have been able to come out of the closet the way I did in 2010. I would've been too dependent upon touring and recording. While I did continue to tour after I came out, my earning potential in country music took a serious hit.

Money earned, grown, protected, and cared for—it gives you choices.

As a woman on a planet that is built for men and continues to tip in favor of men at every turn, we women need choices more than most. Whether it's leaving an unhealthy, potentially abusive relationship, changing a situation where you're just not happy, or maybe you're living in a town where you can't fulfill your life's ambitions... it's usually a lack of resources that makes the difference. Money can and often does equal choice, and choice is a required ingredient in any person's happiness. Does money matter? Hell, yes, it matters.

Alright, we've finished the why—and now it's time to use what we've learned about ourselves as momentum to take action and get control of our financial health. You can't manage what you don't monitor, and what's coming in and what's going out is where it all begins.

CHAPTER 2: WHERE THE F IS MY MONEY GOING?

"Too many people spend money they earned to buy things they don't want—to impress people they don't like."

Will Rogers

IF IT FEELS like your money is disappearing and you can't really pinpoint why you struggle to pay your bills or to save money, what I'm about to walk you through will answer those questions and more.

I promise, it's not as overwhelming as you may think. Also, it doesn't matter if you're age 18 or 50, it's never too early or too late to turn the ship around and get your money shit straight.

There is a way to set aside money for expenses, emergencies, savings, investing and, yes (!), even the fun stuff too.

How?

By choosing a strategy to balance your income and your cost of living.

I know what you're thinking.

How the heck do I do that?

It involves spending with intention, or with purpose. Or being more mindful with your money. Whatever you want to call it.

I mean how easy is it to just use your phone for Uber, Grubhub, or Walgreens, and spend spend spend—and lose track of just how much money you're shelling out? I feel ya.

Even if you're spending on the stuff that makes you feel happy, like a latte at a café, or the necessities like groceries, or an impulse buy, this is about paying attention to how you're spending.

By the time you finish this chapter you will not only know how much money is going out—and coming in—you will also be armed with a 360-degree view of how you may be spending too much, what kinds of things you're spending your money on, and where you can save more. You'll have an overall better understanding about what is happening with your money.

This is the step before you begin budgeting. What you're about to do is necessary because you can't manage what you don't monitor. Think of it as creating a roadmap. You wouldn't set out on a road trip from New York to San Francisco without knowing the route to take. You'd look at Google maps or GPS. Your money needs a roadmap too.

To draw this roadmap, you first have to get up close and personal with your money—just in case you need to figure out where to course correct.

Come with me as I show you how to do it.

THE EXACT PLAY BY PLAY OF HOW TO MAKE YOUR BUDGET

This is a two-step process:

Step 1: Take an inventory of your money situation and evaluate what you need to do to get where you want to be.

Step 2: Choose a budget and stick with it.

For the first step? We will assess what your financial picture looks like and figure out what you're doing right and what you're doing to sabotage yourself.

Second step? I will walk you through three budgets (helpfully characterized as shoe styles) and you get to choose one that suits you best.

- Are you a sneaker kind of gal? Then choose #1: Put a Percentage on It.
- Are high heels more your style? Opt for #2: Envelope System.
- If you love the ease of flip-flops, then go for #3: Reverse Budget.

But it's not quite time yet to decide which shoes to wear (that's for Chapter 3). Here, in Chapter 2, we'll get started with step one.

GET DOWN IN THE TRENCHES WITH YOUR FINANCES

You'll want to first survey your situation and understand where your money is going. This means knowing exactly what your expenses are, versus your income. Only then can you figure out where and how to cut your spending.

Now, I know it's tempting to turn to a budgeting app and let your phone do this for you, but I think if you put pen to paper and do the actual work of running the numbers—really looking at where and how you spend your money—you will feel more compelled to stick to your budget. If you come up with a money plan all by yourself, you will have a better understanding of why it's important not to stray.

Humor me. Get out a pen and paper. Use Alison's No BS Budget Worksheet and fill in the numbers as you go.

Alison's No BS Budget Worksheet
What makes up your budget?

To reach your goals, you need money left over at the end of the month. Consider these categories that make up your budget:

1. Average Monthly Income

_____ $
_____ $
_____ $
Total: $

2. Fixed Expenses

_____ $
_____ $
_____ $
Total: $

3. Variable Expenses

_____ $
_____ $
_____ $
_____ $
_____ $
_____ $
Total: $

4. Non-Monthly Expenses

_____ $
_____ $
_____ $
_____ $
_____ $
_____ $
Total: $

5. Here's What's Left:

Average Monthly Income $
Total Expenses   -$
Money for Goals: $

Money for Goals =
(The amount of money to allocate towards goals after you take expenses away from your income)

$ Income	Fixed Expenses	Variable Expenses	Non-Monthly Expenses
(take-home pay After taxes and benefits)	− (Monthly bills that are generally the same)	− (Typical everyday living expenses that can change month to month)	− (Typical everyday living expenses you know you're going to have, but don't happen every month)

Now, as we run through this, even if it hurts, you have to be honest with yourself about how you spend your money, and how much you have coming in, as you fill in these next key questions:

- **Average Monthly Income**: How much money is coming in on average every month?

- **Fixed Expenses**: How much do you spend on things like rent/ mortgage, insurance premiums, gym membership?

- **Variable Expenses**: What's your outlay on things like groceries, gas, and utilities?

- **Non-Monthly Expenses**: Don't forget to factor in things like car maintenance, repairs, and gifts.

Don't faint. I'm going to now walk you through step by step and help you get those numbers.

HOW MUCH DO I REALLY MAKE?

Let's tackle your income first. This includes all of your incoming money, whether you make a regular salary or your earnings are more inconsistent, meaning irregular income.

The goal here is to figure out your average monthly income. As you do so, make sure you're using your net earnings (what you actually bring home after taxes are taken out) and not gross earnings, which is pre-tax.

All the salaried ladies

It's much easier to take a snapshot of your income when you get a regular salary. Many of you who are salaried have earnings directly deposited into a bank account, usually into your checking account. Certain expenses, like taxes, health insurance, and retirement savings are taken out of your paycheck before you even receive it.

For example, in my case, when I was with CNN, money towards my 401(k) was sliced out of my salary and plopped into an investment account. (If you're salaried and you don't have this set up, let me tell you, you *have to*! More on the importance of the 401(k) in Chapter 9.)

There are some budgeting methods that have salaried folks include the amounts taken out for taxes, health insurance, and 401(k) contribution in that monthly income number. I say leave them out. The money comes out of your check anyway and you're not going to see it when your pay hits your bank account, so why should you include it in your monthly income? Later, make sure you don't add those things taken out of your paycheck, like taxes, monthly health insurance premiums, and retirement savings when you create your expenses list.

Now answer this question: Are you paid twice a month or bi-weekly? If you're paid bi-weekly—or 26 times a year—there will be two months each year where you will have an extra paycheck for the month. So, in order to find your lowest possible income for the month, use your earnings from a two-paycheck month rather than a month that has three paychecks since it's not an every-month occurrence.

If you're paid twice a month, or 24 times a year, every month will have two paychecks. So, just add those two paychecks to get your lowest possible average monthly income. Boom. Done. Write that number in the box 'Average Monthly Income' on the No BS Budget Worksheet.

If you have an additional income stream—say, from a side hustle or rental properties—you will want to include that in your income figure. We're looking for an average here. So, add up the income you've made doing your side gig or gigs over the past three months and divide by three for your average monthly side hustle income. Now add the final income number you figured out from your salaried job to the final income number from your side hustle, and that will be the number you should write in the box 'Average Monthly Income' on the worksheet.

All the gig economy girlies

I was a gig economy girl for a long time. I freelanced for years in TV and made a decent living. I often had at least four different on-air jobs at once, all on unpredictable schedules. I was always hustling for extra gigs, just in case my current ones suddenly dried up. And I rarely said no to anyone, out of fear they'd never call me again. At that stage in my life, I didn't budget because I thought: How the heck do you budget when you have zero consistency in your schedule and in your income?

Well, now I've learned. Yes, there is a way!

I'm currently back doing the freelance grind now, so I know that if you're a freelancer or just have an irregular or inconsistent income, you'll want to figure out a lowest monthly estimate of what you bring in. Most freelancers should look back at the last year of their income. But if your income is as erratic as mine is right now, or if you're not working at the same gigs you were nine to 12 months ago, use the last six months, so your figures are the most up to date.

Add up the total income for each of the six or 12 months, depending on your situation. List each month's totals separately. Then from that list of six or 12 months, pick out the three months where you brought in the least amount of income. Add those three tallies together and then divide by three to get the average.

So, if you add up your three lowest monthly incomes and come up with $8,800, that amount divided by three would equal $2,933 for your lowest average monthly income. And that's what your budget should be based on. Write the amount on your No BS Budget Worksheet.

The idea here is to underestimate your average monthly income so you're able to pay your expenses without freaking out. Then if you have money left over, give yourself a big pat on the back.

WTF is FICA

Even if you're not a fan of the sitcom *Friends*, you have to watch the scene where Jennifer Aniston's character asks the question that just about anyone collecting a paycheck universally understands: "Who's FICA? Why's he getting all my money?" (To find it, search 'Friends, Who's FICA?' on YouTube.)

In the United States, FICA stands for the Federal Insurance Contributions Act. It's made up of two payroll taxes: Social Security tax and Medicare tax. Some think of it more as a tax; others see it as an involuntary contribution—6.2% for Social Security, plus 1.45% for Medicare. If you're a college student and are also employed by the university you attend, your wages are exempt from FICA taxes. Otherwise, every working American has to pay them. For some workers, FICA is the biggest chunk taken out of our paycheck, beyond other tax withholding like federal and state income taxes.

So, if you're an employee, 7.65% of your total income goes to good ol' FICA taxes. Your employer, meantime, pays an additional 7.65% on your behalf. How nice of them, I know.

If you're self-employed, you have to pay the whole shebang, 15.3%, at tax time (or via quarterly estimated payments to the IRS).

Now for the good news. There's a limit to how much of what you earn can be taxed by these programs. The amount is capped and often changes every year. For example, the FICA cap for 2023 kicked in when your salary reached $160,200. So, if you earn $185,000 a year, you'd have $24,800 that would not be taxable for Social Security. If you track your income like a hawk, as you should, it may feel like you suddenly got a little raise after you hit the cap in 2023.

Unfortunately, the Medicare portion of the FICA tax does not have a limit—you always have to pay it. And if your income is over $200,000, your Medicare tax is actually 2.35%, because as a high earner, you pay 0.9% more.

GETTING A GRIP ON YOUR EXPENSES

Now let's dig into your expenses.

This is where mobile banking and online billing come in handy. But if you're not part of the digital world, you can still do this exercise. Pull out your bank and credit card statements—and if you write paper checks, get out your checkbook. Review all your debit and credit card expenses, your bill payments, your non debit card expenses (maybe you keep receipts?), and your ATM withdrawals.

Go back and look at three months of your spending and literally write down Every. Thing. You've. Spent. Money. On—from rent and utilities to the coffee on the go.

As you're recording the expenses, divide them into the three categories on the No BS Budget Worksheet: fixed, variable, and non-monthly expenses. Make columns as shown on the worksheet—you will probably need to add additional lines. Ultimately, all of your expenses will be subtracted from your income.

Let's start with fixed expenses.

Fixed expenses

Fixed expenses are the ones that are the same amount every single month—the things you can probably rattle off right off the top of your head, because you pay them so regularly. Like what it costs to put a roof over your head—your rent or mortgage payment. Your health insurance premium (if it's not being taken directly out of your paycheck). Student loans. Childcare. Car payment. Car Insurance. Gym membership. Cable/streaming. Cellphone. Apps/subscriptions, like Netflix and Apple Music.

List all of these monthly expenses with their amounts under the column 'Fixed Expenses' on the worksheet. Once you've listed them, add all of them up and write the total amount in the Fixed Expenses box.

Variable expenses

Take a deep breath. The real work is about to begin. And yes, it may be tedious, but I promise it's worth it. Put the worksheet aside for a minute and grab your calculator or whatever works best for you in these next calculations. That may be opening a spreadsheet or writing it out on paper. I want you to go through the last three months of your variable expenses.

These are things you spend money on every month, but the amounts change. Think groceries, meals out (don't forget to include breakfast and lunch, not just dinner), utilities (electricity, gas, water), dry cleaning, gas for your car, veterinarian visits, transportation other than your monthly car payment (so Uber or taxi, bus, or subway fare), manicures/pedicures, and clothing. Do you regularly withdraw money from an ATM machine? Include that here. (The problem with taking out cash is often it's hard to keep track of where it goes. Start paying attention to that!)

Look at all of your bank and credit card statements, and pick out each variable expense over that period.

Yes. Each. Variable. Expense. Let's get granular!

Give each expense category a title—for example Gas, Groceries, or Meals Out. Then in that list write the amounts you've spent over the past three months in each category.

So, if you've been to the gas station to fill up your car ten times over the past three months, jot down those ten different amounts under the Gas heading. The goal is to figure out your average monthly cost for each category. For our gas example, add the ten amounts and divide by three (three months). That final amount is the average monthly amount for that expense category. Go back to the No BS Budget Worksheet and write Gas with the final amount in the 'Variable Expenses' section.

Phew! One down, many more to go!

You're ultimately going to make separate lists of each type of expense and tally each of them up for separate three-month totals of each expense.

One more example: Let's say you have developed the habit of picking up a green juice on your way to work. Add up everything you spent on juice over the past three months and divide by three. If you're like me, your jaw may drop when you see this figure. These kinds of expenses are where you can quickly become painfully aware that you're unintentionally overspending. Don't freak though. There's good news here. This exercise will also likely reveal where you have some room to save money. More on that shortly.

Write Juice and the final average dollar amount in the variable expenses box of the worksheet. Now repeat with all your other variable expenses. This will take some time. Tally up your Ubers, manis/pedis, the lunches out (yes, even lunches by yourself count), then divide by three and put the final number in the appropriate box on the budget worksheet.

Coming up with a three-month average of what you've been spending on specific items can be a great eye-opener—you really learn where your money has been going. And, if you decide later that you want to make any changes, it will be easier to come up with a reasonable goal.

> "You know, I realized what I was spending on Starbucks was adding up to about $5 a day, so about $35 a week. And when I added that up, that was $140 a month, almost a small car payment. So, I bought a percolator for $30 and now I make my own organic coffee at home. And I enjoy it even more."
>
> *Mia Carson, real estate agent, New York, NY*

Non-monthly expenses

Exhausted yet? Don't be. We're almost finished.

The last type of expense is the non-monthly expense. These can be tricky because they're hard to track and some can be real budget busters. You know they're going to happen, but most of us don't plan for them, since they don't happen every single month. Suddenly they're a surprise when they shouldn't have been. These are things like predictive car maintenance—an oil or brake change—updating your car registration, quarterly or biannual insurance premiums, charitable donations, after-school activity fees.

The idea? Prepare ahead of time as best as you can. This is a no-denial zone—you know they're coming! Now is the time to plan for those expenses.

Look back at the past year or two for these kinds of expenses and see what the total annual cost of each usually is. Add all of the expenses together. Then divide by 12 to get the monthly amount you should be setting aside for these expenses.

My suggestion? Open a savings account where you can set aside this money for the non-monthly expenses. Give the account a name, maybe 'Seasonal Expenses.' Set up an automatic transfer from your checking account each month into the Seasonal Expenses savings account like you're paying a bill, and forget about the money until you have to use the funds for the non-monthly expenses. This is a long-term solution that allows you to plan and save in advance for big expenses that can creep up on you very quickly.

Additionally, sometimes there are sporadic expenses that you know are around the corner. For example, you know you've got a friend's out-of-town wedding coming up, or a vacation that you are planning for next year. Maybe you've got an appliance that is starting to show signs of age and you know you will have to purchase a new one in the coming year. Estimate the costs for each. And then divide by the number of months there are before you have to pay for it. The final figure is the amount you should set aside every month to put into the Seasonal Expenses savings account to meet that expense.

Taxes can be a non-monthly expense. If you're a freelancer and your employers don't take out taxes from your paychecks, this is a way to get organized for tax day. Say you earn $60,000 a year. Depending on which state you live in, that could mean a tax bill between $10,000 to $13,500. If you're at the higher end of that scale, you would look to set aside $1,125 per month in that account ($13,500 divided by 12 months). So, write $1,125 in the non-monthly expense box next to 'taxes.'

Feel like you always come up short for gift-giving around the holidays? Or find yourself out of funds for birthday presents for your nearest and dearest? Look back at last year's holiday and gift spending to estimate. You may not spend the same amount, but it's a good starting point. Take that amount and divide by 12. That's how much money should be siphoned from your checking account to your Seasonal Expenses savings account each month. It's just more manageable that way.

Here's another example for how to handle the bigger recurring purchases that happen throughout the year. Let's say it costs a total of $300 for a haircut and highlights and you do both four times a year (sorry, not sorry!). That's $1,200 a year. If you budget $100 each month for your hair, you won't stress about this expense and will actually enjoy getting your hair done! (I know, I've been there.)

Keep listing all your non-monthly expenses and their amounts on the budget breakdown worksheet in the 'Non-Monthly Expenses' box.

Before we start tallying up all the numbers you've listed, let's take a breath and assess for a moment.

What surprised you about your spending? What did you already know but not admit to yourself? Did you recognize spending habits you've known deep down need to be adjusted?

Guess what? This is where the change can happen.

THE MOMENT OF TRUTH

Alright ladies, now it's time for the big reveal. I recommend you take a seat.

Take your No BS Budget Worksheet and use the 'Easy Equation' that you see in the box below to plug in your numbers. Start by listing your total monthly income. Then add up all the averaged fixed expenses you've listed in the box. Write the total. Next, total up each of the averaged variable and non-monthly expenses. Add the three totals from the three categories of expenses and, voila! You've got your average total monthly expenses. Now take that number and subtract it from your average monthly income. The answer you get is the money left over, which is the money for your goals.

Easy Equation

Income − Fixed Expenses − Variable Expenses − Non-Monthly Expenses = Money for Goals

---

If you discover that you spend more than you make, don't freak out. You're not alone. And I'm not trying to shame you. Tons of women are struggling to make ends meet, feeling like they're working and working, and barely managing to cover the bills. And if you've happily revealed a surplus each month, it seems like you have your shit together! Go along, skip ahead to Chapter 4 where I've got lots of suggestions on how to have even more money left over.

MARIA, MBA, FORMER SENIOR PARTNER

A cautionary tale

I've been told I'm extremely bright and accomplished, professionally. I've got an MBA from Harvard. Over a

20-year career at a very well known professional services firm. I rose to a senior partner and helped several CEOs of fortune 100 companies make multi-billion-dollar business decisions.

I have a fabulous marriage. My husband is in the financial world and very successful. Our marriage is mutually respectful, and we have good communication.

But my financial house was collapsing, and I didn't even realize it. Or maybe I did.

For the last three or four years I've had a strong gut feeling that we were living too large, and way above what we were earning. But I have always delegated all the balance sheet decisions to my husband. For some reason, I still don't know why, I was completely uninvolved in our finances and embarrassed to challenge him or ask him for details. It was certainly easy to live in the dark and I trusted him to make good decisions. On the rare occasions I commented about our spending, he kept telling me that we were "on the verge of never having to work again" and that I shouldn't worry.

But he recently came to me and admitted that we have a big problem. It turns out we are in a major cash crunch, and it's worse than I ever imagined it could be. I am embarrassed to admit that I had no idea how much we were spending and how our credit card debts were piling up. I guess I didn't really understand how much debt he was accumulating in order to finance the business or make additional investments. Our affluent lifestyle is so high, and we have a lot of fixed expenses—private school tuitions at elite institutions, two expensive homes with mortgages, charity pledges, expensive cars that are financed, household help. And now I've found that we also have credit card debt that's in the hundreds of thousands of dollars, a margin loan on our investment account, an added line of credit on one of our homes. To cover our latest tax bill, we've had to scramble and have pulled from retirement accounts and trusts meant for the kids' education. We have to dramatically change our lifestyle. I don't know what the future looks like.

How did this happen? My husband kept telling me that the payout for a big deal was around the corner—but the deal collapsed. And while we have a long list of investments on the balance sheet, most are illiquid, and we have no control over whether and when we will see our money or a profit. But he was so confident in this big payday that we spent the money like we already had it in the bank.

I'm embarrassed and ashamed that I didn't feel confident early on to get involved in the balance sheet discussions or to ask my husband more about the details of our cash flows. My therapist saw the angst this was causing and told me I had to confront my husband, but I dragged my feet. For some reason I didn't feel comfortable questioning his judgment. I am very smart, but I thought he was very smart too and I couldn't imagine that he would make decisions that would put our family's finances at risk.

For years I quietly asked myself whether he was right in making these decisions. I should have listened to that inner voice.

CHANGE STARTS NOW

If you are living paycheck to paycheck, change has to happen. Amy Dolan, a 55-year-old optometrist I talked with, lives this way. She stresses daily about being unable to earn enough money to meet her expenses. And by the way, she earns a pretty good living. As I gave her advice on how to break out of the cycle, I heard lots of excuses: "I don't want to do that." "It's not the right time." "It's impossible." I get it. It's hard to change your lifestyle. But getting in a better place financially won't happen unless you change your mindset—and realize adjustments have to be made.

If you're like Dolan, and you've realized there's not much money left over for saving, investing, or paying off debt after taking care of your expenses, it's time to figure out where you can cut back and cut out altogether. Chapter 4 has lots of ideas on how to do it.

VANESSA, SURGEON

A cautionary tale

Vanessa is a divorced mom of two teenage children. She's a brilliant, Yale-trained surgeon who has a lot of insecurities and fears around money. She was married for 13 years, and her ex-husband has been horribly sneaky both during and after the marriage.

Here's her story, in her own words:

About a decade ago I thought my life was great. I had a career, had my two kids, thought I was in a good marriage. And then basically came to find out that my now ex was leading a double life—he had been having this affair for a year while married to me. And the affair was with one of the nurses assigned in my operating room!

Normally when people find out that their spouse is having an affair, that person is in another location. And this person was with me day in and day out and had created this whole sort of fatal attraction scenario.

I came to find out by discovering things in my house. I was in one of the closets and I came across this envelope and I was like, this is weird. And it was a bank card.

There was a handwritten note from his father that said, "Here's a card for the account that I set up for you in South Carolina." And then I found bank statements. Over time I realized he had set up these bank accounts where he was siphoning money, which I didn't know about because I assumed that I was in this trustworthy marriage.

I came to find out that his father actually enabled him in this situation with his accounts.

I was working full time and had two small children. I did most of the daily money stuff, like I wrote all the checks and paid the bills. But I viewed him as more savvy financially because, being a physician, I didn't really get any real financial education. They never taught us any of that in medical school.

He was a math major, and I just perceived him as being the stronger financial person. So I would put all the stuff together for the accountant for the taxes, but then when the return came and needed to be reviewed, I kind of delegated that to him because I was doing all the children's stuff and the daily grind. So I never checked the returns. If I had, I could have known about the bank accounts earlier, or seen that the numbers in our account weren't adding up with the W-2s. As an intelligent female, I probably should have thought, 'If I am doing the day to day, why aren't I checking this?'

Then there's the life insurance. We had two term insurance policies for like a couple million dollars that he ended up, without telling me, converting into a whole life policy.

He was siphoning money into these whole life policies. I'm assuming his plan was to eventually loan the money to himself. So now he's got this whole life policy that also has cash stored in it.

Particularly as professional, intelligent women, we need to protect ourselves and we need to go into it eyes wide open. We shouldn't feel intimidated or less confident than our husbands. We need to really be involved, financially aware, and financially literate.

Fully understanding your financial picture and admitting you have to make changes is the first step toward no longer living paycheck to paycheck. There is a way to get a handle on your spending. And it starts with managing your money differently—maybe even a complete overhaul of where and how you spend.

You just created a full picture of your money. This will make it easier to identify how to begin your money makeover. Turn the page for some ways to do just that.

CHAPTER 3: BUDGETS AND SHOES DO GO TOGETHER

"Don't tell me what you value, show me your budget, and I'll tell you what you value."

Joe Biden

I F YOU'RE TEMPTED to skip this chapter because the word 'budget' at once chills your heart and makes you fall asleep, I get it. And I understand that being disciplined isn't necessarily fun. It's even less fun putting restrictions on how much money you can spend. But there are so many benefits to getting your money shit straight:

- Paying your bills will feel less stressful.
- You could improve your credit.
- You could down your debts.
- Being more organized helps you toward growing your wealth.
- You can plan for vacations and actually enjoy them.

The list goes on and on.

But most of all, by putting yourself on a budget, you will take control of your own financial well-being. And there's something really sweet and satisfying about that. Remember the roadmap?

Soon you could even be calling your budget your road to financial freedom.

When I finally took control of my finances, I just felt better, more at ease, and more confident. However, getting to that point? Ugh, it can be a drag. It's uncomfortable limiting your spending. But the discomfort is worth it. And if you're like me, it wouldn't be the first time you've endured discomfort for the prize at the end of the tunnel.

So, let's try to make this fun, shall we?

I like to think of budgets as shoes. And we all know that many shoes can take time to mold to your feet. Like a pair of super sexy boots you spot on display at Bloomingdale's. I mean sexy cute! And you've just gotta have them. When you try them on, they're a little uncomfortable, but you want them so badly, you're willing to feel the pain of breaking them in. So, you buy them, knowing there will be some discomfort at the beginning, until you get used to them.

Like a new pair of boots, at first, your budget may feel limiting and restrictive, but over time you'll get used to it.

> "The best kind of budget is the one that works for you. A budget is of no value if it doesn't fit your lifestyle or personality."
>
> *Bola Sokunbi, CEO Clever Girl Finance, Queens, NY*

IT ALL COMES DOWN TO GOALS, GIRL

Before choosing shoe #1, #2, or #3, let's reflect on why you're doing all of this work.

Ultimately, you're coming up with a budget because, girl, I know you've got goals and I know you want to reach them.

Don't think you do? Stop and think for a second. No calculator needed here—just a willingness to ask yourself what you're hoping your money will do for you—beyond 'I've gotta pay my bills and save for retirement.' If you come up blank, pose the question this way: 'What am I working my ass off for? What am I really trying to save for?' This goes back to the visualization we did in Chapter 1.

The reason it's important to figure out your goals is because they're ultimately what you're going to look to when you're having a hard time sticking to your budget. Your goals are what motivate you to succeed. They hold you accountable.

Goals don't have to be a big production or a reflection of your inner soul, although I want you to think about it. Maybe you want to save to be able to travel to your girlfriend's upcoming wedding. Or to take a vacation to Costa Rica. Maybe you want to buy a car. Or pay off your credit card bills. Or your goal could simply be, 'I don't have a goal, but I want to put away money for when I have a goal.'

Articulating your goal will keep you motivated because you know what you're aiming at. It will inspire you to stay on course. It'll be the voice in your head redirecting you when you're feeling tempted to blow a portion of the money you're supposed to put into savings on a pricey new blouse or a fancy dinner with friends.

It helps if your goals have specific deadlines and amounts. For example, 'By the end of the year I want to add $1,000 to a 529 college-savings fund for my daughter.' Make your goal visible— post it on the refrigerator door or make a dollar sign the screensaver on your phone. Make it stare at you, silently saying, 'This, darling, this is what I'm working toward.'

FIND A BUDGET STRATEGY THAT WORKS FOR YOU

Now that you have a better idea of how much money is coming in and going out (Chapter 2), you're ready for step two, making a plan, a.k.a. a budget.

Budgeting means tracking your finances so you don't spend too much or save too little. I'm going to offer you three approaches to budgeting in the hopes that one works for you. I've chosen three that seem the least time-consuming because, ladies, I know we're all strapped for time. The last thing I want to do is add one more thing to your to-do list.

As you choose which budget is right for you, consider this: The trick to sticking with a budget is choosing one that fits your personality. I like to think of the different budgets as different types of shoes—which one fits you? Will it be shoe #1, shoe #2, or shoe #3?

SHOE #1: THE SNEAKER

Put a percentage on it

If your income and expenses are pretty stable, but sometimes your spending veers off course, you may be able to slip into this budget like a comfy sneaker.

The idea here is simple. Split up your income into percentages—a portion for essential expenses, a portion for desired expenses, some for your Seasonal Expenses savings account and a retirement account, and some for your emergency fund. I'm a real believer in saving money and my idea is a little heavier on the emergency fund than other plans you may see out there.

Think of your income as a pie and carve it up in four ways: for example, 50–20–15–15. Split it up so 50% of your income goes toward your essential expenses—meaning your rent, car payment, and debt payments. Variable expenses, like groceries, plus non-monthly expenses, like car maintenance, should also be part of this percentage, because they can be considered essentials. This is where you will move a portion of money into your Seasonal Expenses savings account for those non-monthly expenses.

Twenty percent goes to 'wants' and everyday variable expenses, like clothing, meals out, coffee, Uber. Fifteen percent goes to long-term investments, meaning towards retirement funds/401(k). Freelancers? You've got some retirement options too: Roth, Traditional, and SEP IRAs are for those who work in the gig economy. (More on these to come in Chapter 9.)

And, until you've built it up to the level you want, 15% goes toward your emergency fund. The 15% directed for your emergency fund is a good start and once you put enough money in a liquid, or easily accessible, high-yield savings account for emergencies only, then you can slow down on the emergency fund a bit, by putting less in it and adding more to your investments or your Seasonal Expenses saving account. At the end of this chapter is my whole monologue about what an emergency fund is for and where it's best to keep it. (Hint: Keep it separated from your other accounts to avoid the temptation of dipping into it.)

About that 'high-yield' savings account

Contrary to conventional wisdom, high-yield savings accounts do exist. Well, sort of. I mean, just by going onto Bankrate.com or Nerdwallet.com, you can find the top banks—mostly online banks—that beat the national average interest rate. It means you can get ten times that much or more with a higher yield, just by googling 'banks with the high yield savings.' And though it may not make a huge difference with smaller balances, it can add up over time. Especially with the cash just sitting there in your emergency fund and your Seasonal Expenses savings account. Why not get the highest interest rate out there? Plus, online banks that offer those higher yields make it easy to set up accounts. The point? Don't leave money on the table.

Now about those percentages—most of us don't spend exactly 50% of our income on needs. Maybe you spend more, maybe less. Because you've already filled out your expenses on Alison's No BS Budget Worksheet, it's all laid out before you. Is the total of your average monthly fixed expenses half, less than half, or more than half of your average monthly income?

From there you can play with the numbers on my suggested budgeting method. If your essential expenses are less than half of your average monthly income, go to 40% on the fixed expenses and 30% on wants. Or split the extra 10% between your savings or emergency accounts. If your essential expenses take up 60% of your income, then tinker with the percentages allocated to wants and the two savings categories and make the numbers work for you.

Wherever you land, organize the budget so it's comfortable enough for you that you will actually stick to it. If it's too demanding, it's unlikely that you'll follow through.

One more thing about those percentages—notice that I break the Seasonal Expenses savings account and emergency accounts into separate distributions because these are different buckets— both are priorities and your contributions to them shouldn't be skipped as you get paid. Thinking 'Oh, I'll get to the emergency and savings accounts later this year,' simply doesn't fly anymore. You want that safety net if you completely lose your income.

That said, let's be realistic here. I do believe in 'paying yourself first' (putting money in your Seasonal Expenses savings account, investments, and emergency funds before you do any other spending), but if you're not rolling in dough at the moment, the most important thing is paying your bills. Sometimes you won't have extra money to put into savings. Don't beat yourself up about it. Number one is taking care of essentials. But, if you do skip a month or two of contributions to those accounts, don't forget that you 'owe' those accounts money and you should 'pay them back' as soon as you are able. Investing, saving for seasonal expenses, and for emergencies are priorities, okay? Alright, I will step down from my soap box.

Should I build savings or pay down debt?

Do both. Walk and chew gum. Strike a balance between saving and paying off debt. You might be paying more interest over time, but having savings to cover sudden expenses will keep you out of the debt cycle.

Think baby steps. Pay at least the minimum (ideally a little more) on your credit cards while sending $15 to $20 per paycheck to your savings account. You'll begin to see the amount build—that will feel good—and it will get you into a groove to help you to create good habits.

Why go with the sneaker plan?

This budget is especially good for those of us who don't want to have a budget line item for every dollar spent. There are five ways to split up your money (essential expenses, desired expenses, seasonal expenses savings, retirement, and emergency fund). If you're not into the traditional methods of rigidly budgeting every area of your spending, but you *are* disciplined, then give this one a shot.

But watch out because you could wind up overspending with this method. Since you're not directing a specific number of dollars to every category (food, car, gas, dinner out), it can be easy to spend a little too much on something like food and then forget you've got to fill up the tank in your car, going a little over budget. That's where constantly tracking your spending should kick in, to keep you in line.

How do you track your spending?

Literally monitor it. If you mostly make purchases on a debit card, those purchases will come up in your bank statement. That's why having half-hour weekly dates with your money is so important. Log in and review all your transactions. See what you're buying. Notice your balance. Do you also use credit cards? Log in and review those accounts as well.

By diligently tracking your spending, you become your own watchdog. Being conscious of your spending is important for any budget, but especially this one, because it doesn't impose strict spending limits for each category. For example, with this budget, even if you've allocated $450 per month for groceries, you may let yourself spend $550 one month. But, if you're tracking your spending, you'll see this and know that the next month you'll try to spend $350 to make up for the overage.

SHOE #2: THE 3-INCH HEEL

The envelope system

This method will take some time to get used to, much like wearing a stiletto. But if you've discovered you're spending too much or you're carrying a load of debt and really need to track every dollar, this is the budget method for you.

It's related to the days when we used actual cash for most transactions. Back then, you literally had an envelope for every expense category in your budget and you put the designated amounts into each envelope. Once an envelope was empty, that was it for spending in that category, until you refilled it with more money (and not money from other envelopes). And if you did run out of money in one of your envelopes, it showed you were overspending.

I like this method because every dollar is being allocated, but I actually don't recommend you use cash, because it's just not practical for the 21st century. Fortunately, there are some cashless ways to pull this off. There are apps created specifically to bring envelope budgeting into the modern day: Goodbudget, Mvelopes, and Simple Budget. You can link your bank accounts to the apps and allocate money from your bank account into the 'envelopes' that you create. These apps let you pay bills and manage your envelope budget right from your phone.

If you don't want to go the app route (they carry annual fees and aren't perfect), envelope budgeting will also work with 'digital envelopes' you can create through online banking. This automated way of budgeting is practical because many bills are paid online anyway.

This digital envelope method will combine different expense categories but still have guardrails in place to keep you from overspending.

Do this by having two checking accounts. Checking account #1 for all of your regular bills—mortgage, streaming services, utilities, etc.—essentially anything with a due date. Use checking account #2 for all variable expenses—groceries, gasoline, fun money, etc. I would recommend leaving a small buffer of around $100 in each account as well. Your third account is your savings account for seasonal expenses.

Here's the play-by-play of how to make this work for you:

Your income is deposited into checking account #1. Make sure to leave enough money to cover bills in #1 and use automation or your bank's online bill pay system to pay all your bills with due dates automatically out of this checking account.

Then transfer the money you've budgeted (see the No BS Budget Worksheet) for your variable expenses into checking account #2.

Allocate the money left over and split it between your emergency savings account, your Seasonal Expenses savings account and your long-term investing account.

This automated version of the envelope budgeting method can give you a good visual of your money literally going from one place to another—and may help you with more purposeful spending. The great thing about this? By physically moving your money from account to account, you're more involved with your money and thinking ahead to what you'll need to spend in the coming weeks, instead of robotically shelling it out.

If you want to have more envelopes, open additional accounts that are linked with the others. Most banks don't charge you for having more than one account and you can label them 'Bills,' 'Expenses,' or whatever name is relevant. Your categories or buckets are up to you. Just make sure you remember which expenses come out of each account, or digital envelope. When it comes time to use the money from each account or 'envelope,' you can use a debit card associated with that account.

Having this electronic view of all your spending money and savings in separate envelopes can be helpful in tracking how you're spending and can help you to stay within your budget. Plus, now that you have a better idea about your spending habits, it may be easier to figure out how much you want to allocate to each category. If you find yourself spending more than you've budgeted in one category, you will see it in the zero balance in that category (or, if you keep the suggested buffer, you're left with a $100 balance) and probably need to adjust how you're spending.

Why should you give the 3-inch heel a try?

If you find yourself constantly overspending, this kick-yourself-in-the-ass method (because you're literally putting limits on your spending) is a great way to give yourself some control over your budget categories. You track your spending in real time, and once the money is gone, there's no more until you get paid. Whether you use an app or online banking, with one glance, you can scan all of your spending activity and know where your money stands at that moment.

A bonus with this method? If you use the online banking version of envelope budgeting, you can take advantage of rewards debit cards, many which offer cashback and travel points.

What to watch out for with the 3-inch heel

With the money moving around in and out of your accounts, make sure the balance of your main checking account stays at the minimum required level, so you don't incur overdraft fees.

And don't let the debit card fool you—swiping plastic can make it way too easy to spend. But, if you're regularly tracking your spending, that knowledge will hopefully keep you from feeling like you're on a shopping spree every time you whip out the debit card.

Keep in mind that 'tracking your money fatigue' may set in with this method, because it requires constant monitoring.

Finally, one other drawback to this method, whether you're using the online banking or app envelope system, is the temptation to 'borrow' from the other envelopes. If the month isn't over but you're seeing a zero balance in one or more of your accounts, hold yourself back from moving money from the other accounts. That zero balance (or ideally buffer balance) should be your wake-up call that you're overspending and that you need to rein it in.

SHOE #3: THE FLIP-FLOP

Reverse budgeting

Whoo hoo! Hello, shoe #3.

This is where I fit in. I really don't budget because I live on less than I earn and am all about conscious spending. At the same time, because I have a fear of running out of money, this is how I make sure I don't overspend. If you're not a crazy spender but rather the girl who's got goals and is working toward them, this budget method could be for you.

This method is much less structured than the others—you know, like a flip-flop. But, before you say, 'I'm on board,' ask yourself, are you the type who can live pretty bare bones, so as to not overspend? Can you make a plan and stick to it, without cheating on your budget?

If you answered 'yes' to all those questions, then shoe #3 is for you.

This kind of 'no-budget budget' still requires serious discipline. It's a reverse budgeting method that says, yes, go ahead, pay yourself first.

What does that exactly mean?

Well, most budgets are built around your expenses. But a reverse budget revolves around making savings your priority. It's got three steps.

- First, when you get paid, immediately set aside money for your seasonal expenses savings for all of those non-monthly expenses and contribute to your investments, and emergency accounts (that's called paying yourself first).
- Second, pay your bills and expenses.
- Third, if you have remaining money, that's what you have to spend on fun stuff—you can do anything you want with that money.

With reverse budgeting, you don't have to build your savings with whatever scraps are left over after everything else is paid. You make regular contributions to your Seasonal Expenses savings account, retirement account, and emergency accounts first. Plus, there aren't any line items with this one, so you have a lot more discretion with the money you spend after you've paid yourself.

I'm able to live this way because I automatically put money away as soon as I'm paid. Via automatic transfer, I move my retirement savings out of my (now severance) paycheck. I move another bit of money into my kids' college funds, my Seasonal Expenses account, and then another chunk into my emergency savings fund. I give myself a mental allowance that I stick to for lunches and coffee out every week, and I carry a zero balance on all my credit cards. The way I see it, if I can't pay the bill off each month, I have no business buying it—even with a high limit on my credit card.

Why the flip-flop is a good one to try

This method is pretty low maintenance as you don't have to categorize or have line items for every expense. And, because this budget method puts savings front and center, it forces you to figure out how to work with the leftover money for everything else. Plus, the focus on saving can help you to cut down on impulsive purchases.

When the first thing you do out of the gate is sock money away, it means you have less to spend, which pushes you to use the remaining money on things you need. If you're able to follow this method, consistently saving will pay off by allowing you to feel more secure in your financial future.

Why the flip-flop is tough

No way to sugar coat this one. Reverse budgeting takes commitment and discipline. It means you'll probably have to sacrifice some of the fun stuff, like splurging on new clothes or dinners out. You also need patience—you make regular contributions to savings over weeks, months, and years, and it takes time to see the money start to build up.

This method may not be for you if your total average monthly expenses exceed your average monthly income, in which case it's difficult to save when you're trying to just pay the bills.

WHATEVER BUDGET YOU CHOOSE...

Of course, with all budgets, the key is to stick with them. So that's why it's so important to select one that works for you. Ideally, it'll be structured so you're excited to adhere to the plan. And when you do, you'll reap the benefits. Or, mix and match parts of the budgets to suit your lifestyle. Everyone is different and budgeting is not a one-size-fits-all.

If your financial situation is something you worry about, having a handle on your money will ultimately help you sleep better at night.

A strong budget that you're able to truly follow is a way of telling your money where to go rather than wondering where it went.

"My husband and I regularly have money conversations—he calls them money summits. We recently started a monthly list of everything we spend—from groceries to our mortgage to fun nights out. It gives us a clear picture monthly of what we spend and allows us to ask if we can afford to spend this way. If we can't, what should we start cutting until we can afford to spend that way."

Rebecca Minkoff, fashion designer, fashion mogul, author, and founder of the Female Founder Collective, NY

By the numbers

It's tough for women to save. Here are few of the reasons why:

- On average women earn less than men: Women earn 84 cents for every dollar men make.[20]

- 50% of women say they are behind on retirement savings vs 35% of men with 24% of women saying they are "very behind schedule" vs 14% of men.[21]

- Women participate in retirement plans in greater numbers than men, but they contribute less to their 401(k)s than men. The median household retirement savings for women is $23,000 vs $76,000 for men. And almost one-third of women say they've saved less than $10,000 for retirement, or nothing at all.[22]

- 37% of women have $100 or less in their savings account

vs 28% of men. In addition, 42% of women say they let their minimum checking account balance reach $100 or less vs 31% of men.[23]

- 49% of women have saved less than $25,000, compared to 36% of men.[24]

- Of the 43% of Americans who say they live paycheck to paycheck, 85% are women.[25]

EMERGENCY FUND

One way I've met my money fears head on is to build up some savings for emergencies.

I know, I seem mildly obsessed with the emergency fund, as you can see that it's in the fabric of all the budget strategies. That's so that we aren't blindsided by events and circumstances. None of us knew we'd be living through a pandemic with the economy at a standstill. Covid-19 taught us that life isn't predictable, and we should be prepared. If the pandemic wasn't a wake-up call about the importance of having money set aside for the unpredictable, I don't know what is. There's immense security in having a separate account for things you just can't anticipate. As best we're able, we should have a cushion. I know it's not easy and that savings will take time to accrue. But the time to begin is now.

Once again, the fund is in addition to your Seasonal Expenses savings account and your retirement account. It's money set aside in an account all by itself for the things in life that can come out of nowhere and throw your whole financial world out of whack—the biggies, like:

- losing your job or income

- unexpected medical or dental expenses
- sudden major home repairs
- sudden major car repairs
- death in the family
- the refrigerator decides to stop working

The point is to stash away money for the unexpected. You don't want to be forced into selling long-term investments to pay for these things. When to dip into this fund depends on what you think an emergency is, which is different from what I see as an emergency. You have to make your own call on that. Especially once you hit your emergency fund goal, if you need to use it, use it. That's what it's there for and you can rebuild it again.

You should contribute to this account as you're able. If you're living paycheck to paycheck, it's understandable that it will be difficult to throw money into the fund. (Hopefully budgeting will help you get out of that lifestyle.) If you're unemployed it will be difficult too. I get it. But you need this fund. A Bankrate survey shows a quarter of Americans said their biggest financial regret during the Covid-19 pandemic was not having enough emergency savings to weather the crisis. This shit is real.

And one more thing? Once you put the money in, forget about it. Act like it's not there. Don't break the glass on your fund in case of a non-emergency like buying the Lana Jewelry hoop earrings you saw J.Lo wear, or for a spur of the moment vacation. You're only cheating yourself. And why would you want to do that?

How much to have in the emergency account is up for discussion. Financial experts in the pre-pandemic world often suggested having three to six months of essential living expenses in a liquid savings account. After what we went through, I'm recommending more. I believe setting aside nine to 12 months of essential living expenses is super important. When I was laid off from CNN, I was still able to sleep at night because I knew I had a year of expenses saved up in my emergency fund.

And I know, nine to 12 months sounds like an insurmountable amount of savings to build up. It is a big number. But this is essentially insurance for your budget—and your life. Look, with the global pandemic the unexpected happened. And the repercussions are still with us. Having a financial cushion that will allow you to weather that kind of storm, in my mind, is our new benchmark.

What's the right dollar amount to have in there for you? Add up your monthly costs for all the essential things you spend money on, what you need to survive—rent or mortgage, car payments, gasoline, electricity, cell phone, food—then multiply by nine. And then take the same number and multiply by 12. Those two numbers are the range of money you need to build up in that fund.

It can feel like it will take forever to reach that goal. But slow and steady wins the race. Just like a squirrel, keep putting away the little nuts and eventually you will set aside enough of a cushion to feel financially secure.

Where should you keep your emergency fund?

Savings accounts aren't the best choice for growing your money. So having a chunk of cash sitting in a savings account may not be as profitable as an investment in a fund or stocks that earn dividends, but this a different kind of investment. It's an investment in yourself, it's your safety net if the shit hits the fan, and it's the foundation of a strong financial plan.

So where should you put your emergency fund money?

Whatever you choose, the money should be liquid, meaning you have instant access to it if you need it. Here are some options:

Online bank savings accounts

Online banks, including credit unions, typically have better interest rates than a lot of the big brick-and-mortar banks, partly because they have lower overheads. Some include Ally Bank, Marcus by Goldman Sachs, CIBC Bank, and Alliant Credit Union. At least the money will earn a little interest as it sits there. Make sure your money is in an FDIC- or NCUA-insured account, which means your savings will be insured up to $250,000.

Money market accounts

Stashing the emergency funds in a money market account is also an option. This type of account may also earn higher interest than traditional bank savings accounts. There are several differences. Money market accounts usually come with a debit card and with the capability to write checks from the account. So, that's convenient if you need the money in a hurry. A money market account generally requires you to have a larger minimum deposit to start the account than other savings accounts. And you have to maintain a higher balance in order to receive the higher interest rate.

Certificates of Deposit

Another option is a Certificate of Deposit account (or CD). CDs typically offer higher interest rates than other savings and money market accounts. The catch is your money is tied up for a period of time and so it's less liquid. And while that period could be as little as a month, how do you know an emergency won't come along during that time? You can still withdraw your money before a CD has matured, but you'd be stuck paying an early withdrawal penalty fee. That penalty could either be a flat fee or a percentage of the interest earned on your CD.

That said, if you've got a good chunk of money already saved up in your emergency fund, you might consider layering CDs in what many call a CD ladder. It basically means you split up *some* of your emergency money—leaving some of it in a savings account or money market account, and putting the other part into a bunch of different CDs that have different dates of maturity. The idea is you put part of your money in a one-month CD, another chunk in a three- or six-month CD, and another chunk in a 12- or 18-month CD. This way, your savings earn better interest and become available to you at different times. A CD ladder takes a little planning to set up and to maintain, as you'll have to keep rolling the CDs over as they mature.

And a little tip: Because many CDs just automatically renew, I set a reminder for myself on my calendar a few days before the CD term is up. Because who remembers the maturity day? Not me. I want to know ahead of time when I need to take that money out. And if I miss it, that money could get locked in again.

T-Bills

Don't skip reading this one! I know what you're thinking: 'I don't understand bonds, how they work or where to get one.' Jump to Chapter 9 for all the exciting details about bonds and how to get into these baby bonds. For our purposes at this point, I want to include T-Bills on this list because, like CDs, they're a good place for you to put *part* of the money in your emergency fund. These investments can last as little as one to six months, and upwards from there, and they generate a higher return than a savings account.

A final word on the emergency fund

Now that you have some ideas on how to get your emergency money to work for you, let's talk about where to physically leave it. Out of sight, out of mind, right? It may be a good idea to keep your emergency fund at a bank separate from your main accounts. That way you won't feel tempted to dip into it for a new Apple watch you think you need.

Alright, I did my budget, now how do I make this work?

Now that you've meticulously crunched the numbers and know what your financial picture should look like, how do you get there?

If you've said to yourself, screw this, there's no way to make a budget work, or you're stumped on how to get your spending under control, stop for a moment and take a breath.

There is a way to get a handle on this. In fact, you're already moving in that direction! It may not feel that way at the moment, but you really have just taken the first steps to fix your financial situation: You've taken a good look at your finances and you know what's going on.

The trick to sticking with it?

I've found it's super important to get into a groove of being conscious about how you're spending and saving. Over time, it will become a habit—a good habit. You will actually seek out ways to save money and think twice before you pull out your credit card.

It's also important to check in with your budget every week. It only takes 30 minutes.

This weekly weigh-in will make sure you're on the right track. If you're not, you can see where you need to redirect beginning the following week, instead of resetting a month later.

30-minute weekly money meeting: your budget

10 minutes to look over the past week's transactions.

10 minutes to review your budget—how'd you do? Do you need to adjust?

10 minutes to see/plan what's coming up—bills, events, etc.

It should feel empowering to now know the steps to get your spending and savings in order. If instead you're feeling overwhelmed or anxious, know that it's not that you can't do this. Perhaps it's that you have never tried. It could be fear of the unknown?

Maybe you used to rely on your dad, your husband, or your boyfriend to manage the money. Maybe you thought you couldn't wrap your mind around figuring out your finances. Or maybe you ignored it all, hoping it would just go away. But now that you've created this snapshot of your financial situation, you know where you stand and what you have to do. That's a win.

As you move forward, all these little wins of taking control of your spending are going to add up to big wins that will brick by brick build your confidence in how you handle your money situation. I know because I've been there. I've had to tackle and come to terms with the reality that there was no one to delegate the money stuff to anymore. It's up to me.

JESSICA ALBA, ACTRESS AND FOUNDER OF THE HONEST COMPANY

In her own words

It's not that hard to live within a budget, at the end of the day. It really isn't. There's the money that you need to live, and then, if you are lucky, you'll have only so much money left over that you can save. And always take your taxes out first. That's rule number one. I learned that one early, as a teen, from my Grandpa Jose. You don't want to be stuck owing taxes at the end of the year. And don't live beyond your means—also a lesson from Grandpa. Ultimately, if it all blows up, then what? Once you get your head above water, having a safety net of assets is also important. There are incredibly smart people in banking that you can sit with and work out various scenarios to reach your financial goals. Ask questions and know there are no dumb questions—I've had to get comfortable with that one for sure. And I kind of always live with the mentality of doing what's right for me, rather than trying to keep up with the Joneses or trying to 'flex' or 'floss.' I was never that person. Truthfully, when you die, you can't take any of this stuff with you. So who cares? It's about quality of life really. Can you look in the mirror every day and be happy? And now that I have kids, I want them to be okay and set them up as best I can for their future.

No matter where you are in life, I think you can genuinely start to visualize yourself being financially independent. See yourself living without financial burdens, moving through the world freely, without having to always be in survival mode. Have gratitude for your financial independence, see it, know you are moving in that direction. It's all about the practical day-to-day execution—don't focus on the finish line. Concentrate on what's right in front of you and take that first little step. Be consistent—consistency is key—and be relentlessly optimistic. Every little step you take matters, eventually you'll look up and all those little steps will add up to something much bigger. Sometimes people just want the end goal to happen right now and they forget that it takes a lot of tiny, micro moves, habits changing, a mental shift and oftentimes a reprogramming to achieve the end goal you are striving for. And the journey is never over—every time you hit a milestone, there is another major one farther ahead. Embracing the journey can be hard, but it's important not to be afraid of the challenge. Try to get excited about what you can learn along the way.

Start with deciding that you're ready for change, that you're ready for that first little step, and trust that the universe will show up. For me, at this stage of my journey, I still make mistakes... but I'm doing my best to be my best and I try not to dwell on the challenges or missteps. Instead, I learn, pivot and move forward optimistically.

DASHA KENNEDY, THE BROKE BLACK GIRL, FINANCIAL ACTIVIST

In her own words

When I got control of the loans, I became very proactive with my money. I practiced once a week with what I called a 'money date.' I sat down every single week to go over all of my finances, anything that came in, anything that went out. I am completely in tune with my money. I am looking at my bank statements. I have an Excel sheet on my computer and I'm just calculating what happened over the week. I'm trying to see if I notice any trends like, I'm noticing for the last few weeks, every Wednesday I'm spending an extra hundred dollars—what's happening on Wednesdays? So that keeps me aware. And I want to put myself in a position that nothing catches me off guard.

I do this manually. I like to be involved. I think these different mobile apps sometimes make us lazy. If I rely on these apps to do all of the calculations for me, I get lazy and I'm relying on something else to tell me what's going on. I like to be involved because now that I can do it manually I can teach my children how to do it. I know it step by step, which is much better than me saying, 'Hey, download this app,' and sending them on their way. I can have those conversations with them, talking them through what I'm doing word for word, conversations that my parents didn't have with me.

If you've found that you're burning more than you earn, in the next chapter I'm going to walk you through some ways to cut down on your spending, whether it's renegotiating a loan payment or examining each expense differently—like manicures: Do you really need one every week? There are lots of ways to trim back so that overall, you win big, and still have some money left over for fun. Let's go there now.

CHAPTER 4: TIGHTENING YOUR BELT ISN'T TORTURE

"The only place where success comes before work is in the dictionary."

Vidal Sassoon

NOW THAT YOU have the numbers showing how much money you spend and what you spend it on, you may be faced with the harsh reality that you spend too much and come up short every month. Or that you just meet your bills and have only a little left over. All of this can feel overwhelming, and you may just say to yourself, screw this, there's no way to get this under control. I'm telling you there is. You're already taking steps to fix your financial situation, because you've sat down and taken a close look at what's going on.

BUT HOW DO I LIVE LIKE THIS?

If you're deep in the red every month, you may need to make big changes. What about selling your car? Is public transportation accessible and realistic for you? If you're renting now, do you have space for a roommate? Or what about moving to a different house or apartment with lower overheads? I know, that's drastic. But it's something I had to do during my first year out of college, because I literally ran out of money. I was working freelance at CBS Newspath, an affiliate services division of CBS News as a producer. I earned $100 a day and I lived in New York City, sharing an apartment with four other girls.

After a year on the job, with student loans and living expenses piling up, I literally couldn't afford the Big Apple anymore. I was young and single and was able to pick up and move out of Manhattan to my first on-air gig in Corpus Christi, Texas. At $13,000 a year, my new salary was still nothing to write home about, but my living expenses were so cheap I could handle it. Back then, the last thing I thought about was budgeting. I was just trying to survive and follow my dream of being a journalist.

If you're in a less dire situation, you can begin making cuts in your spending with small steps. Once you get used to living within certain parameters, and budgeting becomes a little more second nature, take bigger steps. The idea here is to set yourself up for success and stay motivated. If you rip the band aid off and take away all the fun money at once, you're less likely to stick to the plan.

Let's go through your expenses and see where you can trim. Little tweaks can add up to a lot, and can become especially noticeable if you make a bunch of little adjustments all at the same time.

NEEDS VS WANTS

If you've discovered that you're in good shape and are meeting your expenses with money left over, I'm over here cheering for you with my arms up in the air! However, even if you have that surplus in your budget that we discussed in Chapter 3, you'll probably find there are ways to save even more money. Keep reading!

On the other hand, if you've taken a good, hard look at your expenses and realize you spend more than you earn, let me help you figure out how to spend less. Breaking the paycheck-to-paycheck cycle begins with prioritizing your expenses. Here's where you have to be brutally honest with yourself. Start by asking, 'What do I *need*, and what do I only *want*?' Yeah, yeah I hear you groaning. This is not always an easy task. If you made wants and needs into a Venn diagram (no, I won't make you do that), I bet many of your wants and needs would overlap. But let's attempt this anyway.

Most of your fixed expenses are probably needs, so most likely there's very little for the chopping block there. But the variable expenses? Now we're talkin'! Yes, that's where the wiggle room is.

Use the following Needs vs Wants Worksheet for lists you're about to make. Food, clothing, shelter, transportation, cell phone, insurance... those all go under the 'Need' column.

Needs versus Wants

Item	Cost	Need?	Want?	Alternate Item

It's easy for wants to enter a gray area, because everyone's needs and wants are different. You need clothing, but does it have to be designer clothing? What if you fall madly in love with a pair of sandals in the store, but know you've got five other pairs at home? Raise your hand if you'd convince yourself to buy them anyway, because you could justify how you 'need' them. 'Well, I can use them for a party this summer.' And just like that, the sandals have become a 'necessary want.' Deep down you know you don't need them, but you cave. So then our list goes out the window. So how do we make sure that doesn't happen?

Trust your instincts

Are you a sucker for an impulse purchase? Can't resist that latest designer bag you just walked by? But a voice in your head says, 'Wait, don't do it.' Follow my five-day rule. It's best to leave the store and wait five days before buying the item. Use the time to shop around to see if you can find it at a lower price. Think carefully. Does the purchase fit into my budget? Do I need this, really? Maybe after cooling off for a few days, you will feel differently.

DECIDE WHERE YOU CAN CUT BACK, GO WITHOUT, OR FIND CHEAPER ALTERNATIVES

The reality is, if you need to reduce your spending, you're going to have to cut some things out. But hopefully you don't have to cut *all* of your wants. Slashing everything is too much like crash dieting— it doesn't bode well for longevity. Instead, take small steps. Let's say you eat lunch out five days a week. Cut back to three days out and bring lunches from home the other two days—it means you'd be spending 40% less. Consider downsizing some of the extras and even some of the 'necessary wants.' Do you have to buy designer for every piece of clothing? Or can you find fashionable alternatives at Amazon or Zara? Did the Covid-19 pandemic help you discover you don't need as much as you thought you did before it, and that you can eliminate some wants and still live and be happy?

How about an affordable Airbnb on your next vacation instead of a hotel? A little trim here, a little trim there, adds up to savings. I'm not trying to tell you what's important and what's not. You do you. I just want you to live below your means and have money left over so you can feel confident and financially independent. But if your spending is sabotaging your goals, then you've got to make an adjustment. We all have areas of spending where we can either make cuts, drastically reduce, or eliminate altogether. So find those areas!

How to reduce fixed expenses

It's difficult to eliminate fixed expenses, but there are ways to save some money here. Zero in on your fixed expenses, starting with the roof over your head. Earlier, I suggested looking to downsize or take on a roommate if you're renting. It's also worth asking your landlord if you can renegotiate your rent. If you don't ask, you don't have a chance of getting. But what if you own? Should you refinance? I'm going to get into this topic in Chapter 6, but depending on your situation, it may be good to refinance if interest rates are at least 1% below your current mortgage rate and if you plan on staying in your home for another five years or so. That way you can recoup your closing costs and see some real benefits.

Health insurance

This is another biggie, but this one is likely hard to reduce. Still, when the term policy is up, shop around for cheaper insurance premiums. Or, if you get insurance through work, spend time to see if there's a better option. Also, be aware of your coverage details— like your deductible and what you're responsible for after meeting the deductible. It's easy to get into the habit of going on autopilot with your employer-sponsored health coverage. But don't. Take a minute and assess what has changed in your life last year and whether your needs are different, and then make your selections.

Childcare costs

There are some ways to lower childcare costs, if you're willing to part with the nanny or group childcare situation you have now. Oftentimes, this is the biggest hurdle to overcome, because the caregiver bond has already been created along with familiarity of your routine. But if your financial situation dictates a change is needed, then start shopping around. Find out what the going rate is for traditional daycare and a nanny. Check out community centers and religious schools that offer daycare. Nanny-sharing is also a popular option. How adjustable is your work schedule? Could you reduce the time your child spends at daycare? See if a family member can pitch in, even for a few hours during the week. Also, check with your employer about whether they offer a dependent care flex spending account. This kind of FSA allows you to fund thousands of dollars towards daycare costs, tax-free. Make sure you only fund the DCFSA with as much as you plan to spend and make sure to use the money before the end of the tax year, so you don't lose the money.

The gym

It's easy for me to say find a cheaper gym, but I hear ya screaming 'No way!' Okay. Maybe you love your gym, not only because it's clean, but because you have friends there or because it offers crucial childcare. Then how about looking at a lower cost membership? It might mean there are limited days or times you can go—fill in the other days with free online workouts that you can do from home. YouTube and Instagram are rife with them. If you don't have hand weights or resistance bands, invest in some if you're into that. You may wind up loving the variety and not always having to leave the house to work out.

Memberships and apps

Think about all the stuff you pay for every month. It's time for some spring cleaning. Do you really need to subscribe to Disney+, Netflix, *and* HBO? Are you actually reading the print magazines that come to your house? If you no longer use them, cancel them now! I recently realized I had a Consumer Reports membership I'd forgotten to cancel, and the monthly cost added up. Look over your cable bill. Do you really watch or need all of those channels? Ditching traditional cable or pay TV is an option worth exploring. If you choose a basic plan and stay away from premium features, you can reap the rewards of cord cutting. But you have to be willing to give up some channels, learn a new interface or deal with a little technical buffering.

Cell phone

Most of us don't look at our cell phone bill when we get it. But if you track and monitor how you use data, you may find you can change to a cheaper plan. Do you have an unlimited plan, but don't use all the data? Do you pay for overages every month and *should* change to unlimited data? Or is there a way you can stay on your plan and use Wi-Fi whenever possible?

- **Opt-in for auto-pay:** Most wireless carriers will slice some money off your bill if you sign up for automated payments. To go to paperless billing, you will have to link a checking account or debit card.

- **Change or remove your cell phone insurance:** This may be risky, but removing insurance coverage is an option if you need to save some money. If you have a premium protection plan, you could instead go for standard insurance, which protects you if your phone is lost, stolen, or damaged. However, if you're prone to dropping your phone like the klutz I am, keep the insurance.

- **Get rid of the extras:** Look at your bill. Do you pay for extra features? Are you paying for a hotspot feature that you don't use? Do you pay to stream HD video but don't even use it? Cancel those add-ons if you don't need them.

- **Keep your phone longer:** You don't have to keep up with the Joneses. I've kept phones for four to five years and they work fine. They're not as cool, but they do the job. And you avoid being locked into another 18 to 24 months of stretched out payments for a new phone. Wait til your phone *really* needs to be replaced before upgrading.

- **Switch to a pre-paid plan or go with a smaller wireless carrier:** Pre-paid carriers charge you for a set amount of voice, text, and data. With a pre-paid plan, there are often lower costs and there's no credit check. But as with everything there are tradeoffs. You may have to pay full price for a new phone, instead of spreading the payments over 24 months. But almost all pre-paid providers have inexpensive phones. The pre-paid brands run on the same networks as the big guys—AT&T, Verizon, T-Mobile, and Sprint—so the drawback is, when a big carrier like Verizon experiences network congestion, it slows down the service of the customers who are on the smaller carriers. But if you are serious about lowering the cost of your cell phone bill, this can help you right away.

- **Have a yearly check-in with insurance carriers and your cellphone provider:** Call your insurance—home, renter's, auto insurance, and negotiate for better deals. Same with your cell phone company. If they're unwilling to do anything to trim even a little off your bills every month, shop around. If you find better deals, consider making a switch.

Which variable expenses can I reduce?

Utilities

Cutting down on energy use is not only good for the planet, it's good for your bill. Your utility bill often comes with a comparison to the same month in the previous year. Make a goal to reduce your utilities bill by 10% each month compared to last year. How?

- **Turn off the lights:** I know, I sound like your mother. And sure, keeping the lights on in your home may not be expensive on a per-watt basis, but the cost adds up over time. To save as much as you can, take advantage of natural sunlight and only turn on lights when you need them. Similarly, instead of turning the heat on or up every time you feel a chill, try putting on a sweatshirt or layer your clothes. And when you're having good weather, instead of turning on the air conditioning, open some windows and take advantage of natural air.

- **Install a programmable thermostat:** This is an easy solution if you want to cut down on energy usage while you're not at home or if you just want to regulate the temperature in your home. That way you can make sure utilities aren't being wasted while you're at work, asleep, or on vacation. And you can save money in the process.

- **Your lightbulbs matter:** Energy-efficient lightbulbs might cost a bit more at first, but they have a much longer life than incandescent bulbs and use far less electricity. That means more money in your pocket in the long run. So try to light up your house in LEDs.

- **Do a maintenance run on your appliances:** This is stuff I pawned off to my husband to do, and when we divorced I had to learn how to make the appliances last in our home, because they need a little TLC. Even if you rent a place and don't actually own the appliances, this pertains to you too! Your landlord may not be in a big rush to replace appliances, and if something breaks, the landlord may drag his or her feet in getting a new one.

  - **Refrigerator:** Clean your refrigerator coils! Who knew that this is a common problem? If your fridge stops working on a hot day, suspect the coils. On many refrigerators, you get to the coils by removing the front grille. Then push a coil cleaning brush (buy it at hardware store) into the coils, pull it back and vacuum it clean. If the coils are located in the back, pull out your fridge to clean them. Cleaning the coils will not only help the refrigerator last longer, but because it will cool more efficiently you will save more on your utility bill!

  - **Dishwasher:** Finding food on your dishes? Don't be so quick to think the appliance is a goner. The filter is most often to blame. If it's clogged with food bits, water can't make it to the spray arms to clean the dishes on the top rack. So you've got to remove the filter inside the dishwasher and clean it. I couldn't find mine, so I googled the make and model and a video on YouTube showed me where to find the filter, how to get it out and clean it.

- **Oven:** If the temperature in your oven seems off, you can recalibrate the temperature setting. Go online and search for a version of your manual by using your oven's model number. Place a good-quality oven thermometer on the center shelf and wait for the oven to maintain a constant temperature. Then follow the procedure outlined in your manual to match the temperature setting to the thermometer reading.

- **Washer/dryer:** If you've got a front-loading washer, there is a filter that needs to be regularly cleaned out every two months. Maybe every month if you run more washes. Old water that didn't drain sits in there, same with the lint and other dirt and it is stinky! The drain pump filter is usually located at the front bottom of the washer. Now your dryer. To keep your dryer working at its best and to keep it from becoming a fire hazard, once a year clean out the dryer vent. Allowing dryer lint and dust to build up, along with the heat, can cause a fire. A clogged clothes dryer can also cause your utility bill to increase by requiring longer drying times for your laundry.

Shopping

- **Groceries:** Here's where I overspend. I justify it by thinking, well, food is a necessity. But that doesn't mean I should be buying everything in sight. Buy what you truly believe you and your family will actually eat. Buy generic. Even supermarkets make their own organic products. I realize this could be a tough area for a big win, when it comes to saving money.

- **Clothing and all things shopping:** If you're on a tight budget, you may want to shop your closet first. Figure out how to live with the clothes you have, at least until you get a handle on your spending. Give yourself a challenge: Only shop if you actually *need* something. Meaning, if your bathing suit is saggy and all the elastic is gone, you'll need to get a new one. Otherwise, wear last year's. If you need something fancy for a wedding, consider borrowing or renting a dress (Rent the Runway comes to mind).

- **Sign up for free customer loyalty or rewards programs with retailers you regularly buy from anyway:** These are the bomb! Whether it's clothes, make-up, skincare, they'll send you emails containing electronic coupons that you wouldn't otherwise get. What's more, the points you earn with retailers often result in dollars toward other purchases. The idea though is *not* to buy just because there's a discount. Don't fall into that trap! Only use these when you actually need something. One thing I did is set up a separate email account just for these rewards programs. When I need something, let's say clothes, I will go to that inbox and see what discounts are being offered.

- **When you do buy online, try to avoid paying shipping fees:** Retailers often have minimum purchase amounts in order to give you free shipping. Review the return policy. Be aware of any restocking fees for items that you return—sometimes there's a fee for each item so you may want to reconsider ordering too much if you're just 'trying on.' If you're allowed to make returns, take note of what the time frame is that you can return items. Make sure the retailer offers free returns via mail or can accept the return in person. Buy the minimum amount, get the free shipping and just make sure to return the extra item or items before the deadline. This strategy calls for someone who is willing to invest the time to make the return.

- **If you must spend, give yourself an allowance:** By breaking down your monthly variable expenses, you already have an idea what you spend every month on clothing. How much should you carve out for clothing? One suggestion from financial planners is that you should spend no more than 5% of your average monthly income on clothing. How do you get that? Multiply your average monthly income by 0.05. So, if you figured out earlier that you take home $4,000 a month, you can spend $200 per month on clothing. That's for a four-person household. If you're single, this 5% clothing allowance assumes you're debt-free.

I get that retail therapy is a thing. I am right there with you. It makes me feel good browsing through websites for clothing or hunting for a fantastic deal on a cute pair of shoes. If I'm feeling blah, buying a little something just brightens my mood. That's all well and good if you have disposable income. And if you know your expenses exceed your income, sadly this therapy method will be of no help. I know that's not what you want to hear. Look. I'm super guilty of impulse buys, but one way I think about it is, how is digging myself into a deeper hole by making this purchase going to help in the long run? Try to distract yourself with something else. A movie. An online workout. Call your girlfriend.

Shop differently

- Consider cheaper/bulk grocery stores
- Avoid convenience stores
- Avoid fancy prepared meal stores
- Take advantage of sales

Mama was right

If you want to save money...

- plan your meals
- check fridge and pantry before going for groceries
- make a list
- don't shop when hungry

Dry cleaning

I go to a local dry cleaner, and boy does the owner smile when I walk in. He knows me by name. How could he not? Until recently, I singularly must have been paying half his rent. I'm trying to be better. Now, before I purchase clothing I look at the washing instructions to see if I can handwash the item. And that information factors into the decision of whether I will buy it. I already notice how much money I'm saving. Baby steps. Baby steps.

Meals out

I realize we have busy lives, and planning for meals is just one more thing to add to the list. But if you're trying to budget, there's a good bit of wiggle room here to save money. If you can't have breakfast at home, bring it from home. Same with lunch. Especially if you just spent a bunch of money at the supermarket, then to continue to eat your meals out sounds like a lot of extra money going towards food costs. Don't laugh, but I bought a cute little insulated bag that I take with me. I fill it with breakfast, whether it's yogurt or overnight oats that I prepare the previous night. I also have coffee already made that I can just grab and go. I know I'm the type to graze all day so I also include snacks in that little bag, so I limit my food purchases that day. Because the little expenses can add up.

Coffee drinkers, I'm looking at you. A $4 latte every workday is $20 a week and $960 a year. Yeah yeah yeah, you've heard this all before. So I'll stop picking on you. It's not just coffee. Do you grab an iced tea, bottle of water, bag of chips? If every day you pick a little something up to snack on, it will take a bite out of your wallet.

If you do eat lunch out, keep a weekly lunch allowance. Unless I'm having a rough day and want to 'eat' my feelings, I stick to a lunch allowance in my head and I make sure I don't order the most expensive item on the menu. The driving force with this is discipline. My motivator? I don't want to eat all my money, literally. It will feel like a drag at first, because you may be restricting yourself from what you really want on the menu, but just give it a try. If you do this every day, you will build some momentum. And you will be astounded by how much money you will save with just these 'rules' you put on breakfast and lunch.

If you eat most of your dinners out and go to the grocery store and buy food for dinner at home, then you are wasting money. Plain and simple. Why not invite friends over for dinner instead on some of those days? Potluck dinners are fun. Or if you just enjoy eating dinners out, buy fewer dinner items at the grocery store. Make yourself a dinners out budget and try to go to less expensive places or fewer pricey ones.

Me time

Do your own nails. I know. How dare I suggest this? I used to go every week for a manicure and every three to four weeks for a pedicure. Then the pandemic happened, and with nail salons closed I soon realized I can do my nails myself. I bought some lovely polish colors at the drug store, along with cuticle and nail clippers, nail files, and top coat. And the bonus? My nails are actually healthier because the products I'm using aren't as harsh as those in the salons. I'm not saying don't ever go to the nail salon. I still love to go every now and then. But I'd rather save some money. Now when I get my nails done, it's more like a treat and I appreciate it more.

Expensive make-up

If you regularly buy make-up from Chanel or Tom Ford, you may want to reconsider how you shop for make-up in the future. I'm all for treating myself to an expensive lipstick because it's *that* color, but you'd be surprised to see the drugstore has a lot of great make-up and dupes of the high-priced items. Give it a chance. Same for hair products and skincare. There are lots of cheaper alternatives, (just google dupes of your favorite colors) so don't feel compelled to buy the most expensive stuff.

How to reduce non-monthly expenses

Part of the reason for stashing money into your Seasonal Expenses account every month is for when the big surprise expenses come up. If you have money set aside already, you don't have to freak out about not having any money to pay for them. I wanted to give you some ideas on how to save some money on a few of those non-monthly expenses.

Negotiate medical bills

A medical crisis can quickly turn into a financial crisis. Knowing this, it may also be possible to negotiate your medical bills and pay a lower amount.

If they're hospital bills

I consulted Jared Walker, the founder of Dollar For, about what to do when you come face to face with a ginormous hospital bill.

Dollar For is a national non-profit that helps people with ways to trim, negotiate, or eliminate their medical bills. He says the biggest misconception about medical debt is that people see the bill and there's a sense of urgency—they think they have to pay it quickly. Not the case, Walker says. He told me that the amount on your hospital bill, that exact amount, *can* be changed.

First, always check to see if you're eligible for Charity Care, or a financial assistance policy. Almost every non-profit and for-profit hospital in the U.S. offers it. So first find out if you qualify. If you do, the bill can get written off. How do you find out? Google the hospital name plus the words 'financial assistance.' The income range should be on the hospital's website. Or go to the website for 'Dollar For' and search the database. You may be surprised to see the income ranges to qualify are quite high. Hospitals won't come out and tell you about Charity Care. If you think you're eligible, you have to be the one to take the reins. Fill out the application, send it in, and see what is determined.

If you're not eligible for Charity Care because your income is too high, call the hospital billing department and ask for an itemized bill. It will be a long receipt and will have codes, called CPT codes. Those CPT codes identify what happened and the procedures that were done. Then you should go online to FAIR Health or Healthcare Bluebook and look up the codes, cross-referencing with what you received from the hospital. You may see you were overcharged. You will see if you were charged $100 for a Tylenol. When you call hospitals out on those ridiculous charges, they should adjust them. The next step? Call the hospital back, tell them what you found, and ask for a reduction. Many times, hospitals will offer you some type of settlement.

Walker says when he's done this for people in need, if he didn't like the settlement amount, he'd hang up and call again the next week and ask for someone else and get a different amount. He says he did this over the course of several weeks until finally he got the lowest settlement amount.

When you get to a final amount, keep in mind that the three credit bureaus have changed their rules on medical debt and how that can impact your credit score. Bills under $500 are not able to impact your score. And if it's over that amount, you have a year until an unpaid medical bill can impact your credit score. It means you have some time to pay it—so take a deep breath, take the time to put money aside, knowing it won't impact you negatively for a year. The collection agencies will make it sound like it's an urgent matter, but the law says you have a year. Just don't lose track of the bill during that time. Maybe set some alerts on your calendar as you pay it down.

If they're doctor's bills

Before you go see any medical professional, make sure that provider is in-network (meaning they basically have a contract with your health plan provider to give you services at a rate that's already been negotiated). It means that as a patient, you'll typically pay less for services, than if you saw a doctor who is out of network.

A word of warning about group practices: It's easy to assume that if one doctor or dentist in the group takes your insurance, that they all do. I've learned the hard way that's just not true. So double-check.

Also, doctor billing offices make more mistakes than you may realize—roughly 80% of all medical bills contain errors. I recently had a dental procedure and through a little research (just calling the insurance company) I discovered the dental office not only over-billed the insurer but charged me half of the bill when I was only supposed to be charged 10%. Now I just need to be reimbursed the almost $700 that I overpaid. The real rub? If I didn't catch this mistake, it's unlikely I would have been reimbursed. The insurance company told me no one would have notified me about the error. The lesson? No one is going to hold your hand here and give you a heads-up.

Look over your doctor's bills closely and understand how your health insurance coverage works. Don't just pay your medical bill without scrutinizing it. Ask your doctor's office for an itemized bill that shows each specific charge broken down, along with the billing code. Then call your insurer to go over the codes with you to make sure you weren't charged for a procedure you didn't receive or if you were double charged. Much like with hospital bills, you could also go to FAIR Health or Healthcare Bluebook and look up the procedure codes there and cross reference with what you received from the insurance company and the doctor's office. If the amounts don't match up, there's probably room for negotiation.

Even if the numbers do match up and you're having trouble paying the bill, you can still negotiate. Call your doctor's office to see if they offer discounts for financial hardship or if they have relief programs. If there are fees on the bill, ask them to waive those charges. If all else fails, offer to pay in full if they can come to some sort of settlement amount that is lower. Also, many doctor's offices offer payment plans at a lower interest rate than your credit card or no interest rate. They ultimately want to get paid, and may be willing to cut a deal if there's a settlement amount they can count on.

Car maintenance

Along with the family finances and maintenance around the house, car maintenance is another area I delegated to my husband. Oil changes and putting gas in the car were pretty much all I did. That all changed when we divorced. The idea here is to keep your car in good shape and stay on top of issues so they don't get worse. Just like how you should do a maintenance run on your appliances.

- **Know the vehicle's scheduled maintenance:** You will find this in the owner's manual. So dig it out of the glovebox and you will see what the schedule is for preventative maintenance. Changing the oil on time is one of the most useful maintenance steps you can take. If the mechanic then hands you a laundry list of added maintenance services that are 'needed' make sure it coincides with the mileage on your vehicle, which is found in the owner's manual. If you can't afford it that day, find out which services are most important and which can wait. Come back another time for the others, allowing you to budget for those.

- **Inflate your tires:** You lose gas mileage if the air pressure in your tires is low. So just by inflating your tires if they're low, you can improve your gas mileage. Just read your car's manual to see what the recommended tire pressure is, then head to the gas station. Ask the attendant if they have a tire air gauge you can borrow, then stop over by the air pump. Check your tires, then use the pump to fill them up to where they should be.

- **Change out your air filter:** A clean air filter can improve your gas mileage by up to 7%, saving you more than $100 for every 10,000 miles driven in an average vehicle.

- **Find an auto repair shop:** Yes, even if you don't need one at the moment, now is the time to scope one out because you're not frazzled about needing an auto repair at this moment. Ask family, friends, people you work with, if they have a mechanic they trust. Look for a place that's convenient and that specializes in your particular car. Or you can call your auto insurance carrier to see which auto repair shop they support. You'll probably want to make sure it's in a convenient location for you. Once you decide on a shop, put the name in your phone so you have the number on you. And when you're in a pinch, you would have already done the research and there's less of a chance you'll be ripped off by a mechanic that you were rushed to find.

- **Don't ignore the lights:** If your check-engine light comes on, don't wait weeks to get it checked. Take it to get checked within a few days. It could be nothing, but it could also be something serious. If it's serious and you wait, that could mean a big price to pay.

- **Get an idea of charges for repairs:** Women get taken advantage of all the time when they bring their vehicles in for repair. It helps to know the usual charges for car repairs in your area. There are a couple of websites that give estimates for common repair jobs on your make of car where you live. RepairPal and AutoMD provide a range of fair price estimates in your zip code.

- **Sometimes do it yourself:** Yes, some things you can do yourself! Changing the wiper blades or the air filter are two that come to mind. Go to a local auto parts store to help you choose the correct wiper blades or air filter. Then ask to get help installing the parts. I've found they're more than happy to help, because they want to keep your business. And you save money.

- **Dents and chips:** Repairing dents, chips, and dings will help your car maintain its value and can help to prevent rust, so you'll want to get those taken care of. But you don't necessarily have to go to an autobody shop, which can be very expensive. It may be worthwhile to check out used car lots to see if you can find out who makes those kinds of repairs on the used cars that come in for resale. You may find a better price.

Unexpected home repairs

The problem won't just disappear, so don't ignore it. When a repair pops up, take care of it. A report from NerdWallet says just 55% of us would handle a repair right away and 9% of millennials would wait until the problem started causing damage. An issue that starts small can quickly escalate into an expensive headache. For example, a leaky pipe under the sink could eventually lead to a rotten subfloor, hiking the cost of your problem.

Consider doing it yourself

A caveat here, first give your skill level a reality check. You don't want to screw up a DIY project and then the problem becomes more expensive for you to fix. But if you can handle it, DIY projects generally cost less than hiring a professional, especially since you aren't paying for labor. YouTube is often very helpful with many projects. Nothing like a video play-by-play of what you need to do, to do it right. I never thought I would put my hands inside toilet water the way I do now (thank goodness for gloves) but I've saved a good bit of money fixing various toilet issues with the help of online videos.

In Chapter 6 there are some great tips for what things around the house need routine maintenance, which will help maintain value.

Gift-giving

If you're on a tight budget, gift-giving has a way of getting costly, not just during the holidays, but throughout the year. And you can't always plan who you will buy gifts for. Here are some ways to approach gift-giving that can save you money.

- **Shop online:** Shopping online can help you stay within your budget. You shop under no pressure and see how much you're spending before you actually buy.

- **Give a shared gift:** Sharing the cost of a gift can allow you to afford a more expensive gift or to give that person something they've wanted but can't afford. Split the cost with friends or relatives who were also going to give that person a gift.

- **Don't leave it til the last minute:** If you're pressed for time in getting the gift you have a better chance of spending more money, because you will be up against a deadline. If you shop in advance, you will be able to compare deals and avoid the need to pay higher shipping charges to expedite packages.

- **DIY your gifts:** Gifts that you put together or make yourself for someone else can often be better than the ones you buy in the store. Seriously! So don't be afraid to tap into your creative side and make something that can wow the gift recipient.

MADISON ALCAREZ, CAKE SHOP OWNER

In her own words

I feel more confident and just better about myself when I'm saving money and seeing it build. I put small amounts away whenever I can.

Sticking to my budget would help me be more consistent. I think this time I'm going to make a spreadsheet so I can see everything in front of me.

I know that I've been spending on things I don't really need. My biggest splurge is anything related to health or fitness. So new hand weights or organic make-up from Whole Foods and those little purchases that I make from things I see on Instagram and Amazon. You know, needless things. It adds up to like $50 to $75 a month.

I've decided to use my money more wisely now and less frivolously.

Can you feel it? You are well on your way to taking control of your finances. You've probably figured it out already, but as you continue on this journey you're going to require discipline and self-control in terms of how you spend your money. Now it's time to formulate a battle plan to tackle your debt. If you're debt-free and you have great credit history, skip Chapter 5—and congratulations!

CHAPTER 5: A CAN-DO ACTION PLAN FOR PAYING DOWN DEBT AND BUILDING UP CREDIT

"Do or do not. There is no try."

Yoda

WHILE IT'S OKAY to have *some* debt, carrying loads of it can undermine everything you're working for as you get your financial shit together. Making endless payments with high interest rates means you're losing money that would otherwise go to your savings, investment, and emergency accounts. Excessive and badly managed debt also hurts your credit score, which makes it harder to qualify for a loan, and when you do, your interest rate is significantly higher—this goes for credit cards too.

What's the first thing to do to get out from under a mountain of debt? Make up your mind that this time you're really going to straighten out your debt and credit situation. It's pointless to read advice on how to handle it unless you make the commitment to change it.

Change begins with dipping your toe in and starting.

So, let's start by making sure we understand credit, debt, and how one affects the other.

UNDERSTANDING CREDIT

Credit is the ability to borrow money with the promise that you'll pay it back in the future. That arrangement often comes with interest. Like it or not, we run on credit. It's not easy or convenient to pay for everything with cash. Whether you want to get a mortgage for a house, a student loan to pay for college, or use your credit card to charge some drinks with friends, you're going to need a lender to extend you a line of credit, a.k.a. money. Before any of that happens, you have to have already demonstrated that you are capable of paying it back. That's where your credit report and credit score come into play.

Your credit report

Your credit report contains a history of your financial behavior, including your personal information like your employer and current and previous home addresses. It also covers:

- the number of open accounts you have, along with their current balance
- your payment history, including any late or missed payments
- loans you've taken out and the remaining balances
- any financial disruptions like a bankruptcy or foreclosure

How does your information get there? Financial institutions report your activity to some or all three of the major credit bureaus: Equifax, TransUnion, and Experian. Each bureau produces a credit report that you can see for free by going to AnnualCreditReport.com.

The Fair Credit Reporting Act in the United States gives you free access to your reports—but they do not include your credit score. More on that in a moment.

You should review your credit reports at least once a year, but depending on your situation, you should probably check more often. Each of the three credit bureaus produces its own report and I'd suggest checking them all as often as once every quarter. Why check all three? Because although the bureaus collect similar information and offer similar services, they can be different because credit bureaus may not receive all of the same information about your credit accounts. There are also different scoring models in calculating your credit score. The only way to know if there is a material difference is to check all three.

Why should you check?

Monitoring what's happening in your credit world can alert you to problems like a payment you forgot to make, fraudulent activity, or even identity theft—this could mean there's a credit card open on your record that *you* never actually opened. Keeping tabs also lets you track your own behavior and catch incorrect information. If you find errors, file a dispute online. The credit bureaus will investigate and have to remove the information they can't verify.

Your credit score

Your credit score is not just the number that tells a lender whether you should get a loan and what interest rate you will be charged, it also determines whether you can get access to the most rewarding credit cards on the market and at what rate. It's the number that tells landlords if they should rent to you, and some potential employers whether they should hire you. The list goes on.

Your credit score paints a picture of your overall financial health and your creditworthiness.

How creditworthy you are boils down to a three-digit credit score and, like it or not, it is the key to your financial life. It represents your history of borrowing and paying back money. So if you want to borrow money, rent an apartment, open an account for utilities in your apartment, those places will pull your credit score.

Who or what is the keeper of your credit score?

FICO and VantageScore are the two main credit scoring systems. FICO is an analytics company and lenders use its credit scores the most. FICO produces credit scores based on the information in your credit reports that are compiled by Experian, Equifax, and TransUnion. VantageScore is newer on the scene and is a competing model for FICO scores.

The higher your score, the better chance you have of borrowing money at the lowest interest rates available. A poor credit score could mean paying high interest rates on credit cards and loans if you get approved at all. If you've got bad credit, you might be asked to pay an upfront deposit just to open a cellphone account.

Credit scores are grouped into bands ranging from 'exceptional' to 'poor.' These are:

Exceptional: 800 and above

Very Good: 740 to 799

Good: 670 to 739

Fair: 580 to 669

Poor: 579 and below

Before you start stressing, let me point out that you don't need an exceptional score to get the best interest rates. Generally, a FICO score above 760 gets you access to the same rates and terms as someone with perfect credit.

What factors go into your credit score?

The actual formula for your score is secret (of course it is!), but your FICO score is calculated using different pieces of credit data in your credit report. There are five main credit score factors. The list starts with the most important factor.

- **Payment history (35%):** Paying your bills on time not only means you avoid late fees, it's also the number one factor to maintain a good FICO score. Payment history accounts for more than a third of your number. Even if you miss one or two payments it can seriously hurt your score. The lesson? Pay your bills on time.

- **Amounts owed (30%):** This is the second most important factor. And here, size matters. In this case it's the proportion of your available credit that you've used. The lingo for this is the 'credit utilization ratio.' The lower your ratio, or utilization percentage, the better your credit score.

- **Length of credit history (15%):** Lenders want to know you've been in the credit game a while. Your credit score will continue to improve as your credit history grows.

- **Credit mix (10%):** A wide variety of accounts helps to boost your credit score. This shows you can handle different kinds of debt, like credit cards, student loans, and mortgages. Whatever the mix of debt you have, all of the accounts need to be in good standing.

- **New credit (10%):** Too many 'hard inquiries'—when a creditor checks your credit before making a lending decision—within a short period of time can hurt your score even if you don't get approved for the credit card or loan. So don't exceed five hard inquiries in two years. Try to space them out to no more than one every six months. If you get rejected for a credit card, don't try your luck somewhere else immediately. You're better off waiting several months and improving your credit first. But a single hard inquiry is likely to have a minor effect unless you have other negative marks. Otherwise, your score could recover or even rise within a few months. If you're new to credit, though, the impact of a hard inquiry may be more significant. Additionally, if you're rate shopping for loans, be speedy about it. Do it within about 45 days so all the credit inquiries are treated as one.

How to look up your credit score

Let's put the myth to rest: Checking your credit score doesn't damage your credit score. Check it every week if you want! It's known as a 'soft inquiry.' Some companies provide scores for free, while others charge a fee. To access your score, you may need to provide some personal information like your date of birth, address, and Social Security information. Here are some places to go to get your credit score:

- **Credit bureaus:** You can get your scores from the three credit reporting agencies: Equifax, Experian, and TransUnion, but you may be charged a fee.

- **Credit card companies:** This may be the easiest way. Plus it's free. If you have a credit card, the lender may provide access to your credit score on your monthly statement or on your online account. Peruse your online account. You may be surprised to see it's in plain view!

- **Your bank:** If you're signed up for online banking or through a bank's app, you can see your credit score.

HOW TO BUILD YOUR CREDIT FROM SCRATCH

If you're just starting out and have no credit or a low credit score because you have no credit history, it's easier to build your credit from scratch than it is to rebuild after a misstep. How do you start? Here are some ways.

Become an authorized user

Get on a parent's credit card as an authorized user if they have a positive credit history. This can really jump-start your credit journey. The benefits can be pretty immediate—within a month or two—especially if you're starting from nothing. But be aware that if your parent takes you off of it, your credit could take a substantial drop. So it's best to have a path in mind, like maybe you're on there as an authorized user and then that helps you get a student credit card or a secured credit card. So you're on both of those simultaneously for a bit and then you eventually drop the authorized user relationship.

Open a secured credit card

Secured credit cards are easier to get if you have no credit or bad credit. When you open an account, the card requires a cash security deposit. The credit limit you'll be given is often equal to the deposit amount. And then here's how these cards work:

1. Apply for the secured credit card—be aware if there are any fees to have the card.

2. Pay a deposit.

3. Use the card, build credit.

4. Get your deposit back.

5. Move on to an unsecured card that doesn't require a security deposit.

Secured cards work like any other credit card. Your bill comes monthly, and you pay for the purchases you've made. No, your deposit is *not* used to pay for purchases. You do incur interest if you carry a balance. You can build your credit by using the card responsibly and paying your balance on time. It can take six months to a year to build your credit score enough that you're able to qualify for an unsecured card, or a credit card that doesn't require a security deposit.

Alternative credit scoring

Being an authorized user will give you a chance to establish some accounts in your own name. You could take advantage of alternative credit scoring systems like Experian Boost, which gives you points on your credit score for things that haven't historically counted, like rent payments, streaming services, utilities, and cell phone plans. With Experian Boost, you give Experian permission to scan your bank account and let these types of payments 'count' toward your Experian credit score. Experian says Boost counts only positive payment history, so missed payments will not hurt your score. To sign up for this service, you'll need to have at least one active credit account like a credit card or personal loan. The average boost in your credit score is about 13 points, which is potentially significant. If you're on the border of a higher credit score band, every little bit counts.

Buy now, pay later

The industry is in the process of incorporating buy now, pay later (BNPL) credit into credit scores. Whether you're shopping online or in real life, instead of paying full price for your item, you often have an option of buying now and paying later in installments. You'll make the initial payment on your credit or debit card and then you'll pay the rest at regular intervals, usually split into four payments due every two weeks. So if you buy something for $300, you'll pay $75 when you check out, and you'll be billed for the other three payments over the following six weeks. If you make all your payments on time, you won't have any fees or interest to pay. But there are longer BNPL plans that may charge an annual percentage rate of up to 36%. The fees could also be hefty. If you're late making a payment or you have to reschedule a payment the fees range from $1 to $15.

Here's where I will put up a big red flag. It smells and sounds like a credit card, but isn't. Yet it carries risks. This method of paying can be a slippery slope where you overspend and don't even realize it. There's mental accounting that goes on where it doesn't feel like a $200 pair of shoes anymore. It's just four easy payments of $50. Also, if you have multiple BNPL plans running at the same time you could lose track and then slip up and pay late. The interest and fees can add up fast.

If you've got to use this method of payment, I suggest that you only use it for essentials—like a computer for school or to replace an appliance that just broke. Just be sure that you can pay back the cost by the time the installment plan ends.

HOW TO RECOVER FROM BAD CREDIT

Building your credit back from bad to good is possible. Just remember that credit building is more of a marathon than a sprint. But if you've got a low score, you're more likely to improve your score faster than someone who wants to go from good to excellent.

Small changes could make a big difference. How big? I'm talkin' a 100-point increase pretty quickly.

Here are some ways:

Be strategic in how you use your credit cards

Credit utilization—there's that phrase again. It's the portion of your credit limits that you're using versus how much credit you have available. Experts say use less than 30% of your limit on any card—and the lower the better. So much of improving your credit score is about the long game, but something you can do quickly is to lower your credit utilization ratio. That's the credit you're *using* divided by credit *available* to you. The goal is to make sure your balance is low when the card issuer reports it to the credit bureaus, because that's what is used in calculating your score.

One trick is to pay down the balance even before the billing cycle ends. Make an extra payment or two during the month so you can knock the balance down before the statement even comes out. The results are fast. As soon as your credit card reports a lower balance to the credit bureaus, that lower utilization will be used in calculating your score.

Call your credit card issuer and ask for a higher credit limit. The results are fast with this one too. When your credit limit goes up and your balance stays the same (although I hope you're paying it down!), your overall credit utilization will instantly be lowered. That in turn will improve your credit. But this isn't the time to flex and go on a shopping spree because your credit limit is higher. Resist the temptation! A quick tip: When you contact your card issuer, see if it's possible to avoid a 'hard' credit inquiry which can temporarily make your score drop a few points.

Pay your bills on time

Yes, I know this one is obvious, but no strategy to improve your credit will work if you pay your credit card bills late. Even one late payment drags down your score. That's why I encourage you to automate your bill payments—from your utilities to your rent to your car payments. Paying your bills on time is one of the biggest factors in your credit score. Set it up, but don't just forget about it. Check regularly to see whether those bills have suddenly gone up and to make sure you have enough in your account to cover them.

If you miss a payment, call the creditor immediately and be ready to pay as soon as you can. Especially with missed payments of 30 days or more, ask the representative if the creditor will consider no longer reporting the missed payment to the credit bureaus. Late payments can stay on your credit reports for seven and a half years.

You don't have to just wait for the statement close date to pay. You can also pay bi-weekly. That will help you improve your payment history and keep your credit utilization low.

Use a secured credit card

You don't have to be new to the world of credit to reap the credit-building benefits of this type of card. If you use it and pay on time you will add more positive credit history to your record and dilute past missteps. The goal is to build a record of keeping your balance low and paying on time. Try to find a card that reports your credit activity to all three major credit bureaus.

Get credit for rent and utility payments

This too helps to rebuild your credit. Look for free services like Pinata that report rent payments to credit bureaus (Pinata reports to TransUnion). If your landlord signs up for a specific partnership with Pinata, your rent payments can be reported to all three bureaus. Experian Boost may also help.

Don't rush to close or cancel your credit card

If you want to close your card, just do it with a plan in mind. If you're looking to take out a loan in the near future, for example, wait until you've secured the loan before closing the card. Cancelling your credit card can lower your credit score. Why? For one, it lowers your credit utilization ratio, meaning it shrinks your available credit. The more credit you have available and the less you use, the more responsible you look. Second, if you're looking to cancel an old card, especially if you've had it for years, you will lose all that cred, pardon the pun. In other words you will lose all that credit history you've built up, showing for example, years of on-time payments. Generally, the longer an account has been open and active, the better it is for your credit score. The same goes for paying off a loan. It's a little twisted thinking, but closing that line of credit might lead to a drop in your credit score. The good news is that drop should be temporary.

DIGGING YOURSELF OUT OF CREDIT CARD DEBT

Not all debt is bad. Mortgage debt, paid on time, for instance, helps build your credit score. But credit card debt? It's not the kind of debt you want to carry. If you don't pay your full balance every month, that's the kind of debt that can pile up and pile up fast. That revolving debt means the outfit you were so psyched to buy on sale for $100 could wind up costing you double or triple if you have a high interest rate on your card and you don't pay off your balance when you get the bill.

The average interest rate? It's a real whopper: 21%. That's easily three, four times—maybe even more—the rate of other debt like mortgages, car loans, and student loans. For most of us it's the highest cost debt we're paying.

ABBY, EXECUTIVE ASSISTANT

A cautionary tale

A lot of my issues stem from generational upbringing. We weren't affluent. My dad took over his family's trucking and warehouse company and that's all he knew. He never pursued anything else. He doesn't have any schooling and did not go to college. My mom was a hard worker, but she also did not have schooling. So both of them lacked financial literacy. I don't blame them. It is what it is.

I got my first credit card out of high school. I was working at a bakery and my dad was trying to teach me about credit cards and establishing credits so that when I got older I could buy a house, get a car, and make it in society.

But what we both lacked was knowledge of how to maintain and actually use a credit card. I knew I had to spend on the credit card to build credit, but I never knew how to pay it off. I didn't know what interest rates and APRs and cash advances were, or how to pay them in full while still covering my important bills. I was spending more, not making enough.

By the time I graduated college, I was already in so deep that I just lived on credit. I would pay a certain amount to the credit cards, but I used them to live—to buy food, water, and gas and to pay utility bills. And then the snowball effect started to happen.

I'm honestly at my breaking point right now, because interest rates are just so high and I fell so behind on paying the minimum payment—I don't even think I've hit any of the principal. I'm just paying the interest. I have four credit cards and three personal loans. The total revolving debt is $53,000. My debt is almost as much as my income. I'm bringing in $70,000. That's after a 10% raise. But I'm not making any progress. My take home is only $900 a week.

I do have a 401(k), a Roth IRA, and a high-yield savings account. I used money in there for a car battery that just went.

I'm putting 7% of my income into my 401(k). My employer doesn't offer matching. My accountant advised 7%.

I feel ashamed and a little guilty. I'm making decent money, but my financial situation is not changing.

(Can you tell where the most wiggle room is for Abby to pay down her debt? I talked with a Certified Financial Planner™ who suggested that Abby should find a way to bring in more income, stop contributing to her 401(k), seek credit counseling, and possibly even file for bankruptcy.)

If you're sitting on a mound of credit card debt, I get it, it's really, really hard to come up for air and feel like you're paying it down. But you're not alone. About half of all credit card holders carry debt from month to month. So before I preach your new rules for the road, let's tackle that existing debt.

Follow one of these three ridiculously simple strategies to say sayonara to your debt

Especially if you're carrying a high amount of debt on your credit cards, getting rid of it takes some planning and even a strategy.

Think back to the shoe personalities we used when trying to decide which budget would best fit you. We can use those same personalities for different debt payment strategies. The key is to not get discouraged. Here are three ways to start.

The sneaker—focus on the highest interest rate debt

If you're an athlete, you know that your sneakers are essential to your ability to perform—and with sneakers you can really cinch the amount of debt you're carrying. The focus here is on paying off debts with the highest interest rates. Even better, pay twice in your billing cycle to really cut through the interest charges on top of the original debt amount.

The 3-inch heel—go for the highest balance

This one is for the woman who wants to stand up to her biggest balance and who's able to stay motivated over the long haul. Focus your energies on paying off your debt on the card that carries the highest balance. This may take a while, but it will help improve your credit score faster.

The flip-flop—target the lowest balance

Like a comfy pair of flip-flops, this is a more easy-going strategy to dig into your debt. It involves tackling the lowest balance first. This approach is less likely to noticeably impact your lifestyle and it does provide small wins, but it'll also take you longer to get out from under and improve your credit score. But if conquering one debt will inspire you to stick with the program, it's worth it. Once you pay off your smallest debt, take the payment you'd put towards it and add it to the payment you're already making towards your next smallest debt. That way with each debt you pay off, you'll chip away faster at the next larger one you owe.

Whatever strategy you choose, you must still pay at least the minimums on all the other accounts.

Once you've picked your approach, choose one or more of the following options to accelerate your debt repayment.

Option 1: move your debt to a 0% balance transfer card

If you've got a ton of debt and you're on the fence about a balance transfer card, I say hell yes, just do it! Getting a zero-balance-transfer credit card is the quickest way to get out from under the debt mountain. It sounds almost too good to be true. You take your 20% credit card rate on average and trade it for a 0% rate, which can last for anywhere up to two years. And with all of your money going towards paying off your debt instead of any interest, it means you can pay off your debt faster. It also means you can save hundreds, even thousands of dollars in interest payments. But zero interest doesn't last forever. You have to pay off as much as you can during the limited time that you have. Also take notice if there's a balance transfer fee. Many cards charge one, but not all cards have this fee. So shop around online for the best option for you.

Here's how it works:

Apply for a card

Search online for cards with an introductory 0% annual percentage rate (APR) offer on balance transfers. To qualify for the best offers, you generally need to have good or excellent credit. But try anyway if your credit is fair—there are some offers out there for you, too. And make sure the new card has at least as high a credit limit as your old card, or your credit score could be negatively affected—you want to have the same available credit as you did before or more (even though the plan is to *not* use it!). By opening a new card you'll also get the added bonus of a positive uptick in your credit score, since you'll be increasing your total credit limit. These 0% balance transfer deals are typically for people with good to excellent credit. So if you have a lower credit score, maybe work with a reputable non-profit credit counseling agency like Money Management International or Green Path. They can often negotiate something like a 6% or 7% rate over four of five years, which is actually very similar to the terms that somebody with really good credit could get on a personal loan, which is another form of debt consolidation.

Be aware of the terms

Once you find a card you think you'll qualify for, read the fine print for how much you will be charged to move your money. When you transfer a balance to a new card, you will typically have to pay a balance transfer fee of 3% to 5% of the total balance that you're moving to your new card. It means you could pay $30 to $50 for every $1,000 transferred.

If you need time to pay off your balance, paying the fee is definitely worth it because it is less than you'd pay in interest with your original card.

There are some credit cards without transfer fees. Also it is possible, though difficult, to negotiate the fee if you call the card provider.

If you're approved, initiate the balance transfer

Whether online or by phone, you'll need to provide information about the debt you want to move, like the issuer name, the amount of debt, and the account information.

Wait for the transfer to go through

The balance transfer could take two weeks or more, and once it's approved, the issuer will generally pay off your old account directly. That old balance, plus the balance transfer fee if there is one, will show up on your new account.

Pay down your balance

When the balance appears on your new card, you're responsible for making monthly payments on that account.

Here comes the strategic part. With the terms of your new card, you'll probably have a good runway of a year or more to pay off your balance. Dare to be among those who can pay it off within that time frame! With these kinds of cards, banks are betting that a good number of people are going to carry debt beyond the term. Without any interest, don't add any new purchases to that card—even if you're tempted because of the 0%. Just don't! You already have existing debt. Pay that off. How to do it within the time frame? Divide what you owe by the number of months in your 0% term and stick to that level of monthly payment.

And remember...

The 'free ride' doesn't last forever! Make sure to read the fine print for how long your 0% interest rate lasts. When the promotional period ends, you're going to get hit with a high interest rate— maybe with a rate higher than your previous card. This is especially important, because if you're unable to pay the whole thing off by the time the term ends, you will be back to accumulating interest— at that rate.

Option 2: take out a personal loan

If you have a lower credit score, it could be tough to get a balance transfer card. Another option is to take out a personal loan in order to get a lower interest rate. The interest rate won't be 0%, but it may be lower than what your credit card is charging you. It could also help you get organized, because you'll be given a set monthly payment for a particular time frame, which can allow you to budget it out. A couple things to watch out for here: A personal loan may have higher monthly payments than credit cards and may have additional fees attached.

Option 3: negotiate with the credit card company

You can ask your credit card company to do the following:

1. Reduce your monthly payment.
2. Lower your interest rate.
3. Remove past late fees.

These changes may be good options if you have some money coming in, but not enough to meet your monthly payment. If the credit card company agrees to significantly lower your interest rate, that in itself may help to reduce your overall debt. Then ask for the other changes.

You may be surprised to learn that many credit card companies are even willing to negotiate a settlement with customers. So if your debt has become unbearable, there are some settlement options you may be able to work out over the phone. When you call, ask for the department that handles debt settlements or collections. Clearly and politely explain your financial situation and ask for what you want. If you get a no, I wouldn't stop there. Be persistent—you can call back in the days ahead and get someone new to talk with.

Here are a couple of things you could ask for:

Lump-sum settlement

This involves negotiating with your credit card company to pay less than you owe. So if you owe $15,000 they may be willing to reduce that amount to $10,000. This option only works if you can pay a significant amount of cash upfront to the credit card company.

Hardship plan

If your financial difficulties are because of a job loss or serious illness, your credit card company may be willing to put you on a hardship plan. The arrangement may lower your card's minimum payment, interest rate, and fees. It will most likely include a structured payment plan.

Strings attached

With many of these negotiation options there a catch—isn't there almost always?

If your credit card company plays ball with you on any of these options, they may cut your credit line. Ask them not to do that. If they do, your credit score may take a hit because lowering your credit line lowers your available credit and increases the proportion of credit you're using.

If you make a lump-sum settlement, the credit card company will most likely report the action to the major credit bureaus. And depending on how it reports the action, it could negatively impact your credit. You can ask the company to report the debt that's 'forgiven' as either 'paid as agreed' or 'current' so it may not negatively affect your credit score. But if the credit card company reports the debt as 'settled' or 'charge-off' then your credit will likely be negatively impacted.

There's also a tax impact to consider. Forgiven debt of $600 or more may be considered taxable income.

A few thoughts on credit cards

Credit card debt is some of the worst debt you can carry, because the interest rates are really high. At least with student loans, you're increasing your earning power and lowering your chances of unemployment. Or with a mortgage you're building equity and the loan is giving you a place to live. But with credit cards, you're really just paying for the past. You're not building equity and there's no underlying asset, which is why I never charge stuff on my cards that I can't pay back by the time my bill is due. I pay off my cards fully, every month. Interest can compound very quickly and get out of control fast—for me, it's not worth the stress that goes along with it. So don't charge what you can't afford, and pay off your card in full every single month.

If once in a while you do have a big spending month, and can't pay it in full, try to pay way more than the minimum. Try to not drag that balance out for too long. What really gets systemic is just making the minimum payments. The average credit card balance in the U.S. is $6,000. If you just make minimum payments, that's going to keep you in debt for almost 18 years. And on that $6,000 balance, with a typical APR you're going to end up paying almost $9,000 just in interest. So that's when it really becomes harmful, and it's a difficult cycle to break. Also, make sure you make your payments on time.

JOANNA MATIS, ENTREPRENEUR

In her own words

Despite growing up with privilege and feeling secure financially in my family, I also was taught that you can't get what you want all the time. But that being said, it was a very old-school environment. We did not learn about finances. We weren't really given an allowance. I wasn't taught how to make money, how to save money, or even the basics of how to pay off a credit card. I have guilt growing up with privilege because so much of what I do is rooted in helping people and advocating for those who don't have a voice. I know how lucky I was, and not everyone has that opportunity. Unfortunately, the lack of education around money led to some challenging road bumps when I first started my business.

Right now I owe $40,000 in taxes from last year and the upcoming year because I hadn't put aside enough money for last year. So now I have to go on a payment plan. I owe $15,000 on my credit cards. That's down from about $40,000. The sad part: I wasn't even spending much money; the debt just accrued over time. It's almost all interest. Plus, I was just paying the minimums on the cards. And then I'd spend more money, pay the minimum, and repeat the cycle each month. It made me feel terrible, embarrassed, and also ashamed—this should be taught in school!

Something I've learned about myself is that my ADHD can create impulsivity with money, especially during different times of my cycle. Here is a real stat: When women are premenstrual, they spend on average $600 more during that part of the cycle.

Now that I have educated myself and actively worked on my finances, I know I will never get to that place again. My biggest lessons: Pay your entire credit bill in full each month and don't buy things you can't afford. I definitely spent above my means for a long period of time, which led me to this point. Plus, I now put aside a 30% minimum out of every check and put it in a tax account.

While it is possible to live without a credit card, having one is a good idea. The trick is to know how to use it responsibly. While you're at it, find a credit card that works for you. Credit cards are like power tools. They can be really useful or they can be dangerous. And really, it's all about how you use them. Be strategic about how you spend. Credit cards give buyer protections. You also can get rewards on your favorite airline or money back. Understand what the rewards are. So if a card gives you triple points for grocery purchases, use the card for that and then pay off the balance before your statement closes. But the trick is to use the cards—don't let them use you. Avoid paying interest, and you can be the consumer the credit cards love to hate—because they're not making any money off of you!

If your credit card balance is $5,805 and you only make minimum payments with your credit card rate at 19.93%, it will take you 208 months (more than 17 years) to pay it in full and it will cost you a jaw dropping $8,205 in interest!

REBECCA MINKOFF, FASHION DESIGNER, FASHION MOGUL, AUTHOR, AND FOUNDER OF THE FEMALE FOUNDER COLLECTIVE

In her own words

I've had periods where I'm carrying more debt than I like, whether it's a loan or a credit card. And now I'm just of the mindset that outside of my mortgage, I don't carry debt. So my Amex is paid off every month, I don't take out loans on anything.

When I was younger, I had ConEd (a utilities company) after me. It was 2004 and I couldn't pay the electric bill. I thought, what's the worst thing that can happen if you don't pay your bill? I thought they would just shut it off. But I heard this pounding at the door and two very large musclemen from ConEd were like, "We're here to collect a check." I said I don't have any money in the account. And they're like, "We'll be downstairs until you figure it out." And they waited and I wrote them a check that I didn't know how I was going to cover, but at least they went away. It was very unpleasant. The lesson I learned? That minimally you've got to keep the lights on.

At my worst point I was personally $60,000 in credit card debt and I didn't know how I was going to pay it down. I wish I hadn't gone into debt the way that I did.

Fun fact: I turned that debt into stock and ownership in my company. So I had someone pay it off and then they got an exchange, a very good deal, early on—the first shares issued of my company. And then when we did take on investors in 2012, that person got a nice payout. It was a good deal for them.

YOU CAN DIG OUT OF IT

Getting rid of debt and building back your credit is all about the long haul. Do your best to find a balance between paying off your debt and saving for emergencies and retirement. Get disciplined, keep your ultimate goal front and center and take a good, hard look at your spending habits. Just because you've got your paycheck in hand, doesn't mean it's all meant to be spent. Question why you're spending your money on the things you're buying. Do you really need them all? Try to have a conversation with yourself before making purchases, so you can become more intentional with your spending.

Once you get into a groove of being conscious about how you're saving and spending your money, thinking twice before you pull out your credit card will become habit. And before you know it, you will build a nice financial foundation for yourself and feel proud about it. And who knows? Your next step could be buying a home. But how do you know if that's the right move? Let's dig into that next.

DASHA KENNEDY, THE BROKE BLACK GIRL, FINANCIAL ACTIVIST

In her own words

Divorced, two kids.

When my husband and I got a divorce, I lost his income. I got trapped in the cycle of payday loans, taking on multiple loans with the expectation that I'd be able to pay them back. But pay day would come and I would not be able to afford to pay the loan back in full. So I would make those small installment payments. And I probably had like three to four payday loans out at once. This is what I was having to do to make up for the loss of income. I racked up thousands of dollars in interest owed. That was the bulk of my debt. I did not know much about personal finance at the time, but I had heard enough about credit cards that I knew to stay away from them. What I didn't know enough to realize was that payday loans are just as bad, or even worse.

I was taking out those loans to cover living expenses, things like rent, emergencies, utilities. I don't think I ever took them out for something like leisure. At the time I was making like $10 an hour. And that income just wasn't cutting it with my two kids and an apartment to pay for. I was taking out the payday loans just to make ends meet.

But knowing what I know now, what I should have done was downsize immediately when me and my husband separated. The extra expense of daycare and housing were my next biggest expenses. I should have moved to a smaller space right away. But I didn't do that until years later. It's hard though, to realize that you *have* to move.

I think that for me, I was afraid of being uncomfortable. I was afraid of facing the reality that divorce changes you, it changes your income. It changes your plan for life, changes your outlook, and it definitely changes your finances. I wish I would've faced that much early on instead of trying to hold on to something that I could not afford.

Once I realized I was in way over my head, I also got a second job. So for a while I worked two jobs and then, eventually, I found a better-paying job. I decreased my living expenses and increased my income and was able to take care of those payday loans.

Downsizing is a hard choice to make. These are life-changing decisions. And many women have trouble making these decisions, like who wants to go and work a second job while raising two kids? What do we say to women who are really drowning in debt? How do you convince them that they need to make these extreme, excruciating decisions? You say, 'This is how to take back power over your life.' If I am proactive and I make these tough decisions, I still feel like I have some sense of control over my life. That gave me some type of dignity.

Then I became proactive with my money. I practiced every week with a money date, where I sit down and go over all of my finances. I am completely in tune with my money.

GABRIELLE BELLI, VINTAGE STORE OWNER

In her own words

Before I owned my vintage store, I worked for an NGO, a working group on women, peace, and security. I lived in New York and was being paid $60,000. I quickly learned that really wasn't going to work. So I worked multiple jobs to make ends meet and wound up working 80 hours a week. I was horrified at the thought of living paycheck to paycheck, that was everything I was trying to avoid. I didn't know it at the time, but it was my fear of living paycheck to paycheck that fueled the almost toxic culture I was thriving on, though it wasn't sustainable.

With the extra jobs I finally had money. I was also saving money and I had good credit. I started opening up credit cards, and that's when the trouble started.

I'm like, oh my gosh, I can start traveling again. I opened up a Chase Sapphire card, got great points, great benefits— quadruple points for booking travel and all these other kinds of things on it. I had a $5,000 cap, right off the bat, which was huge for me at that point in time.

It was so easy to put one big trip on the credit card. And it was really easy to escalate from there, really. It started with extra fun experiences I would charge. And I was paying it down with just that one card. But by two or three years down the line that spending had became a habit.

I've always had poor impulse control. I have ADHD, and that's one of the main elements of the condition. So when I would make purchases, it would make me feel untouchable, like nothing else mattered and there was nothing that I couldn't have. I went impulse shopping, and with credit cards it became harder to keep track of and I thought it would all be fine.

It was easier to just focus on that beautiful bag, or that wonderful weekend to the Poconos. I didn't want to miss out on life. I didn't want to miss out on anything. While I was spending, I felt great. It felt good to have that decision-making power without having the immediate negative impact of seeing my real capital go down in a checking account. There were no guardrails. I ultimately had four credit cards, and within a couple of years they were all maxed out and I was carrying $25,000 in debt.

I wound up having to quit my full-time job, and that's when it occurred to me—holy shit, what am I going to do to get out of this?

I was ashamed. Absolutely ashamed and embarrassed, because the interest was starting to get me. I thought, how did I get myself in this position? I was angry at myself.

To start chipping away at the debt I signed up for an app that tracks your spending. But I realized I didn't know anything about budgeting. It was really hard to ask for help. I didn't know who to ask. That kept the whole horrible situation going, because while I came to understand where my money is truly headed, I still didn't really know what to do about it. That added to the shame.

I started upping my credit card payments and stopped spending on everything aside from essentials. But it didn't completely work because I was needing to charge them to my credit cards—I didn't have enough in my checking account at the end of the month. I wasn't able to save, and I didn't know calling the credit card companies to try to make a settlement deal was even an option. But it's been four years and now I'm down to $10,000 in debt.

I've gotten a handle on my spending. Now, before I spend, I ask myself, do I actually need it? Like, I have two sets of cups, I don't need a third to have guests over.

I have this rule of thumb, but sticking to it is hard. If I'm walking by a store or I see something online—if I think wow, that's a beautiful dress—I wait and see if I still think that way about it three days later. If I do then, okay, it might be worth just looking at it again. But if I'm not thinking about it three days later, it really wasn't that important. And even if I look at it again, it may have lost its luster, so it really highlights the impulse problem.

I've also deleted my credit cards from all of my web browsers, which puts up an actual physical barrier. It was too easy to just click, click, click. You can buy whatever you want and have it delivered whenever you want in three clicks, without interacting with a human. But it's harder to type in the 16-digit card number, expiration date, and the code on the back.

CHAPTER 6: HOW TO BE THE QUEEN OF YOUR OWN CASTLE

"If you don't like where you are, move. You are not a tree."

Jim Rohn

THINK YOU'RE READY to buy your next home? Well, then, I'm excited for ya! But before you begin the process, let's really make sure you're ready to become a homeowner, without putting yourself into a financial prison.

TO BUY OR NOT TO BUY, THAT IS THE QUESTION

It's a no-brainer. If you can afford to buy a home then you should; paying rent is like pouring money down the drain—right? Not so fast. There are plusses and minuses to both.

RENTING MEANS...

Pros	Cons
The landlord takes care of repairs and maintenance	After paying tons in rent, you have no equity
More freedom to move	There may be lots of restrictions involving decorating, pets, etc.
You don't have to pay property taxes	Your landlord could suddenly raise the rent... by a lot

OWNING MEANS...

Pros	Cons
Pride in owning your own home	Property taxes could be an annual jaw-dropper
Mortgage-interest tax deductions and other tax benefits	Extra and sometimes unforeseen home maintenance and repairs
Freedom to do as you wish... you get to decorate and renovate the way you like	Requires a big financial commitment that includes a down payment and closing costs
Have a pet without fees and hassles	Did I say it requires a *big* financial commitment?

Assuming you decide you *want* to go head and buy, I'll take you through 15 steps to buying a home, starting with some critical questions to ask yourself and taking your through the entire process blow by blow.

1. DECIDE WHETHER YOU'RE REALLY READY

How's your debt situation?

How much debt you're carrying especially matters when you're thinking of buying a home. You'll likely need to take out a mortgage to buy the house, which is a loan agreement between you and a lender that gives the lender the right to take your property if you fail to repay the money you've borrowed plus interest. For lenders to decide how much money you can borrow, they look at something called your debt-to-income (DTI) ratio. That's the percentage of your monthly gross income which goes toward paying your debts. A DTI ratio of under 36% gives you a good chance of getting approved for a mortgage. A higher ratio could mean you'll pay more interest or be denied a loan. If your DTI ratio is high, it may make sense to wait to purchase a home. Not only do you want your finances in a place where you can get the best possible terms on a loan, you also don't want to struggle to make your monthly mortgage payments.

My advice? Even if you can afford the down payment, get rid of the bulk of your debts before even considering buying a home.

What's your credit score?

If you're trying to get a home loan, your credit score also matters. As we've seen, a higher credit score is better than lower. As you pay down your debt and prove that you're a dependable borrower over time, your credit score will go up. You can qualify for most mortgages if you have a credit score of at least 620.

Got money?

A potential lender will also be looking at how much money you have in the bank and the value of other assets like investments. Long before you decide you're ready to buy a home, you'll want to rev up your savings.

Ready to put down roots?

Money and credit aren't the only factors to consider when buying your home. Are you able to stay in one place for a while? Picking up and moving is a lot harder when you've already signed on the dotted line. Ideally you want to stay in your home long enough to recoup costs and to make a profit from selling. Although, if the housing market is booming, you may reach that profit or breakeven point sooner.

How to get to that breakeven number? You'll need to wait until the appreciation of your home's value surpasses the cost of the transactions at closing. So if closing added 15% to your purchase price and the average home in your area appreciates 3% to 5%, it's reasonable to estimate about five years until you reach breakeven point. If you can't commit to staying at least five years, you should probably rent.

Do you have a reliable income source?

Lenders want to make sure you have a regular income when they decide how much money they are willing to lend you. They'll also want to see a two-year work history to make sure you've got reliable income.

Do you have an emergency fund?

You're responsible for fixing the stuff that breaks down in a home you own. If you don't have an emergency fund, you could quickly find yourself struggling with debt. Have a fund that has at least four to six months' worth of living expenses before you buy a home.

Did you answer those questions with an 'I'm good'? Then move on to the next consideration for buying a home.

2. UNDERSTAND THE COSTS OF OWNING A HOME

No joke, it's really expensive to own a home. Whatever you think it costs once you've moved in, I guarantee it costs more. Consider that a reality reminder. Plus, you don't need me to tell you this, but what the heck: Buying a house is a major commitment. So before you get sucked into the dream of a white picket fence and imagining how you will decorate your new place, I want you to have a deep understanding about the major expenses related to purchasing and owning a home.

Down payment

You'll benefit if you put a 20% down payment on your home. That's a big, one-time payment. Anything lower and you will have to pay for private mortgage insurance (PMI). PMI protects your lender if you default on your loan. You can save thousands of dollars in insurance costs over time with a solid down payment.

Closing costs

You'll also need to pay for closing costs, or fees for the mortgage loan, before you move into your new home. The amount depends on where you live and the type of loan you have. It's a good idea to be ready to pay 3% to 6% of your loan amount in closing costs. So if you're borrowing $200,000 to buy the house, you may pay $6,000 to $12,000 in closing costs. You may be able to roll part or all of those costs into your mortgage or arrange for them to be paid by the seller as part of agreed-upon seller concessions. In some circumstances, a seller can pay some or all of the buyer's closing costs. In a buyer's market, where there's more competition for sellers, buyers have more leverage to request concessions. Sellers who are eager to get their homes off the market may be amenable to this.

More costs

You'll need to pay property taxes every year and maintain homeowner's insurance. Right there, those are some hefty bills on the regular. You may also need to budget for homeowner association (HOA) fees. HOA fees can range from a few hundred dollars a year to thousands of dollars. Home utility expenses like heating, cooling, and lighting your home can quickly turn into larger bills than expected. Maintenance and repair costs can also add up.

3. IF YOU'RE STILL GOING FOR IT, THEN HERE COME THE CALCULATIONS

How much home can I afford?

You don't want to be house-poor. What do I mean by that? You don't want your housing expenses to make up such a large portion of your income that you're left accumulating debt or unable to pay bills or even go on vacation. No home is worth that stress! You want it to be your sanctuary. Okay, with that in mind, how do you figure out how much house you can afford?

Managing your mortgage

There are two rules to think about when you're considering how much mortgage you can handle.

The first is that the ideal mortgage shouldn't be more than three times your annual salary. So if you make $80,000 a year you should think twice before you take out a mortgage that's more than $240,000. Also, just because you're approved for a certain loan amount doesn't mean you should buy a house that costs that much and accept that much debt. The bank wants to push that on you. Instead, if you take a loan below your max, you'll have more financial wiggle room to pay bills and to invest your money without feeling like you're being suffocated by your home.

The second rule focuses on your monthly income and spending. You want to make sure that your monthly mortgage is no more than 28% of your gross monthly income. So if you bring home $5,000 per month (before taxes), your monthly mortgage payment should be no more than $1,400. That goalpost of 28% should include all the other big housing costs including property taxes, home insurance, and HOA fees. Keeping your mortgage payment and all the other housing costs at 28% (or even less) of your income ensures you have plenty of room for the rest of your needs.

Use a mortgage affordability calculator

Go online and find a mortgage calculator. Not just any mortgage calculator, though. You want one that will take into account all the monthly costs that go into a mortgage payment. These costs are added together to estimate your total monthly payments as well as the interest you'll pay over time.

Inputs should include:

- home price
- down payment
- interest
- private mortgage insurance (PMI)—if you put down less than 20% down payment
- mortgage type: 30-year, 20-year, or 15-year
- homeowner's insurance
- property taxes
- HOA fees

Use the calculator to compare different combinations and how they affect costs. By changing input amounts, you can see how borrowing more or making a smaller down payment impacts what you pay per month. Or, by changing the loan term, you can see how a shorter or longer payoff time affects loan costs.

4. CHECK YOUR CREDIT REPORT

Deal with any potential issues like fraud or errors before a lender digs into your background. You'll want to check your reports at the three major bureaus: Experian, TransUnion, and Equifax. Yes, this is free. If you go to AnnualCreditReport.com, it's the only website that is federally authorized to provide official reports for free. You can request a copy once per year without impacting your credit score. At the website, you can select which reports you want. You should select all three.

Here's what you should look for:

- **Personal information**: Check for identity errors, like an incorrect name, address, or phone number, accounts with similarly named owners and accounts that have been subject to identity theft.

- **Account status**: This might include closed accounts reported as open, accounts mistakenly labeled as delinquent, or debts that wrongly appear more than once.

- **Data management**: Look for false information that reappears on a report after you corrected it or accounts that show up several times and list different creditors.

- **Account balances**: Review your reports for incorrect balances or credit limits.

If you notice an error on your credit report, it's important to notify the credit bureau right away. If you're reviewing your credit report online, there should be a button on the page to submit a dispute. You should also send a written letter to the agency so you have proof that you're contesting something on the report. Under the Fair Credit Reporting Act, the credit bureaus have to investigate any disputed items and correct the information if it can't be verified.

Before you begin the house-hunting process, you'll want to make sure your credit is in a good place—620 or higher. So in the months leading up to the hunt, don't apply for new credit and make sure you pay your bills on time—something you should be doing anyway!

5. PREPARE TO SHOP FOR A MORTGAGE

Mortgage loans come in several different flavors. Before you shop, figure out which one suits your situation.

Fixed-rate mortgage (FRM)

This is considered a 'traditional' mortgage. It's got a set interest rate that doesn't change during the term—or time frame—of the loan. The 'term' of the loan could be 10, 15, 20, or 30 years. If your loan term is longer, you'll have lower monthly payments. But you'll pay more in total interest costs over the life of the loan. Why go for a fixed rate? It gives you the certainty of knowing what your monthly mortgage payments will be for years into the future.

Adjustable-rate mortgage (ARM)

Also known as the 'variable-rate' mortgage, which means the interest rate on this type of loan fluctuates. While the initial rate is generally lower than the rate on a fixed-rate mortgage, the catch is that the rate can go up after that, according to the terms of the loan, also known as the fine print. But most ARMs have caps or limits on the size of each rate adjustment and how high the rate can go in total. Why would you want this kind of loan? But ARMs can be a good choice for homebuyers who expect that interest rates will fall in the years ahead or for those who plan to move before their loan's interest rate is adjusted.

6. READY, SET, SHOP FOR A MORTGAGE

There are a couple of important factors that should be buzzing in the back of your mind as you try to get a mortgage.

First, remember the two types of credit inquiries that lenders will be able to make to see if they want to lend you a bunch of money.

Hard inquiry

We saw in the last chapter that a hard inquiry can hurt your credit score and you could lose anywhere from zero to five points each time you apply and the lender requests your report. Getting pre-approved for a mortgage is an example of a hard inquiry. Since a few points on your credit score can mean the difference between getting the lowest interest rate or the next-lowest interest rate, don't allow just any lender to do it.

Soft inquiry

This kind of inquiry doesn't affect your credit score. This is more of a brief look at your credit report and is used for getting pre-qualified for a mortgage.

The second factor to keep in mind is how much time you have to shop for a mortgage before you impact your credit. This is a no-dawdle zone! Although getting pre-approved generates a hard inquiry, you can get as many mortgage estimates as you want, with the minimal damage of 0–5 points to your credit, if you get your shopping done within a 14-day window. Credit checks from lenders within that window will count as a single inquiry on your credit report.

If you want to start out slower and test the waters to get a sense of how much home you'll be able to afford, then get pre-qualified for a loan. It won't impact your credit, and having a better idea about how much money you can borrow could be eye opening. You will also learn if there are areas in your finances that you need to fix, which may help you qualify for a bigger loan or better terms. A pre-qualification, though, doesn't guarantee you will get approved. But it is an important step in the process.

Alright, let's get a good interest rate!

There are a bazillion lenders out there, so where to start? Well, you can start the process online. And it pays to shop around, because each lender can offer a different mortgage rate—yes, even for the very same type of mortgage—the differences could mean you keep hundreds to thousands of dollars in your pocket. What are you shopping for? You're trying to get the lowest mortgage rate possible.

I talked with Yale Professor James Choi, who said the biggest mistake prospective homebuyers make is not shopping around for the best mortgage rate. He suggests getting at least three quotes on a mortgage.

Banks, savings and loan associations, and credit unions are the traditional sources for mortgages. Non-bank financial companies are also gaining a major share of the market. Those companies aren't regulated or overseen by federal and state authorities, but they play a key role in meeting the credit demand unmet by traditional banks. Those companies include Rocket Mortgage, PennyMac, and SoFi.

You could also start with a financial institution you already have a relationship with. They may have a special offer for established customers.

A mortgage broker is another option. They work with a number of different lenders and sometimes can find a better rate than you could get on your own. However, they're often paid commissions by lenders, which may give them an incentive towards going with their guy or gal even if it's not the best lender. To find a reliable mortgage broker, ask your real estate agent, lawyer, or another knowledgeable source you trust.

7. GET PRE-APPROVED FOR A LOAN

Once you've estimated your budget, you might start looking for homes within your price range.

You also may want to find the right real estate agent for you. Technically, real estate commissions have always been negotiable. Now that a legal settlement has been reached in the U.S., the way real estate agents get paid has changed—that commission is now truly negotiable. It is possible to buy a house without a real estate agent, but the process can be emotional and complicated, especially if you're a first-time buyer. There are also online and discount real estate brokerages that offer lower commission rates.

This is also when you may want to take the first step toward getting a mortgage: getting mortgage pre-approval letters from three lenders. These letters show how much money each mortgage lender would let you borrow based on your savings, credit, and income.

You'll want to do this before you make an offer on a property. Most sellers and agents won't even consider an offer unless the buyer is pre-approved, because the seller needs solid evidence that you're qualified for a loan to purchase the home. You aren't required to stick with a lender you use for pre-approval when you get your final mortgage. You can always choose a different lender if you find a better deal.

8. FIND A HOME

Now that you've been pre-approved, it's time for the fun part: narrowing down your choice and going house hunting!

Here's some of what to look for when hunting:

- Price
- Square footage
- Home condition and possible need for repairs
- Access to public transportation
- Backyard condition
- What is surrounding the house—are there businesses? Know your surroundings.
- Local school district ranking
- Local entertainment options
- Property value trends
- Property/real estate taxes
- Check out the neighborhood—talk to neighbors if possible to see their thoughts about the 'hood.

Make sure you see plenty of homes before deciding which to make an offer on.

9. MAKE AN OFFER

After visiting properties with your real estate agent and picking out the home you want, it's time to make an offer.

Your real estate agent will know how to structure the written offer. The offer letter should include the price you're willing to pay for the home, and it will include a deadline for the seller to respond to your offer.

Most offers also include an earnest money deposit, which is a small amount of money—typically 1% to 2% of the purchase price—that goes towards your down payment and closing costs if you buy the home. If you agree to the home sale and later cancel, you'll typically lose your deposit.

10. COMPLETE A FULL MORTGAGE APPLICATION

Once you've compared offers and have chosen a mortgage lender, the next step is to complete a full mortgage application. Most of this application process was completed during the pre-approval stage. Now comes the underwriting process. Underwriting is when your lender verifies your income, assets, debt, credit, and property details before approving your loan application. The underwriter assesses your finances and history to determine your creditworthiness and your ability to repay the mortgage. It's the underwriter who makes sure that you don't close on a mortgage you can't afford.

Your lender may request updated income, liabilities, and asset documentation, like pay stubs and bank account statements. If you're self employed, expect the process to be more complicated. You may need to show tax returns. You will receive a loan estimate which will list the exact rates, fees, and terms of the home loan you're being offered.

11. GET A HOME INSPECTION

As you work through the mortgage process, you should also order a home inspection. Some buyers choose to waive them in a competitive market—but remember, a thorough home inspection gives you details about the home beyond what you may be able to see on the surface. This inspection will tell you if the property could need costly repairs. If it does, you may want to look for another home. And if you want to continue with the purchase, what may be uncovered in an inspection can become part of a sales negotiation between buyer and seller.

12. HAVE THE HOME APPRAISED

Your lender will also arrange for an appraiser to provide an independent estimate of the value of the home you're buying. Most companies use a third-party company not directly associated with the lender. The appraisal lets you know that you're paying a fair price for the home.

13. ASK FOR REPAIRS OR CREDITS

After going through your appraisal and inspection results, you might want to ask your seller to address some of the issues that were found. You can do this in one of three ways:

1. Ask for a discounted purchase price in light of the results.

2. Request that the seller gives you credits to cover some of your closing costs.

3. Ask that the seller has the problems fixed before you close.

Your real estate agent will submit your requests to the seller's agent. If you're buying a house that's for sale by owner, meaning the seller isn't using a realtor, your agent will negotiate with the seller directly. The seller might accept your request, or they might reject it. If your seller rejects your request, it's up to you to decide how to proceed. If you have an 'inspection contingency' in your offer letter, you can walk away from the sale and keep your earnest money deposit. A home inspection contingency says that the offer is contingent on the result of the home inspection.

14. MORTGAGE PROCESSING AND UNDERWRITING

Once your full loan application has been submitted, the mortgage processing stage begins. For you, the buyer, this is mostly a waiting period. This is when the underwriter reviews your information in detail. It's their job to pick through the information you've given and look for red flags. During this time, your loan officer may come back with questions. Respond as soon as possible to any requests to make sure underwriting goes as smoothly and quickly as possible.

15. CLOSING DAY AND FINALIZING THE MORTGAGE LOAN PROCESS

You've made it! It's the big day: closing. The lender will send your closing documents to the closing attorney or title company or both—what is required depends on the state you live in and what you prefer. When you show up, expect to have a big stack of papers that you'll be signing. Closing is traditionally done in person, although e-closings are becoming more common and may be an option.

There are things that can go wrong on closing day, and I want to give you a heads-up now so you can have them in mind ahead of time. One of the most common closing problems is an error in the documentation. This could be anything from a minor misspelling of your name to something as significant as the loan amount being incorrect. How to prevent it? Preview everything. By law, you will get your Loan Estimate and Closing Disclosure forms three days before closing. Don't let them just sit on the kitchen counter. Read them carefully. Double check the loan and down payment amounts, interest rates, spellings, and all personal information. Call your lender immediately to make any necessary corrections. Cash flow can be another issue. Banks aren't perfect and sometimes—even if you arrange to have your down payment transferred to the closing agent— the transfer could fail. Avoid this by bringing your down payment in the form of a certified or cashier's check. You cannot use a personal check. Or just arrange to have the money transferred a couple of days early. Another potential problem? It's the day before closing and you're doing a final walk-through of the house you're about to buy. And you notice the seller has left holes in the walls after taking things off the walls and ripped down fixtures they were supposed to leave. How to solve this? Your agent should work with the seller to resolve the issues. One answer—negotiate a credit on your closing fees. Another solution—have an agreed upon amount from the seller's proceeds on the home be put in escrow until the problems are fixed.

One of the more important documents you will sign is the Closing Disclosure. It should look similar to the loan estimate you received when you originally completed the full loan application. The loan estimate gives you the expected costs. The Closing Disclosure confirms those costs. The two should match pretty closely. Laws prevent them from differing too much. If everything is in order, you'll sign all of your documents, get your keys, and boom, just like that—you're a homeowner!

TO REFINANCE OR NOT TO REFINANCE?

When you refinance you're literally swapping out your old mortgage loan for a new one. Usually this is to reduce your interest rate or to cut your monthly payment.

When should you refinance? If mortgage rates are lower now than they were when you bought your home. If you can lower your interest rate by at least three-quarters of a percentage point, it makes sense to refinance. You also may qualify for a better interest rate if your credit score has improved.

You can also tap into your home's equity and use what's called a cash-out refinance to pay off high-interest debt you're carrying from credit card balances that are costing you a fortune.

As with anything, however, there are costs to refinancing. There are fees and closing costs of 3% to 6% of your home's principal balance: If you still owe $200,000 on your home, expect to pay $6,000 to $12,000 in refinance fees. So you should only do this if you plan to stay in your home long enough to recoup the refinance closing costs. Here's how to find the best deal:

Find the best interest rate

- Shop around different lenders to get the best deal, much like you did with your first mortgage. Get a loan estimate from three to five lenders. That's a document that details your loan terms, payments, closing costs, and other fees. Also, before you take the refinancing step, make sure you're not on the hook for extra fees from your current lender. Some lenders charge a fee if you pay off your mortgage in full in the first three to five years after getting the loan. Submit all your applications within a two-week period to minimize the impact on your credit score.

- Choose your lender. Compare the loan estimate documents that are provided—look at the fees and closing costs.

- Use a mortgage refinance calculator to help you figure out how much you'll save on your monthly payment or total interest over time. If you refinance to a shorter term—like from a 30-year to a 15-year mortgage—you will pay less interest over the loan term, but your monthly payments may go up. On the flip side, if you extend the life of the loan you'll lower your monthly payment but will pay more interest over the long run.

- Close on the loan. Here you'll pay the closing costs. Now you'll get the keys!

When will you reap the reward of refinancing? When you get to the breakeven point—when the amount you save exceeds the amount you spent on closing costs.

Here's how to figure that out:

Divide the closing costs by the amount you'll save each month with your new payment. Let's say that refinancing will save you $150 a month and the closing costs on the refinanced loan are $4000.

$$4,000 \div 150 = 26.6 \text{ months}$$

So you'd break even a little over two years and two months from when you refinanced. If you live in the home for five years

---

after refinancing, the savings really start to add up—$9,000 over the five years. But do the math to see if refinancing is worth it for you.

YOU'LL NEED A WRENCH

Like in so many marriages, the unspoken thing in our household was that my husband was in charge of the maintenance of our home. When he moved out, it's not like he left behind a manual of the major things that I needed to know to keep the house running. On his way out the door, all he said was, "You'll need a wrench," and he handed me a mini-belt of five tools—hammer, screwdriver, etc.— but these were crappy tools with feminine pink handles.

He had a smirk on his face. He knew I had an unparalleled cluelessness about the upkeep of the house. As embarrassed as I am that I didn't even know at the time how to properly plunge a toilet, I later discovered I wasn't alone. Plenty of women are disinterested in home maintenance and delegate it to the guy in their life. What a mistake that is. That ignorance is yet one more thing that left me dependent upon someone else. If we don't have an understanding of how our home works and blithely assume it will run itself, maintenance issues can become very, very expensive. Many of these costs can be avoided if we're in the know in the first place.

I came up with a basic checklist of things to have on hand and actively monitor, so you can maintain your property, prevent problems, and ultimately improve your home's value.

An essential checklist to keep your home running and create value

- **Get your heating, ventilation, and air conditioning (HVAC) system serviced:** The heating and cooling system in your home accounts for more than half of household energy consumption. It can also cost thousands of dollars to replace. So keeping it in top condition is important. You may want to schedule two seasonal HVAC tune-ups every year. One in the spring for the AC and one in the fall for the heating.

- **Regularly change air filters:** You can improve the air quality inside of your home and use less energy if you change the HVAC filters every 30 days. Have enough on hand that you don't have to run to the store every month. Figure out the right size and filtration levels by either looking at the filter's number that you're replacing or the owner's manual online.

- **Know where your main water shut-off valve is:** You'll probably find this in your basement, utility room, or on an outside wall. This main water valve shuts off the flow of water to your entire house. Knowing the location of this valve can save you thousands of dollars if you have a plumbing issue. A burst pipe can dump water into your home, and you have to be able to move fast to cut off that water flow. Know where the valve is before any problems occur, so you're not hunting for it while a problem is underway.

- **Know how to plunge your toilet:** Make sure you use the appropriate plunger—there are different types! It should fit with a tight seal in the drain hole, so you get a good suction to clear the clog. The trick is to hold the plunger straight up and not at an angle, otherwise you will lose that suction power.

- **Get to know your hot water heater:** Learn what kind of heater you have and do some research on how it functions. Be aware of its age. Over time it can corrode from the inside and then you slowly run out of hot water.

- **Know where your electric panel is and properly label it.**

- **Have names of service contractors at the ready:** Especially plumber and electrician.

- **Keep a list of the brands and model numbers:** For appliances, your boiler, electric fuse panel, plus a running list of repairs, routine maintenance, upgrades, or renovations done in your home. This helps you to stay on top of preventative home maintenance to protect your investment. Keeping records of these things isn't only important for your own reference but also for tax purposes, future appraisals, and for when you sell your home. The details will show future buyers that your home was maintained and well cared for.

- **Service your fireplace:** If you have a fireplace be sure to have it cleaned and serviced before use. Even if you hardly ever use it, it still needs a check-up every year.

- **Check for water leaks:** Look for leaks underneath all of the sinks, spigots, and any other water connections. This monthly check could potentially save you hundreds or even thousands of dollars because you'll hopefully be catching potential issues early on.

- **Smoke and carbon monoxide detectors:** Test them annually. Replace batteries when necessary. Check that fire extinguishers are fully charged.

- **Dryer vent:** Clean out your dryer vent monthly. Lint in the ductwork can be a fire hazard and can also make your dryer less efficient.

- **Clean gutters and downspouts before every season:** Ensure that downspouts are secure and that the discharge of the downspouts is appropriate. If you feel comfortable getting on a ladder, remove debris with a gutter scoop and use a garden hose to flush out the rest. Check for any clogs in downspouts and clear them using a plumber's snake or pressure washer to clear the rest. You may want to install gutter guards to prevent future debris build-up.

With any home project or maintenance, the decision between calling a pro or DIYing depends on many things including time, budget, results, and yes, confidence that you can do the job safely and effectively.

How many bids for repairs and projects if calling a pro?

Amy Matthews, general contractor and host of HGTV's *Renovation Raiders* and Discovery Network's *Sweat Equity* and *Bathroom Renovations*

I advocate for getting three bids for home repairs and renovations. Make sure all bids are apples to apples. Otherwise there can be a big spread in the cost. I often take the middle quote. All should provide references or have verified reviews on sites like Yelp or Angie's List. If not, run. For big jobs I check a contractor's license on the state Department of Labor & Industry website and the Better Business Bureau site as well.

Other factors are the scope of work and how desperate you are in the situation—if it's an emergency mechanical issue like a burst pipe or your furnace is out in winter, you have to make a fast decision so go with a quality licensed company. They might not be the cheapest, but they will get the job done right.

SINGLE FEMALE HOMEOWNERS BEWARE

Women who are in the market to buy or sell a home on their own are faced with a harsh reality.

A growing number of single women are skipping the spouse and buying the house, but they're apparently getting screwed on both ends of the housing market.

Between 2016 and 2022, 17% to 19% of the homebuying market were all the single ladies. Compare that to 7% to 9% of single men.[26]

You go girls, right? Sorta. Single women homeowners are not reaping the financial rewards like men.

The issues for single women occur at the moments when they buy the home and when they sell. I talked with Yale professor of finance, Kelly Shue, who co-authored 'The Gender Gap in Housing Returns.'[27] She told me there are two potential reasons.

The first is market timing. Since women are often primary caregivers for a child, they may not have as much control as men over when they buy or sell a home. School calendars often dictate timing, for example. So buying a home at a low price and selling when high is often easier for men than women.

The second reason women aren't getting the return on investment that men do is about negotiation. Professor Shue says that female sellers choose to list their homes at lower prices. When you start your price lower, the first offer from a buyer will of course be further negotiated lower. Men benefit from being more aggressive in their listing price. Women prefer a fast, low-risk, and non-confrontational negotiation process.

Also, when women are selling, they offer bigger discounts. When they buy, they negotiate smaller discounts. Shue found that, "Female sellers and male buyers are associated with the largest negotiated discounts relative to the list price, while male sellers and female buyers are associated with the smallest discounts."

Shue examined repeat sales of the same property during the same month. Women would buy the same property for 1% to 2% more than men and sell for 2% to 3% less. That seemingly small discrepancy can add up to significant money.

It's not that women make negotiation mistakes or have a lesser ability to negotiate. Even when women negotiate more aggressively, they get penalized. Shue says if the negotiation results in a deal for anyone, it's the woman who typically gets the short end of the stick.

So what can you do about this?

First, don't be afraid to negotiate. And if you don't feel good about the offer, whether you're buying or selling, just say no. Shue says if you have flexibility in the timing of it all, wait for a tight real estate market so there's less room for negotiation. Finally, Shue says to reduce a single woman's financial disadvantage she should hold her home for a longer period of time, since her annualized returns are divided over a greater number of years.

WHICH IS CHEAPER, RENTING OR BUYING?

It depends. I know that's a lame answer, but it really does depend on a ton of factors. For every person saying it's financially beneficial to rent, there's another person saying buying a home makes more financial sense. And it depends on the city, and interest rates, and whether you're going to stay in the home long enough to at least reach the breakeven point. Once upon a time, renting was seen as throwing away money because you're not building equity. And while that's still true, renting has become more affordable than buying a starter home in 38 of the 50 metropolitan areas surveyed by Realtor.com.

As a SFH myself—that's a single female homeowner—I can honestly say homeownership is not for everyone. I happen to love owning a home—it's comfy, stable, and I have kids who grew up here, so I wanted to build memories. After my divorce I refinanced, and I got a low interest rate and a lower monthly payment. That was important for me because I wasn't earning a lot of money, but I wanted to keep the house. However, I have a 30-year fixed mortgage—currently I pay more in interest than the principle of the loan, so by the time I move I will have probably paid beyond the price of the house, even if I turn a profit when I sell it. Add that to the annual property taxes, HOA fees, and repairs, and I've spent a lot of money living here. Still, I have no regrets. Wouldn't have changed a thing.

ASTRA, RADIO HOST

In her own words

I've been renting my current apartment in New York City for almost nine years. It is a great area, conveniently located in midtown. It's right by the subways. Ironically, it's a huge apartment for New York City standards. It's the biggest in the building. When I first got here, my rent was $2,975, which is a lot because that's basically what people pay for a mortgage.

But I work in the city and for me it was more of a convenience. I'm not paying for commuter trains, or a car, car insurance, gas. So if you compile all of that together, I'm saving that money instead of paying all of it if I owned a home in the suburbs. And I'm only 15 to 20 minutes away from work. I also prefer renting because I want the flexibility of being able to move if my job changes. But my rent just went up $700 a month, which is a 22% increase. It's crazy.

JAMES CHOI, PROFESSOR OF FINANCE, YALE SCHOOL OF MANAGEMENT (AND RENTER FOR LIFE)

In his own words

What are two of the biggest mistakes when buying a home?

I think mistake number one is not shopping around for the best mortgage rate. If you look at national surveys of mortgage borrowers, the vast majority of them think they got the best rate that was available to them. But you can show with data that that's just not true.

There is a lot of variation in the mortgage interest rates that are offered to people who have the same eligibility. So shopping around does pay off. You absolutely should shop around. Get at least three quotes on a mortgage.

Mistake number two is being house rich, cash poor, where you're scraping the bottom of your checking account towards the end of every month because your mortgage payment and property tax payment and all the other expenses associated with home ownership or even rent, frankly, are so large relative to your income. You're just right on the financial edge, and that's a hard way to live.

There's emerging evidence of the psychological damage living that way does to people—distracted at work because you're worried about money, stressed out, and that's not a pleasant way to live.

STRAIGHT FROM SOCIAL MEDIA: WHAT ABOUT HOME OWNERSHIP HAS CHANGED YOUR LIFE FOR THE BETTER?

Thunder_struck85

The first few years are always the worst. More and more of the mortgage payments will go towards repaying the principal each month. But remember one thing: Mortgage payments are for 25 years. Rent is for the rest of your life. As your career winds down and you get on in age, you'll be in a paid-off home with property taxes and maintenance only. As an aging renter you will also have decreasing income and ever-increasing rent payments.

Some people that enjoyed rent-controlled apartments for 15 years and are forced to move are literally facing homelessness because they can't find a place given how far the current market rate has advanced.

I'm 100% certain I wouldn't want to be in a position where I'm 70 and told I have to move for whatever reason. Hell no!

Folklovermore_

I have a secure base. That's really important to me—after my divorce and moving around rental properties, draining my savings on deposits, etc., knowing I've got my flat to fall back on and I won't be in that situation again feels like massive peace of mind. Even though I don't necessarily spend all my time at home, having a space of my own is a comfort somehow, like having a safe place to land that I can always come back to when I need to.

Bonus points: I can decorate it how I like, and I can have a cat (both things I couldn't do when I was renting).

Allyuffy1

The best thing is knowing eventually the mortgage will be paid off and I may be able to have some kind of retirement. Not paying someone else's mortgage for them. My mortgage isn't cheap, but rent prices are awful. And I can do what I want with the place. I can make it really nice, whereas most rentals I lived in had horrible decor that I couldn't change, And I can have all the pets I want!!!

I have safety in knowing it's my choice if I want to move, not someone else kicking me out.

Plus, not having to live in a flat is great. I wouldn't buy a flat unless it was my only option. When renting I used to have neighbors complain about me walking around the flat and I could hear arguments, etc. Owning a house is amazing. I still jump up and down upstairs sometimes.

Eyesontheprize13

For me, it's all about sitting on my sofa, looking around and thinking 'I own this.'

Fenian_ghirl

I have my own space. I don't need to kiss a landlord's arse, can redecorate, knock down walls, have pets. It's all I ever wanted.

TelevisionMelodic340

You don't have to buy property to be financially secure or to build wealth. There are a myriad of ways to do that, and investing in the stock market has historically outperformed every other type of investment (including real estate).

That being said, there are non-financial reasons to value ownership over renting, and I may eventually choose to own again. But for purely financial reasons? No, owning property wouldn't get me as far as my other investments will.

There's a lot to think about when buying a house because there are so many moving parts. Buying a car can conjure up a similar overwhelming experience because it's just not something we are involved in every day. I want to peel back the curtain on car buying to reveal what the car seller is thinking, so you can have more control over the outcome.

CHAPTER 7: HOW TO BUY A CAR WITH CONFIDENCE

"I always did something I was a little not ready to do. I think that's how you grow. When there's that moment of 'Wow, I'm not really sure I can do this,' and you push through those moments. That's when you have a breakthrough."

Marissa Mayer

THERE'S A SUCKER born every minute. I can't take credit for coming up with that line, but I'm almost certain just about every car salesman and saleswoman has thought it at some point in their career.

So much for that female support.

Fresh out of my divorce, turning in my leased car and then getting another car were among the first big money decisions I had to make. What a disaster! I had never purchased a car on my own—ever—yet somehow I felt emboldened to just waltz into the dealer and wing it. Big mistake! It turned out to be the first of many.

From the cringeworthy moment when I announced that I wanted to lease and not buy, to when the salesman asked how much I wanted in a monthly payment—and I told him! I later learned that just with those bits of information I had revealed too much and unknowingly lost all leverage.

A car is one of the biggest purchases we make, but it's one that we least like doing. Look, it is intimidating to buy a car. Especially if you're a woman. All of the industry-speak and smarmy tactics are enough to shake the confidence of even the strongest woman trying to buy some new wheels. Salesmen I've talked with for this book admit the car showroom is very much like a locker room environment, and when a woman walks into a dealership on her own, she is immediately seen as a pushover. And believe it or not, sales*women* are known to be just as ruthless—perhaps even more so as we tend to (mistakenly) assume they're on our side! Once she engages the dealer, if she doesn't appear knowledgeable, savvy, or confident, salesmen take advantage of that opening. Plus, it's tough to go toe to toe with someone who makes deals, day after day, while buyers are handicapped because they go through this process only once every few years.

Here's why this is fucked up. Women either buy or influence the purchase of 85% of all new cars and trucks sold in the U.S. Yet we're ignored when we walk into a dealership. Hello! What about some respect? When the salesperson finally does acknowledge us after we've been standing there for 15 minutes, he talks about car colors and gives us the runaround about price and added fees. It all makes it much easier for them to manipulate us into paying much more for a vehicle than we should.

I've got some good news, though, for women car buyers everywhere. If a woman is knowledgeable, understands the lingo, and is asking for the right things, she may have an advantage because as an informed buyer she would have earned the salesperson's respect and can't be pushed around.

With that in mind, I'm about to walk you through a ten-step guide not just to arm you with information, but to give you the tools and the terms to use to come out on top in a car-buying negotiation. You might be surprised to find that most of the work happens before you even step foot in the dealership!

1. GET INTO THE RIGHT MINDSET

You have to have the right mindset when you buy a new car. It's not just about driving the car, liking it, and trying your best to make a deal. The car-buying process takes a lot of time and work. It requires patience, because it needs to happen in steps—you will have to negotiate separate pieces to get you to the sale price and a final deal. I will warn you now that it is time-consuming. You need to remain focused and dedicated. But if you put in the time and work, you can avoid being ripped off. Car salespeople don't *want* you to know what the heck you're doing. They want the process to remain confusing. Depending on the kind of car you're buying and the dealership, you could be entering a predatory, aggressive environment, and you've got to remain firm under that pressure. Your job is to show them you've done your research and you are aware of what's happening.

2. BUDGET

Figure out your car budget. Now that you've done your overall budget you should have an idea what you can afford. You could also start shopping for a loan to find out what your credit will allow and then you know what you can afford when you're looking for a car. Buyer beware here: You need to budget more than the sticker price on the car because of taxes, dealer fees, the cost to insure the vehicle, and more. Before you decide on which car you want, also check the insurance rates for the kind of vehicles you'll consider so you can factor in that cost early in the process.

3. RESEARCH PRICES

Which car do you want? Scan dealer websites and go to truecar.com to see the comparable prices to get an understanding of the true market value—what other people are paying for the vehicle in your region. This is a bit tricky because what you see on car websites and even at 'reputable' sites like Kelley Blue Book and even Edmunds won't really be the same price you'll get. But by researching you will have an idea. Having trouble narrowing down the car that's best for you? Maybe think of the following: Prioritize your budget. Don't buy a car you know deep down you will struggle to afford. That's no fun if you're stressed out about your monthly payments! What do you need your car for? Is it for a long commute to work every day or road trips you plan to take? In that case you may want to prioritize fuel economy, reliability, and performance (although in any car, those should be somewhere among your priorities!). Should you buy a new, used, or much older car? This goes back to your budget, but there's also a technology factor to consider here. Not just for fun aesthetics, but for the latest safety technology like automatic emergency braking, blind spot monitoring, and a back-up camera to name a few. Do you want an electric vehicle? Pure electric or hybrid? Whether one is right for you depends on how much you drive, if you have access to charging stations and if you can afford an EV's higher price point.

4. GET PRE-APPROVED FOR A LOAN

Approval for a loan is essential to get before you start the process. Being able to get into a negotiation knowing you're pre-approved, that you have cash 'in your pocket,' completely removes a huge part of the negotiation and swings the balance in your favor. Because it means you are not at the mercy of the dealership's interest rate. You can get an auto loan from traditional banks or online lenders. The interest rates will vary between lenders, so shop around for the best rate. Select the lowest interest rate and the shortest term you can handle. Once you're approved, you will be given the total that you can spend and the interest rate. Keep these numbers in mind as you go through the car-buying process. Here's the thing: You don't have to use the loan—the salesperson may be motivated to beat the rate you have in order to keep the financing within the dealership. So if you sense you could get a better deal by financing with the dealership, take their financing and just pay it off or pay it down quickly if there's no penalty for paying early. Never finance a new car for longer than 60 months, and for used cars don't go longer than 36 months. Stretching loans beyond that time frame means you'll pay more in interest, and who wants to make car payments on a six- or seven-year-old car? The harsh reality? If you feel like you need a longer-term loan, maybe you can't afford the car.

Before stepping foot inside the dealership, you also should have figured out how much of a down payment you'd like to make on your new car. You'll want to put down as much as possible. For one, you'll reduce the interest you'll pay on the loan. Depending on how much you put down, this can save you hundreds, even thousands of dollars over the life of the loan. There's no set formula, but if you're looking for a guide, former car salespeople I've talked with say put down 10% to 20% of the price of the car.

5. CHECK INVENTORY

Now it's time to make sure the car you're interested in is on the lot. The great thing is, you don't have to go anywhere to see a dealership's inventory. Especially for women, the idea is to do everything you can remotely. Traditionally, car shopping involves literally walking onto a dealership's lot, but by doing that you give up so much control. Instead go to the manufacturer's website of the car you want. There will be filters there to help you narrow down what you want. You can literally search right down to the dealerships in your area and what the inventory is of the cars that are on their lots. Build the car on the manufacturer's website and find out what the manufacturer's suggested retail price (MSRP, or the sticker price) is. It's actually a fake price, but it gives you a ballpark idea. Once you find exactly what you want—including the color, model, and options—write down the stock number. Then call the dealership to talk with the internet sales manager to confirm the car is still on the lot. You'll want to take it on a test drive and make sure you like it.

What to say to the dealership

Ask for the internet sales manager and say this: 'I understand you have such and such car on your lot. I'd really like to come in and test drive it. I'm not going to buy it today because I'm shopping around and looking at different brands. So I'm going to come in and drive the car and we'll chat. And if I like it and decide to buy it, I'll definitely give you my business.' That's *you* staying in the driver's seat (so to speak!) and putting *them* on notice that you're not going to get bullied into a deal on the spot.

Don't know what to buy?

Narrow it down to a target list of three different cars and try to drive them back to back. Set aside a morning to do this—midweek is a better time at dealerships than weekends. If you drive them back to back, the differences in the cars will become very apparent.

About that test drive

Ask to go alone. But if the salesperson insists on going with you, try not to answer any questions. Just act dumb. Whether it's color or add-ons, 'I don't know what I want and I'm not sure,' should be your answers. Even if the dealer has the exact car you want, you can't let them know that.

The person that does most of the talking in the negotiation is going to lose.

---

6. GATHER INFORMATION

Once you've settled on a car you want to buy, it's time to gather information—most importantly, the price. The only way to get the actual price of the car is to call dealerships. Lots of dealerships. Dealerships in your area and those that are further away from where you live. Cast a wide net to get different prices to use as leverage against local dealers. Make sure you're calling reputable dealerships.

When you call, ask for a high-volume salesperson or the top salesperson who's been at the dealership a while. It's important to work with a good salesperson because it gives you a better chance of having a good experience. Once you get connected with that person, say, 'I saw you have this vehicle [Year/make/model] and I'm interested in it. I would like to give you guys the opportunity to sell me a car today. Is the car there?' If the car is there, ask them for a proposal or a buyer's order or a menu. You want to see the 'out-the-door number.' All car salespeople know what that term is. It's the sales price that includes everything—tax, title, registration, dealer fees. Get it in writing. Have them email it to you.

What you need when requesting proposals

Request that the dealerships provide the following in their proposals.

- MSRP (manufacturer's suggested retail price): Although this is the sticker price, it's basically a number fabricated by the manufacturer. It's unlikely you will ever pay this number. It's only a starting point for your negotiations. If you're comparing vehicles with the same MSRP, then the bottom-line numbers should be the same. If you're comparing a vehicle with a higher MSRP and the bottom-line number is the same, then the vehicle with the higher MSRP is a better deal.

- Cash price: The price of the vehicle before any rebates or incentives from the manufacturer.

- Sale price: The price after all rebates and incentives. This is the final price before adding in all the taxes and other fees.

- Trade-in value: This is what they will give you for your trade-in.

- Price after trade-in: This is the sale price minus trade-in value.

- Documentation fee: This should really be included in the

---

sale price, but dealerships always charge one. Keep an eye out for this number and make sure that it's not too high.

- Taxes: Typically calculated based on where you live.

- Total due: This is the number that *really* matters. This is the loan amount or the cash amount needed to buy the vehicle. It's the out-the-door number. If you focus on this number when negotiating a car deal, you're doing it right. For example, if Vehicle A and Vehicle B have the same MSRP and same interest rate, but Vehicle A has a total due $500 less than Vehicle B, Vehicle A is the better deal.

- Interest rate: Compare this to the interest rate on the loan you've already been pre-approved for.

Comparing the out-the-door number of the same or similar cars at other dealerships is the only way for you to know if you're getting a good deal. So call another dealership and *another* dealership to get *their* out-the-door number. Getting these comparisons is the truest way of getting the fair market value price of a particular vehicle in your area.

While searching for vehicles, be open to cars in different colors (even if you aren't willing to buy them) if inventory is low. This ensures you have multiple quotes on similar vehicles. Tell each dealership you're getting quotes from others and you will buy from whomever gives you the best deal. You may find some salespeople will be hesitant to give you a proposal in writing. Tell them you have a pre-approval letter from your bank and will only consider offers that you receive in writing.

Dealerships that refuse to provide proposals in writing may not be dealerships you want to do business with.

When you find the lowest-priced vehicle that's thousands or even hundreds of dollars less than the competition, you can be sure you're getting a good deal. A lot of it is based on supply and demand. You may find that the dealerships that have a bigger supply of the vehicle you want may be willing to give you a better deal than a dealership that has only one or two of that car. That's because they may be trying to get their cars sold and off the lot.

7. NEGOTIATE

Let's say, after getting multiple quotes, the lowest quote is not for the exact car you want. Maybe it's a color you don't like. So call the dealership that has the color you want. Don't tell the salesperson you actually want that color. Act like you are open about it. Say, 'I'm calling about this specific car. But I'm about to buy this car at another dealership because they gave me a better deal. Their deal was X amount of dollars lower, but I'm willing to buy your car today.' Make them the offer and say, 'This is the number I need to be at so I can buy your car, and if you're not at that price I'll buy the car at the other dealership.' If they don't believe you, ask if they want to see the other dealership's number. You're essentially making them compete against each other and as Mike Rumple of Your Car Buying Advocate says, "It doesn't always have to be the truth, right?"

Once you have a 'deal' for the lower price for the car you want, you want to make sure it's a clean deal. So before you say yes, you want to see what you're saying yes to. You'll need to see the breakdown of the fees that are within that price. Remember, the main fees are sales tax, title, and vehicle registration. The documentation fee (the fee to process the vehicle's paperwork) will also be included. The destination fee (which covers shipping and handling) is usually somewhere in the sticker price, so look for the line. All fees should be included in the out-the-door number or the total cost of the vehicle. It's what you asked for in your original call to the dealership.

If you see fees within the price beyond the main fees, you should get the salesperson to explain them. For example, sometimes they'll charge you 'SNH.' Seeing that on the breakdown, you might be like 'Whaaaaat?' (It's shipping and handling.) So if you see there's already a destination fee on the sticker, including a charge for SNH is an attempt to charge you twice for the same thing.

Although you should be aware of the fees, it's usually hard to get around them and may not be worth your time to negotiate them. It's best to focus on the overall price of the vehicle and try to lower that, instead of trying to chisel a fee off the bill.

Here's an example. Let's say you have a $35,000 budget and you're looking at a $33,000 car with a $500 documentation fee. Add in a 7% sales tax, and this car costs $35,845. In this case, tell the dealer you'd be willing to pay $35,000 'out the door.' So essentially it wouldn't matter if the dealer charges the documentation fee, since you're only going with the total price.

If you're at a point where you feel good about the price, make sure to get everything you and the salesperson have agreed to in writing. That should include the breakdown of how he or she arrived at the out-the-door price. You may need to leave a deposit to hold the vehicle.

With that proposal in hand, it's almost time to go to the dealership. Congratulations! You are now about 75% finished with your car-buying adventure.

Focus on the out-the-door price

To negotiate when buying a car, focus on the out-the-door price. It's the only number that matters. Salespeople try to divert your attention by asking you how much you can afford each month. *Don't tell them!* Because they can play with the numbers to keep the monthly payments in your price range, dealers may extend the length of your loan, actually increasing your total cost to own.

About those fees

A former BMW salesman told me there are many fictitious fees that dealers try to pile on. From the 'dealer prep fee' to an 'admin fee' to an 'advertising fee.' All are fake and pure profit for the dealership. The legit ones are tax, title, and license or registration fees plus documentation and destination fees. Title and license fees are for your proof of ownership of the vehicle, they also register your car for a license plate and get you temporary tags. These fees go to the state and mean you don't have to go to the DMV.

Best time to buy

Car salesmen I've talked with all agree that they're more willing to give a better deal at the end of the month. That's when dealers are trying to wrap up their sales quotas. So time your research and phone calls according to the calendar.

The best days to make a purchase are Monday to Thursday, when there are fewer people buying cars. Try to avoid weekends when dealerships are busiest and less pressured to make a deal.

8. TRADE IN

This next step is if you have a car of your own to trade in. Trading in the car should be negotiated separately from the car sale. This is one of the transactions where car salespeople look to take advantage and avoid giving you what you really should be getting for the trade. (One salesman told me this is where they try to "steal the trade.") Even so, there's a big advantage to trading in your car where you will be buying your new vehicle: Depending on where you live, doing this could reduce the sales tax you pay when you make the new purchase.

Here's an example: Let's say there's a 7% sales tax in your state and you want to buy a $45,000 car at a dealership. You're offered $25,000 for your old car, so now you owe the dealer the $20,000 balance for the new car. That means you will be taxed on only $20,000 instead of being taxed on $45,000. This is a big difference: A 7% sales tax on $20,000 is $1,400, while a 7% sales tax on $45,000 is $3,150.

With that in mind, your first step is to get a good estimate of what your car's trade-in value will be. Get a trade-in offer in writing from the dealer that's handling your new car purchase. Call another dealership or two, look online at Carvana, CarMax, and Vroom. Also check out what you could get if you sell it privately.

But selling this way is also more paperwork for you. Compare the offers and which scenario makes you more money. If you don't accept the trade-in offer from the dealer, you'll be paying $1,750 more in taxes. If you decide to sell your car on your own instead of trading it in, you'll need to get at least $26,750 for it to cover the additional sales taxes.

Finally, trading in your car will benefit you the most if you have positive equity, meaning your car is currently worth more than the amount you owe on the vehicle loan you bought it with. If you trade it in and have negative equity, so you sell the car for less than what you still owe on the loan, you will still have to pay the remaining balance. It may be better to buy a less expensive vehicle to help minimize your losses.

9. FINANCING

To the dealership you go! This will be the first time you meet with your salesperson face to face. And guess what? You're already pretty much done with this piece—the financing part—because you've already got your loan pre-approved in step four... riiiight? Now with your pre-approved loan, term, and interest rate in mind, find out if the dealer can beat that rate—without actually telling him your rate yet. See what rate he brings to you first.

10. SIGN THOSE PAPERS!

Alright, it's time to head into the finance office and sign the papers. Don't be fooled and don't let your guard down, especially if it's a woman handling the paperwork for you. The job of whoever is in the finance office is to make you feel real comfortable and to close the deal with as many add-ons as possible. In fact, once in the finance office, you will be pelted with a million questions about add-ons. This is a major source of profit for dealers, and they will do anything they can to upsell you once you've agreed to buy a car from them.

Just say no

You should say no to just about everything except the car. To make things go more smoothly, you may want to go in there with a pre-emptive strike, putting them on notice about it. You can say, for example, 'I know you need to present these products to me, but I want to tell you ahead of time I just want the car. I want a clean deal.'

Worthless add-ons

Skip antitheft additions, VIN matching, interior protection, fabric protection, pin striping, paint protection, key protection, roof rack accessories, window tinting, nitrogen-filled tires, windshield protection, dent protection—almost anything they're offering you can be purchased later for much cheaper.

Extended warranty

Skip this too. You don't need an extra warranty. There's already one built in for a certain number of years or miles on new and used cars. You can buy an extended warranty later on if you keep the car longer by shopping around to other dealerships or companies.

Add-ons to consider

Wheel protection

For most car buyers, a wheel protection plan isn't worth it. But this depends on where you live and what kind of car you buy. If you live in a city where there are lots of potholes and the roads are in disrepair, it may be worth ensuring you can have damaged wheels replaced—especially if you have specific tires, like run-flats. Those are expensive and can run up to $800 for each replacement. Read the fine print to understand the restrictions, and make sure that you have good access to a repair shop that comes under the policy.

Gap insurance

Gap insurance is an add-on to your auto insurance that's designed to cover the gap between what you owe on your car and how much it's worth. It essentially helps you pay off your car if you total your car or it's stolen. Because cars depreciate the moment you drive them off the lot, it wouldn't be surprising if what you owe on the car is more than what your car is worth. Typical insurance policies cover what your car is worth and if you don't have gap insurance, you'll be left paying the remaining amount out of pocket.

Whether you need gap insurance depends on your situation. If you've paid off your car, you don't need it. Or if you've made a large down payment on your car, or if you've been significantly paying down your loan for a couple of years, you may not need it. But if you've made a small down payment, financed the car for 60 months or bought a vehicle that depreciates faster than average, having this financial bridge may be worth it. The thing is, you don't have to decide in the finance office at the car dealership. You can buy it through most auto insurance companies in the United States and the United Kingdom. Do it when you're not in a high-pressure environment. I'm glad I had it the time I got in a bad car accident a few years ago. My car was totaled, and not only did I feel fortunate because I walked away in one piece, my gap insurance saved me thousands of dollars.

One last word of warning about the finance office: If suddenly when you walk in, the numbers change from what the salesperson told you, be willing to walk away. It may not be easy if you need a car right away, but you shouldn't feel pressured or allow yourself to be scammed.

BUYING VS LEASING

If you're in a business where you can take a tax deduction for leasing, that may be a strong reason to lease. If you like new cars and would like to be in a new one every three years, that's a reason too, I guess. But in the long run, you will wind up paying more for the privilege of driving new cars.

If you're drawn to leasing because you're focusing on a low monthly payment, read the fine print: A huge down payment is usually required, and the monthly amount doesn't include taxes or the first payment.

The way to decide if you should lease or buy a vehicle is to ask the dealership to show you your options for both buying and leasing. They aren't going to volunteer this information. If the vehicle you want has a lease payment of 1% or lower of the sale price with no cash due at signing, that's a pretty good lease deal. But make sure the dealer includes all taxes and fees and first payments—including the exact amount due at signing. Still, the consensus with all the former car salesmen I talked with say buy the exact vehicle you want, don't lease it. Pay it off as quickly as possible and drive it until the wheels fall off.

WHEN THEY SAY THIS, YOU SAY...

They say: 'I'm not sending you a proposal or an out-the-door price. You have to come into the showroom.'

You say: 'Okay, then there's a 0% chance I'm buying a car from you. Either you give me a number or I'll move on, because I've already got numbers from other dealerships.'

They ask: 'What do you do? Where do you work?'

You say: Something vague like, 'I'm in the medical field,' or 'I'm in tech.' instead of revealing you're a doctor or a software engineer. If you're doing well, keep it to yourself. Don't reveal if you're struggling financially either. A car salesperson will take advantage of your desperation and your need to cut a deal.

They ask: 'What's the interest rate you got on your pre-approved loan?'

You say: Don't tell them what rate you have. But make them aware that they are competing on the financing as well. 'I'm approved through my bank and you can pull up rates at different banks and see. I'm willing to finance with you, what's your interest rate?'

They ask: 'What monthly payment are you looking for?'

You say: 'I'm just looking at the price of the car and fair market value. We can always talk through financing later.'

They say: 'I'm not making any money on this car with all the discounts and incentives I've given you.'

You say: 'Sure you are. Manufacturers give dealers 2% to 4% of the sticker price of the car after it's sold.'

They say: 'For you to get the customer cash incentive for the vehicle you need to accept the extended warranty.'

You say: 'I don't believe that's the case. Also, incentives should come off the negotiated price, not the sticker price.'

They ask: 'What color car do you want?'

You say: 'I'm open to any color. I just need to know the cost of the car.'

At the end of the deal, the dealer says: 'In order to get this price you have to finance with us.'

You ask: 'Who are you financing it through? Is there a pre-payment penalty?" If they say no, (typically there isn't) say, "Fine, if you expect me to pay a crazy high interest rate, I will finance with you for a month and pay an extra 2% interest.' Then just refinance it with the bank you got your original loan and lower rate from.

They ask: 'How are you paying for the car?' (This should be the last part of the negotiation.)

You say: 'I don't know how I'm paying for the car. I may pay some cash, I might finance if you give me a good deal on the financing, I'm not sure. I don't even care about that right now. What does the car cost?'

They ask: 'Are you buying today?' or 'When are you buying?'

You say: 'I'm going to buy as soon as I get a good deal. I'm going to buy when I find the right deal.'

DIMINISHED VALUE CLAIMS

When you're in a car accident and your car is damaged, it will probably lose value. Even after you get it repaired perfectly, a vehicle will still be worth less than it was before the accident happened. CARFAX and other vehicle history reports will show that it's been involved in an accident, and its market value will go down. These reports exist to help consumers make more informed decisions when buying a used car.

There is a way to recoup that value. But insurance companies don't readily provide this option, even if the accident was the other driver's fault. It seems most insurance companies want us to believe that trying to claim when we end up keeping the car isn't legitimate, because we haven't actually realized a loss.

I was recently in a car accident like this—it was the other driver's fault, not mine. I'm grateful I wasn't injured. And my car will be repaired. Sure, my insurance company was great about it. But not once did an insurance agent mention that intangible loss—the loss of the value of my car, caused by someone else—not once did they tell me I can file a diminished value claim.

You might not have known about this type of claim either, but that's what I'm for! When your car survives an accident, you need to make sure you tell your insurer you want to file a claim once the vehicle is repaired.

By filing a diminished value claim, you can recover the difference between the value of your car before the accident and its value after the car insurance company of the at-fault driver has covered repairs. The actual claim process depends on in which state you reside in, but will involve you showing the insurance company the values of your car before and after the accident.

Most insurance companies use a calculation and formula to figure this out, which then spits out an amount that they will pay on the claim. But if you feel that the diminished value the insurance company comes up with may be miscalculated, you might be able to negotiate to get a higher value. Or you may want to negotiate anyway, because they may limit their payout to only 10% more than the new value. I've been told to ask for 20–30% more.

But before you make your counter-offer, do your research. The National Automobile Dealers Association (NADA) and Kelley Blue Book (KBB) websites have calculators where you can figure out your car's value. You can also request a third-party assessment of the damage to your vehicle—another repair shop or even a car dealership who will provide an estimate which outlines the full damage that happened during the accident. (The original repair shop has the list of damage and the cost to repair it, too—just ask for it) By asking a third party to inspect and make their own report you may have more room to negotiate with the insurance company, leading to a higher payout.

Every industry tends to have its own language. Hopefully the translations I've given you to use when buying a car will help you more comfortably purchase your new set of wheels.

Just when you thought the industry-speak was over, think again. Buckle up, because in the next chapter I've decoded and translated the world of insurances.

CHAPTER 8:
INSURANCE: PAYING
FOR PEACE OF MIND

"It takes as much energy to wish as it does to plan."

Eleanor Roosevelt

OTHER THAN WATCHING paint dry or waiting for the phone to ring, there are few things more boring than having to figure out what insurances you need. There are so many kinds it's hard to tell which types of insurance are essential and which you can let go. And if you do need it, how much should you get?

I break down some of the more complicated insurances here for you, sifting through the jargon to shine a light on some of the types of insurance you may have glossed over.

Key insurance terms

Premium: The monthly amount you pay for your health insurance plan.

Co-pay: A flat fee that you pay each time you receive a healthcare service or procedure.

Co-insurance: The percentage of a medical charge that you pay; your health insurance plan covers the rest.

Deductible: The amount you pay for covered medical care before your insurance starts paying.

> **Out-of-pocket maximum:** The most you'll pay in one year, out of your own pocket, for covered healthcare. Once you reach this maximum, your insurance pays the rest.

NAVIGATING THE ABYSS OF HEALTH INSURANCE

Who needs health insurance? Literally everyone. Yes, even if you're a single, healthy woman in your 20s. Why? Because any medical help you need has to be paid for, and medical expenses are just too high to cover out of pocket. In fact, medical bills are a leading cause of consumer debt and related financial problems like bankruptcy. In the United States, because of the Affordable Care Act (ACA), health insurance is mandatory for most. You must have a plan that qualifies as minimum essential coverage, or you'll have to pay a penalty on your next federal tax return (when you file your taxes every year, you have to show proof of health insurance).

There are three steps you'll need to take when choosing your health insurance.

Step 1: Decide where to get it

In choosing where to get health insurance you'll want to prioritize cost or monthly premiums. But those aren't the only factors. Just because a plan meets your budget, it may not be the best plan for you. Investigate what the out-of-pocket expenses are. Consider co-payments, co-insurance, the deductible, and the prescription drug coverage—all which are in addition to the premium. Also factor in whether your preferred doctors will be covered. Networks change each year, so you'll want to check.

Employer plans

This is the most common source. Employers offer plans to their employees. You sign up during an open enrollment period. The plans usually cover medical expenses plus other types of insurance like dental and vision.

Directly from an insurance company

Shop around for an individual health insurance policy. You can apply for an individual policy anytime throughout the year.

From the U.S. government

Either from the federal Health Insurance Marketplace (access it at HealthCare.gov) or your state's marketplace. These online marketplaces were created as part of the ACA. Sign up is usually once a year, during an open enrollment period. If you experience a 'qualifying event,' like marriage or losing your job and any associated employer coverage, you can enroll outside the open enrollment time frame.

Medicare and Medicaid

These are health insurance plans available from the U.S. government for people that meet very specific income or health criteria.

More on individual health insurance

If you're out on your own or if your company doesn't offer coverage, finding medical insurance can be difficult, frustrating, and expensive. But there's more you should look for than just comparing premium costs with each insurance company you reach out to. Deductibles, co-pays, and co-insurance might all be different, so you'll want to take a close look at those out-of-pocket costs while you compare.

Look at each plan's deductible—that's how much you have to pay out of your pocket before the plan begins to pay a portion of the costs. You can find this in the paperwork next to the monthly costs or premium of any plan you look at. If someone on the plan goes to the emergency room or needs a lot of healthcare services, you'll likely have to pay the deductible toward care in the next year. For an emergency room visit or expensive treatment, you could be charged your deductible all at once, so there is a risk if you choose a plan with a high deductible.

Pay attention to prescription coverage—if someone in your family relies on prescription medication and that drug is expensive, you may have to pay the full cost for it until the deductible is met, and a co-insurance percentage after that. Ask yourself if it would be a better deal to pay a higher monthly premium in exchange for a flat co-pay each time you need to refill at the pharmacy.

Also check the plan's provider network to make sure there are doctors and hospitals near you that take your plan. If you go out of the network to receive care, you might have to pay full price. If you have a doctor you like, also make sure that doctor accepts your medical insurance plan.

Step 2: Choose from the alphabet soup of types of health insurance plans

The most common types of plan are HMO, PPO, EPO, POS, and HDHP. I realize these acronyms can be confusing, so I've added a summary below.

Plan type	Do you have to stay in-network to get coverage?	Do procedures & specialists require a referral?	Snapshot
HMO: health maintenance organization	Yes, except for emergencies.	Yes, typically.	Lower out-of-pocket costs and a primary doctor who coordinates your care for you, but less freedom to choose providers.
PPO: preferred provider organization	No, but in-network care is less expensive.	No.	More provider options and no required referrals, but higher out-of-pocket costs.
EPO: exclusive provider organization	Yes, except for emergencies.	No, typically.	Lower out-of-pocket costs and usually no required referrals, but less freedom to choose providers.
POS: point of service	No, but in-network care is less expensive.	Yes.	More provider options and a primary doctor who coordinates your care for you, with referrals required.
HDHP: High Deductible Health Plan	No, but in-network care is less expensive.	No.	Offers lower premiums in exchange for higher out-of-pocket costs. Makes you eligible to contribute to HSA (read more below).

What to consider

Weigh your family's medical needs: It's impossible to predict the future, but look at the amounts and types of treatments you and your family have received in the past. Understanding the trend can help when choosing the type of health plan that is best for you.

Plans that require referrals

If you choose an HMO or POS plan, those require referrals. This means you typically must see your primary care physician before scheduling a procedure or visiting a specialist. This can be a pain in the ass and time-consuming. Because of this requirement, many people prefer other plans. However, by limiting your choices to providers they've contracted with, HMOs tend to be the cheapest type of health plan.

A benefit of HMO and POS plans is that there's one primary doctor managing your overall medical care, which can result in greater familiarity with your needs and continuity of medical records. If you do choose a POS plan and go out-of-network, make sure to get the referral from your doctor ahead of time to reduce out-of-pocket costs. (You cannot go out-of-network with an HMO unless it's an emergency.)

Plans that don't require referrals

If you would rather see specialists without a referral, you might be happier with an EPO or a PPO. (EPOs typically don't require a referral, but some do, so read the fine print.) An EPO may help keep costs low as long as you find providers in-network; this is more likely to be the case in a larger metro area. A PPO might be better if you live in a remote or rural area with limited access to doctors and care, because you may be forced to go out-of-network.

Do you have preferred doctors?

If you want to continue seeing particular doctors, make sure they're taking the insurance plan you're choosing. Staying in-network is the goal with any health insurance plan, because it's the most cost-effective.

What about an HDHP?

A high-deductible health plan (HDHP) can be any one of the types of health insurance above: HMO, PPO, EPO, or POS, but follows certain rules in order to be 'HSA-eligible.' HDHPs typically have lower premiums, but you pay higher out-of-pocket costs, especially at first. They're the only plans that qualify you to open a health saving account (HSA), which is a tax-advantaged account you can use to pay healthcare costs.

But buyer beware on this one—or at least understand what you're getting. With this plan, there would be an individual deductible and a family deductible if there's more than one person on the plan. ($1,650 for an individual and $3,300 for a family in 2025. The government sets these amounts every year so they can change.) This means there are more out-of-pocket costs before your insurance kicks in to cover costs. And once the deductible is met, then co-insurance kicks in. So you'll still be paying a percentage there.

But if you're an individual, and you're healthy, you're the best kind of candidate for this plan, for a few reasons. One, because you only have to worry about the individual deductible. Two, because you're healthy. And even in a high-deductible plan, you don't have to pay out of pocket for most preventative healthcare visits. Plus, this plan usually carries a lower premium. So you could have very limited costs.

An HDHP with an HSA

Ugh, so many letters! One of the perks of having an HDHP is the HSA that's 'attached.' If you're enrolled in an HSA-eligible health plan, which is the HDHP/HSA combo, your money can go in tax-free, meaning you can direct pre-tax money to come out of your paycheck into the HSA, which reduces your taxable income. The money can be used for qualified medical expenses and there's no time limit on when you have to spend the cash. You can pay for current expenses or use the money as a cushion for future medical needs, even during retirement.

Once you turn 65, you can withdraw money from your HSA for any reason without a tax penalty. You would, however, pay ordinary income tax on the distribution. And if your HSA is through an employer, the money stays with you even if you switch jobs and rolls over year after year. Another big benefit of an HSA is that it's 'triple tax advantaged.' Your initial contributions are untaxed, you can invest the money, it grows totally tax-free, and the withdrawals are tax-free if you spend the money on qualified medical expenses.

So although HSAs are technically not retirement accounts, they are a great way to save or invest money for both near-term and long-term healthcare needs. The money in the account can earn interest, you can invest it into stocks or mutual funds, or you can spend it right away.

In the U.S. the IRS decides how much you can contribute to an HSA. In 2025, the annual HSA contribution limit for an individual is $4,300. For family coverage, you can contribute up to $8,550. Employers also often contribute to your HSA, which is free money that has the potential to grow over time.

HSAs sound like a dream if you're healthy. But if you have chronic medical issues, you go to the doctor beyond preventive visits, or even if you're planning to have a pregnancy or are expecting to need expensive medical care in the future, you're probably better served by traditional health plans.

Step 3: Compare out-of-pocket costs

When choosing which health insurance plan is best, consider what your out-of-pocket costs would be—in addition to your monthly premium. A plan's summary of benefits should clearly lay out how much you'll have to pay out of pocket for services. You'll probably find that the plans with a higher premium will have lower out-of-pocket costs like co-pays and co-insurance. A plan that pays a higher portion of your medical costs, but has higher premiums, may make more sense if:

- you see a specialist or doctor frequently
- you take expensive or brand name medications on a regular basis
- you're expecting a baby, plan to have a baby, or have small children
- you have a planned surgery coming up
- you've been diagnosed with a chronic condition like diabetes or cancer

A plan with higher out-of-pocket costs and lower monthly premiums might be a better choice if:

- you can't afford higher monthly premiums
- you're in good health and rarely see a doctor

BET YA DIDN'T KNOW YOU NEED DISABILITY INSURANCE

Disability insurance is designed to replace a portion of your income if you become unable to work. So ask yourself this: If you became injured or ill and were unable to work for an extended period of time, how would you support yourself financially?

If you don't have a good answer to that, you need disability insurance.

'It will never happen to me.' That's what all of us think. But the whole point of insurance is to buy it before we need it, to make sure you're covered if the unthinkable happens.

There are two main types of disability insurance: short-term and long-term coverage. Short-term replaces about 60% to 70% of your base salary. Long-term replaces about 40% to 60% of your base salary. Policies vary on how they define a disability. Some policies pay out only if you can't work any job for which you're qualified. Others pay out if you can't perform a job in your current occupation. Some policies cover partial disability, which means they pay a portion of the benefit if you can work part time. Others pay only if you can't work at all.

Do I *really* need it?

If you're earning a paycheck, and you wouldn't have any other way to survive financially if you couldn't work for one reason or another, then you should carry long-term disability insurance.

But it also depends on where you are in your career.

If you're retired and not working, you don't need disability insurance.

If you're in your 20s and are just starting out in your career, you may not need disability insurance, because even if you were unable to work in your current role you'd likely have alternative career options. Let's say you're 25 years old, you're studying to be a doctor, maybe taking a job in a hospital. If God forbid you lose a limb, you're young, you're really smart with a college degree, you can pivot—change careers a bit, maybe become a consultant with pharmaceutical companies. In that case you may not need this type of insurance yet.

As you get further into your career and develop specialized skills, that's when you really need disability insurance.

What you get from your employer may be enough. So if you're earning $65,000 as a recent grad and your employer's basic disability insurance covers up to $3,000 a month, that works. You don't need supplemental disability. But if you're all of a sudden earning $300,000 and your cost of living is higher, you might want to consider finding a supplemental long-term disability benefit outside of the one your workplace provides.

How much is it and how do I get it?

Disability insurance is more expensive for women than men. When you take an individual disability policy you'll typically pay about 2% of your income. So if you're earning $100,000, it could cost you $2,000 a year to insure that salary. If you need to go on disability, you could get $60,000 a year—$5,000 a month.

Getting it through your workplace or through groups like professional organizations, labor unions, and alumni associations is cheaper than taking out individual, private insurance. If you work at a company that offers employer-provided disability coverage you should absolutely take it. Don't poo-poo this part of the benefits package. The little bit that it takes out of your paycheck is not going to change your life. When you agree to your benefits package, checking the disability benefit box is just as important (if not more so) as 401(k) matching. Just make sure you understand the fine print, because every employer's benefit is different. For example, any payout you receive will most likely be taxable. Take note, this type of insurance is not portable, meaning once you leave your job the coverage ends.

If you're self-employed or if your employer doesn't provide it—because not all employers do—you will need private disability insurance. That can get incredibly costly. It's expensive because the risk of becoming disabled and not being able to work for six months or more at some point in a 30- or 40-year working life is pretty high. But if other people are reliant upon your income and you don't have other ways of surviving financially, seek out ways to get into a group plan.

A word of warning: The process for applying for this insurance takes time and energy. Expect to have an online or phone interview with the insurance company. You may also have to take a medical exam.

Be prepared for this. Insurance companies want lots of background information about you. They want a reason to charge you a higher premium or to just not cover you. Sometimes insurance companies need to request medical records from your doctor before they underwrite you, and they will send you a general authorization form to gain access to all your medical records. General authorization forms can be dangerous if you just sign them without reading carefully. Don't just sign it, giving them blanket access. Instead, limit what they can get.

Provide them with a list of the doctors they can contact about you. There may be certain things that may not be relevant at all to the insurance company. You want to know what information they're getting. For example, if you give full access to your medical information, they can track down notes from your psychologist or therapist, where you may have discussed that you had an eating disorder 20 years ago. Once they get those records—even if they don't underwrite you—all those files are entered into the federal court system and become part of the federal record. Remember, you still have a right to privacy, even as you're trying to get disability insurance.

Don't have the illusion of insurance

As with all insurances, the devil is in the details. You don't want to pay for something you *think* you have only to find that you actually don't. The details are there, it's just nobody bothers to read the fine print. But it's imperative when you sign up for disability insurance—or any insurance for that matter—that you understand what you're getting. If you go on long-term disability for mental illness, for example, there's a standard 24-month limit on the benefits you'd get.

Words matter

Understand the disability insurance you've signed up for.

Partial cover vs **full cover:** Partial disability cover is when you can still work but not at the same level as before. Maybe you can do some things—but not everything—your job requires. Or you need to work fewer hours because of your health condition. Full disability cover means you can't work at all because of your injury or illness. You can't do any of your job duties and you can't earn a paycheck. It's very rare for people to suffer total disability. Oftentimes, it's a GI issue or a back issue. So you can still work part time, just perhaps not at the intensity you did before or at the same long hours. Partial is also a cheaper way to get covered. But know the difference.

Own vs **any:** An any-occupation policy means if you're still capable of working, even if it is at a lower-paying job, the policy would not pay you benefits. An own-occupation policy considers you disabled if you are unable to perform the same job as you did before an injury, in which case you would receive benefits.

If you're self employed and you can't afford both life insurance and disability insurance—if you're young, choose disability. Think of it this way. It's unlikely you'll drop dead, but it's more likely you'll have a terrible ski injury or get into a car accident or need time off work for cancer treatment. I know, these are horrible things to think about. But you don't think twice about paying for car insurance or paying for homeowner's insurance. So why not protect your body?

The drawback with disability insurance, as with any type of insurance, is the cost. You're ripping up dollar bills if you don't ever need the benefit. But to me that's a positive, because no one ever wants to get the benefits, since it means some really bad stuff has happened.

Don't disregard disability insurance

Globally, an estimated 1.3 billion people—16% of the worldwide population— experience a significant disability today. This number is growing because of an increase in noncommunicable diseases and people living longer.[28]

Another sobering fact is that more than one in four of today's 20-year-olds will become disabled before they retire, which makes this type of insurance sensible for everyone, even if you're young and single.[29]

LIFE INSURANCE

While disability insurance exists to replace your income if you're alive but you can't work, life insurance replaces an income stream that is lost if you die. You need to get life insurance if you have loved ones who you provide for and who depend on you financially. So a child, your parents, or if you have a big liability like a mortgage with someone else in your life. If there were a catastrophic event, oftentimes people don't want their survivors to worry about a mortgage payment in addition to everything else.

Which kind of life insurance?

I'll make this simple.

There are generally two categories of life insurance policies: term life insurance and permanent life insurance.

Term life insurance provides coverage for a specified number of years (the term). Terms can go from five to 30 years. You pay premiums while the policy is active and if you die during that time, your beneficiary will receive a death benefit. When the term ends, you can choose to renew the policy—if you do it will be for a higher rate. If you don't renew, the coverage ends and there's no payout. Permanent life insurance provides protection throughout your entire life in return for much higher premiums. Very rarely does somebody need permanent life insurance. There are only two instances where you'd need it: If you have a child with special needs who will forever be dependent on you or if you are very, very rich and you want to escape estate taxes. As long as you pay the premiums, this kind of policy lasts a lifetime. Permanent life insurance policies also accumulate cash value on a tax-deferred basis. You can tap into this to buy a home, supplement your retirement income, cover an emergency expense, and more. However, if you withdraw money or have a loan balance, there will be a lower death benefit for your beneficiary if you die.

How much life insurance is enough?

The cheapest way to get life insurance is through a term policy. If you take this route and you have kids, make sure to sign up for a long enough term that it gets you a few years beyond their graduation from college. At 23 years old it's not immediately clear if kids are fully financially independent!

The general guideline is that you need the insurance to provide ten to 16 times your economic contribution to the family.

I realize that carrying life insurance of this level comes with a costly bill every month, and of course the guideline depends on your debt and your goals, but a policy should at minimum pay off a mortgage and pay for your kids' college educations. So let's say you have a two-year-old and a four-year-old. If you're making $200,000 a year, you need $2 million of life insurance, minimum, and you need it for at least a 25-year term until the kids are grown. After that term, you have no more coverage and one less bill to pay.

There's a caveat, though. Isn't there always?

Women are more likely than men to interrupt their careers to have babies.[30] And U.S. Census figures show moms who are married are less likely to go back to work after giving birth to raise the child. Her income will clearly take a hit as her husband goes on his merry way to provide for the family. If this is the case, the husband should have way more than is dictated by that ten-to-16 multiple. He needs to take out enough life insurance to include her income too. And on top of that, she should also have a private life insurance policy.

SUSAN KIM, SOFTWARE ENGINEER

A cautionary tale

I painfully learned that my husband didn't take out enough life insurance, and I learned this only after he died. I wasn't part of the conversation when he signed up for a basic life insurance plan through his employer, so I had no idea he had only the minimum amount for his salary. Later, when he died of cancer, I learned that his policy was only worth $50,000.

One partial positive here: He also had a $1m private policy and a ten-year term. Sounds great on the surface, but it's not. I remember when he got it, he was so proud of himself because he followed through. But you know, if he would've just consulted with me first, I would have told him that $1m is not enough. We have two kids, and the term was not long enough. But he was just so proud he did it.

I had been out of the workforce for seven years, and suddenly needed to return to work to provide for myself and my children, who were seven and nine years old. Finding a high-earning job after all that time was difficult. I needed more of a runway. A $2m payout would have been better. Now I have to figure out how to raise my kids alone, and I probably won't be able to replicate my lifestyle from before, for which I would need $100,000 a year. I also probably won't be able to pay for my kids' college educations. One lesson I learned? This is why your spouse needs more life insurance if you are not working full time.

The other lesson here? You've got to keep your toe in the water when it comes to your career. Don't just check out when you have kids. Even if you work very part time and it takes care of daycare bills or the car payment. You have to have your own earnings history. You have to have your own skillset and network. You could get divorced, he could get fired, or he could die. It's important to have your own safety net.

> ## If you're going to get life insurance, get enough
>
> One in five adults don't have life insurance, and of those who do, about 44% carry an inadequate amount.

Do I need more than employer-provided life insurance?

If you have people who depend on you, yes.

If you have children, you need a private life insurance policy first and then you should view your employer-provided group insurance as supplemental. Employer life insurance policies are not a replacement for a private policy. Especially if you've got a young family, don't rely only on the employer for life insurance, for a few reasons: Group life insurance is often not portable. If you leave your job, or if you're fired, you can't take it with you. By that point you're older, so what if you had a health event that made you less insurable or even uninsurable?

Dragging your feet to get life insurance

Your life insurance premium is not a fun bill to pay, I know. But once you have kids, procrastinating to get life insurance is a risky move. You've got those little mouths to feed. Certified Financial Planner™ Elizabeth Hersch told me a story about a software engineer husband making $300,000 a year who waited and waited to get life insurance—his policy would have needed to be for $3m. Then he was suddenly diagnosed with thyroid cancer. He's going to be fine, but he is now uninsurable for three years. You can always drop or lower the amount of the insurance, but you can't always guarantee you'll be able to get more.

The biggest misunderstanding about life insurance

Life insurance is often sold as an asset management tool. But it's not an investment strategy. It's a risk management tool. It's insuring against a loss of economic contribution to a family. I don't care what the insurance salespeople tell you. They make a lot of money on commission. They prefer to sell permanent life insurance rather than term policies because it's literally ten times the cost for a premium for that same death benefit. It's extraordinarily expensive because the idea is you're building cash value.

Here's an example: A million-dollar term life insurance policy on a 30-year-old female might cost $600 per year. A million-dollar *whole life* policy—a type of permanent life insurance that offers a death benefit and a savings portion—might cost $15,000 per year, and guess what? The insurance agent gets 30% of the first year's commission. Which would you rather sell if you were the insurance agent? You're better off investing in the stock market.

One more thing about life insurance—because this is an area where you can get sucker punched. There's a whole bunch of products and fine print and the contracts can get very complicated. To make sure you get a good deal when you do shop for life insurance, get multiple quotes.

Only insurance agents can sell insurance. But make sure the agent doesn't sell you a policy you don't really need. Don't let them sell you the insurance equivalent of a Mercedes when all you really needed was a Camry. Insurance brokers make commissions— and that's completely fair and reasonable. But when it comes to insurance, the products or policies being sold can be complicated and carry embedded fees and costs that may not be transparent. Don't be afraid to ask questions about anything you don't understand and make sure the brokers don't dance around the answers.

LONG-TERM CARE INSURANCE

At some point in your life, you're probably going to need long-term care, by which I mean a nursing home or a home health aide. This one is tricky—and not fun to think about—but it's essential for women to understand the potential costs of aging and dying (both can be quite expensive!).

Whether you're 25 or 65, you should know there are only three ways to pay for this care.

1. The first way is straight out of your pocket—private pay. Unless you're at a nursing home that serves cocktails at 5 o'clock, private pay does not mean you're going to get any better care than those paying with Medicaid benefits. And the cheapest places are around $7,000 a month.

2. The second way is long-term care insurance, and that's the best way to pay for long-term care. But the premiums can be obscenely expensive. Still, if you're in your 50s or 60s you should see if you can afford them.

3. The third way is Medicaid benefits. Medicaid is a state and federal program for Americans with limited financial means. It provides health coverage if you have a very low income. Medicaid will pay for long-term care, but Medicaid benefits do not mean free money. If you want to qualify for Medicaid, you will have to spend down your assets. And if you own a home, Medicaid

is just a loan. The government will do anything possible to get their money back, including taking your home.

Although long-term care insurance is typically not even considered until you hit your 50s, it is also important for younger female readers to understand the costs—especially if they think they might need to take care of aging parents. It's women who usually wind up doing the majority of the caregiving, typically while working full time. It's not only time-consuming, it's costly.

The rates for aides and nurses can be overwhelming. This section will help you weigh these costs as part of your financial plan, even if you're young.

How do you know if you need long-term care insurance?

Look at your family history. How do people age and die in your family? That's the first question. Do they drop dead of a heart attack, or do they get Alzheimer's and live until they're 95? The second question: What does your balance sheet look like? Could your retirement accounts and investments support the costs of long-term care? That one is more difficult to answer. Hersch suggests you will need at least $2m (which you're not depleting too quickly), a Social Security income, and to own your home to fund long-term care without needing insurance.

The idea then, is about accumulating wealth and coming up with a savings plan where you're going to be okay if there's a long-term need, instead of giving money to an insurance company.

But if people in your family get conditions that require long-term care, like Alzheimer's, and you don't have a lot of money or assets like a home, you'll probably want to get long-term care insurance. For example, Barbara is a 70-year-old woman with no children who rents her home in Manhattan—so has no equity—and has $425,000 in savings. It's too late for her to get long-term care insurance. At about $3,000 per month for a premium, she cannot afford it. But she should have had it. The lesson here is that a single woman in her 40s or 50s, especially one who is childless, has no choice but to save aggressively and possibly consider some long-term care insurance, however expensive it may be. Premiums get more expensive as you get older. This is why it's important to have the long-term care conversation early. And consider buying a long-term care insurance policy in the five years before you retire.

Long-term care insurance costs

It's hard to not repeat how long-term care insurance is incredibly expensive. Long-term care insurance costs are based on many factors, but the average 60-year-old woman is estimated to pay $1,960 per month for a benefit policy that covers $165,000 in care.[31] The only way to manage the cost is to plan early. But I recognize that for many the costs are simply impossible. Plus, the reality is you could buy a policy only to spend tens of thousands of dollars on something you won't use. Long-term care policies pay for nursing homes, assisted living, or home health care. But what if you never need these services? And never mind the opportunity cost of what you could have earned if you invested all of that money instead of it going toward premiums. But that's the nature of insurance, isn't it?

There are different products. There are long-term care insurance-only policies. Those have lifetime premiums that often become untenable for people over time because those premiums will increase. There are no guarantees that cap the premium. And even if you can afford it, activating it can be another issue. The recipient of the insurance has to meet specific qualifications of illness—known as benefit triggers—before being able to 'unlock' the funds.

There are also newer types of policies that combine long-term care insurance with permanent life insurance. These are called 'hybrid policies.' If you don't max out the long-term care benefit portion, then the insurer will pay an additional benefit to your beneficiary upon your death. A hybrid policy also may allow you to pay a family member who provides care for you. If it uses a model that pays cash rather than reimbursement for the actual cost of care, you could use that cash to pay a family caregiver.

With this type of policy, you would typically pay one lump sum premium or a few large annual premiums for about ten years—so a shorter period than traditional long-term care. This can make this type of policy unaffordable for some people. The average cost of a single premium combination policy is about $4,000 to $8,000 per year. For ten years. That can add up to $80,000. Yep, I know, nuts. But the policy provides a pot of money for long-term care. If you use the long-term care expenses while you're alive, the policy's death benefit will be reduced—which means less money for your heirs when you die. If you don't use the long-term care benefit, then the policy can still pay out a substantial death benefit to your beneficiaries.

Get advice before you go for any long-term care policy

Before you decide on a long-term care policy or hybrid, compare quotes from multiple insurers and check the insurance companies' financial strength ratings before you buy. You can look up the information on the websites of independent rating firms such as AM Best, Fitch Ratings, Moody's Investors Service or S&P Global.

The ratings agencies issue grades for insurance companies, and each agency has its own scale.

It's an immensely difficult and personal decision. Women tend to live longer than men and they tend to be the caretaker for their spouse, which can deplete resources. And when the husband dies, doesn't necessarily have someone to take care of her.

So the circumstances often leave women more vulnerable.

If you do decide to buy a permanent life insurance policy, understand the financials of the company you're buying it from. If you're buying permanent life insurance, you are relying on that company to be in business for the rest of your life. If the company goes belly up, things with your policy could get very complicated, because your policy isn't insured by the U.S. government like the FDIC insures deposits in bank accounts.

If none of the long-term care options so far are feasible, there are other things you can do. One way to prepare is to come up with a savings plan where your saved and invested money can go towards long-term needs. This is also where equity in a home can come into play. Damon Gonzalez, a Certified Financial Planner™, says the ace in the hole could be putting your house up for sale. If you need to live in a long-term care facility, you won't need your home. So the proceeds from the house could fund that long-term care need. I know, this stuff is very sad to even think about, but it's important to plan and prepare as best as you can.

Medicaid benefits

Medicaid Long Term Care is another way to pay for long-term care. It's for Americans with limited financial resources who can no longer live independently in their homes. Care can be provided in a nursing home, private residences, or other qualified location.

To financially qualify, there are limits on monthly income, total assets, and home ownership. If you're an applicant and you have assets over the limit, you would have to spend down your excess assets to meet the limit. This could include your house, though there are ways to protect your home from government recovery. If one day you have to go to a nursing home using Medicaid benefits, the first thing you will have to do in order to qualify is give the government a copy of your deed. But you can take steps to keep this from happening. You can put your home in a trust that protects it from Medicaid recovery ahead of time. It's called a Medicaid asset protection trust. Once the home is in that trust, and it's been there for five years, the government cannot get to it. The downside is that if you don't leave it to the trust five years before you need long-term care there is no protection. So look into this early on while the chances are high that you still have five years before you'll need the care.

Three sobering stats

80% of men die married while 80% of women die single.

- By the time a woman is 75 years old there's a 70% chance she will need assisted care at some point.

- Of the 5.3m people in the U.S. aged 65 and older who have Alzheimer's, 62% are female.[32]

SURPRISES ABOUT SOCIAL SECURITY

Social Security is a social insurance plan that offers a basic level of income when you retire. That income is generated by you during your working years. If you look at your paystub, you will see that you pay taxes into the Social Security system.

If you're younger, your two thoughts are probably, 'Ugh why is all my money going to that?' and, 'Social Security may not even be around when I retire!' Fact check: Despite what you might have heard, there's no certainty Social Security will run out. My suggestion though? Don't count on it. Plan for the worst by socking away as much money in investments toward your retirement. The reason for investing is so that money can supplement your Social Security income. Your investments may also give you some breathing room in deciding whether to collect your Social Security benefit early (62 years old) or wait until you're at full retirement age (67 years old). If you can live off your investments and wait to tap into your social security that's one way to do it. Or you can let your investments compound while taking your Social Security benefits early.

Even if you're still decades away from retiring, it doesn't hurt to be aware of what could be coming your way. Lemme ask you this: When was the last time you looked up the estimate of your Social Security benefit at retirement? Never? I feel ya. Who looks at the government's Social Security page, anyway? But you should. Go to ssa.gov to create your personal account. Keep your password information somewhere safe where you'll be able to access it many years from now. Based on how much you've earned so far, you will see the estimated monthly benefit amount you could get if you retire early at 62 years old, at the full retirement age of 67 years old, and if you delay collecting until you're 70. If you drag the bar chart you can see the amounts in the years between 62 and 70.

If you're older, you've probably already looked. But hopefully Social Security benefits aren't your only source of funds when you retire.

Let's assume the Social Security program is still around when you plan to retire. In this section, I've pulled out some reminders about how to get the most out of the Social Security program and some surprising benefits that you may not have realized Social Security offers, because again, who ever visits that website?

If you're far from retiring, file this information away somewhere in your brain until the time comes for retirement. If you're nearing the age of retirement, there may be some things in this section that surprise you. Or just tell your divorced and widowed friends, because they may not know any of this stuff.

You could still get benefits from your ex

Are you divorced? Did you know you can receive Social Security benefits from your ex-spouse, without impacting the amount he or she receives? Hold onto your ex-spouse's Social Security number, and your marriage and divorce certificates, to streamline any future claims.

If you're divorced, you can receive benefits based on your ex's work if:

- your marriage lasted ten years or longer

- you're not currently married

- you're at least 62 years old

- the benefits you're entitled to receive based on your own work are less than the benefits you'd receive based on your ex's work

- your ex-spouse has a work record that makes them eligible for Social Security retirement benefits. If your ex qualifies for Social Security but has not applied for the benefits, you can still claim benefits off of his record as long as you've been divorced for at least two years. If your ex is receiving benefits, you can claim spousal benefits immediately if you meet all the other criteria.

And now this, because I know you're asking...

- if you're going to collect on your ex's record, you'll be eligible for half of your ex-spouse's full benefits if you start collecting at your full retirement age

- claiming won't reduce your ex's Social Security benefits or his current spouse's benefits

- the SSA won't notify or consult with your ex that you've claimed on his record

- you can claim even if your ex has remarried.

Some thoughts on this...

- if the benefits you'd receive by collecting on your own earnings record are more than what you'd collect on your ex's record, consider collecting on your own record

- if you collect Social Security before you reach your full retirement age, your benefits will be permanently reduced whether you're collecting on your own earnings record or your ex's record.

If your ex-spouse is deceased, you can still receive benefits. If you're divorced, you can receive benefits based on your deceased ex's work if you're at least 60 years old (or 50 if you have a disability), your marriage lasted at least ten years, and you aren't entitled to a higher benefit on your own record. You could qualify for 'survivor benefits' of up to 100% of your ex's benefit.

You can remarry at 60 or older and still receive divorced survivor benefits, and you can switch to your own benefit later if that's larger.

You can claim at any age if you're caring for your ex-spouse's child, who is also your natural or legally adopted child and younger than 16, or has a disability and is entitled to benefits. Your benefits will continue until the child reaches age 16 or until the child no longer has a disability. You can receive this benefit even if you weren't married to your ex-spouse for ten years.

If you work part time

Social Security benefits are based on how long you've worked, how much you've earned, and when you decide to start receiving your benefits. Women have challenging choices to make, to say the least, when balancing work and children. Some may spend their entire adulthood in a career or job outside the home. Some may work for a few years, leave the labor force to raise children, and eventually return to work. Others may choose to not work outside the home.

In Social Security speak, most people need 40 credits to qualify for benefits. That's usually ten years of work. Your benefit amount is based on your highest 35 years of earnings.

But what if you decided to be a stay-at-home mom with no outside job? Or if you took many years off from work, leaving that overall earnings amount low? If you haven't worked or you don't have enough Social Security credits to receive benefits on your own account, and you're married, you may be eligible for Social Security benefits based on your spouse's work.

If you're married and have no work record or a low benefit entitlement on your own work record. Consider the following:

- You could receive half of your worker spouse's Social Security benefit, if you wait until the full retirement age of 67.

- You must be married to the worker spouse for at least one continuous year immediately before applying for benefits.

- The worker would need to file for and start receiving benefits in order for spousal benefits to be available.

- You can apply for benefits before you reach your full retirement age as long as you are at least 62. If you apply for benefits at age 62, you would only receive one third of your worker spouse's benefit, instead of half.

- If you qualify for Social Security retirement benefits based on your work records, you cannot also collect the spousal benefit. You would receive whichever is the higher benefit.

- For example: If you are entitled to $500 per month from your own retirement record, and you are entitled to $1,200 as a spouse, your total monthly benefit will equal $1,200.

- If you claim the benefit, it doesn't reduce or change the amount that your worker spouse receives.

The motherhood and gender penalties

Women receive Social Security benefits that are, on average, 80% of what men receive. Benefits are based on the 35 highest-earning years. Women with long career interruptions because they have children or leave work to care for an elderly family member risk not having 35 years with positive earnings. Lower wages or wage gaps further reduce women's Social Security benefits.[33]

Social Security benefits for widowed spouses

If your spouse dies, you are entitled to get benefits based on their work record. If you're in this situation, call Social Security as soon as possible to get your survivor benefits because they don't start until you call. With all the other benefit requests, you have to go online to notify the Social Security Administration. But with a death benefit you cannot notify them online, you *must* call. I understand you would be in the middle of grieving, but if you delayed calling you would lose benefit money during that time. The Social Security

Administration will not give you benefits retroactively to the date of your spouse's death.

To receive Social Security survivor benefits, you have to meet the following criteria:

- Your marriage must have lasted at least nine months (though there are exceptions).

- You are at least 60 years old (or 50 if you are disabled or become disabled within seven years of your spouse's death).

- Your spouse had enough work credits to qualify for Social Security benefits.

- You are divorced from the deceased but have not remarried before 60 years old (or age 50 if you are disabled).

If your spouse dies, you can receive a survivor benefit from your spouse's earnings record while your own Social Security retirement benefit amount won't be impacted. You can also collect a survivor benefit even if your spouse hadn't yet claimed Social Security at the time of his death. In order to get 100% of the survivor benefit though, you would have to wait until your full retirement age. Otherwise you'd receive a reduced amount—anywhere from 71% to 99% of your spouse's benefit, and you can start collecting that portion as early as age 60.

However, if your spouse's benefit is expected to be more than your benefit at 100%, it may be in your best interest to wait for the survivor benefit to grow. You may want to collect your own Social Security benefit at 62 years old, which is early retirement. Then, when you reach your full retirement age at 67, you would stop collecting yours and start collecting his benefit at 100%. You'd then collect that higher benefit for the rest of your life.

The Social Security Administration will not give a double payment if your spouse passes before you. If you're both entitled to a retirement benefit, you'll receive only one—the larger of the two amounts.

Children of the deceased may also be eligible to receive monthly benefits up to age 19, if enrolled in school. If you get married again before turning 60 years old, you forfeit eligibility for survivor benefits on your prior spouse's earnings record.

LAURA, SPEECH LANGUAGE PATHOLOGIST

A cautionary tale

Honestly, what it boils down to is ignorance. For me, I'm just not really interested. Maybe some of that comes from feeling like it's always been over my head, and it's something that maybe somebody else would eventually handle for me.

And now that's definitely happening. He handles pretty much everything.

Off the top of my head, I don't know what we pay every month for our mortgage. I don't know what our electric bill typically is. So if he was gone and I had to pick up the ball and start paying the bills it wouldn't be easy to figure out where everything is. I don't think it's something that I think about or worry about, but it's something I *should* be more concerned about.

Ultimately, I wish I knew more. I just can't get myself interested. Because I think part of me feels like it's too over my head and I wouldn't understand it anyway. Fortunately I have this nice security blanket, and I guess I feel like he's got it. We've started with a financial advisor, and I still thank

God for my husband, because I don't know half the things she's talking about.

It's not something that my husband's overtly keeping from me at all. It's just not something that I access every day. I'm sure that if I just said, 'Hey, you know, what's the password to so-and-so?' he would give it to me, though I don't think he'd ever expect me to ask for that information. I think he'd probably fall out of his chair if I asked him.

If I don't have him anymore, for whatever reason that may be, that's scary to think about. It's terrifying and I'm hoping after this conversation I actually do something about it.

SHOSHI, PEDIATRICIAN

A cautionary tale

In many domains in my life, I am powerful and a go-getter. But money is an exception to that. Sure, I'm the breadwinner, I use my skill to make the money, but when it comes to investment decisions or long-term planning, that's something that I've always deferred to my husband and have just recently started thinking critically about.

Why did I just hand that over? The simple answer is, I don't know. It just didn't occur to me to take control of those finances. It's also that I don't feel confident in it, that I feel like I would be a fool. It was something that I felt embarrassed for not knowing in the first place, and then felt embarrassed to ask about. I find it very hard to break in with the jargon, even though I was able to learn all of the jargon in medicine.

I ceded all investment decisions to him. He also researched and found a life insurance policy; he was the one who set it up. And he actually ended up making a mistake with the whole life policy. Our Certified Financial Planner™ says we probably shouldn't have gotten a whole life policy in the first place, because those are necessary only in specific circumstances. We got the policy when we were young—11 years ago—and I was so overwhelmed with the idea of life insurance and the finances and making such a long-term commitment that I completely deferred it to him.

We still have not changed the policy, but we plan to. But the truth is that even the decision of getting additional life insurance or a different kind of policy is something that has basically become his job. I have shied away from that as well.

I think it's the fear of messing up and making decisions that have such lasting implications. If I had been the one who bought the whole life insurance policy, I would be kicking myself right now. I would feel it was so catastrophic that I would be me talking to myself, saying, 'See, you can't handle money exactly right.'

I still don't know any of the passwords to our accounts. But after this interview I will!

Now we're going from playing it safe to taking a risk. With insurance you might not get back what you put in, but you're spending to protect what you have. With investing, there are no certainties, but the rewards can be great, with the potential to end up with way more than you started with.

CHAPTER 9: BABY STEPS THAT WILL GET YOU INVESTING

"The most important quality for an investor is temperament, not intellect. You need a temperament that neither derives great pleasure from being with the crowd or against the crowd."

Warren Buffett

I'M RIGHT THERE with you. Most of us aren't taught in-depth about investing. Somehow, as we go through life, we're just supposed to learn it. Osmosis, anyone? What makes it even more difficult is there is so much jargon, and so many ways to invest, and when you start digging in and come to that realization it can be quite overwhelming.

We all lead busy lives, so sitting down after a really long day and getting to know this stuff is just not fun—really it's the last thing we feel like doing. (Although I promise it becomes fun when you see your money grow!) It leaves us saying, 'Forget it, I'll let my husband handle it,' which leaves us vulnerable. Or we think we'll figure it out later. Problem is, the longer you put it off, the more time you lose. And in this realm, time really is money. The earlier you start investing, the better off you'll be.

What's a financial-knowledge-challenged girl to do?

Just do it. Sallie Krawcheck says the biggest mistake any woman can make in investing is not doing it. And 'doing it,' by which I mean opening an investment account, takes only about 15 minutes. Sallie told me a little story about a client of hers—of how transformative it was for her to just take that 15 minutes to open an account. Why? Because over time the client finally reclaimed control of her own money. The client went from saying, "I can't leave my dick husband because only he understands and has control of our finances," to "Yes, I can leave my dick husband *and* take back control of my own life!"

She also told me a more serious story about the corrosive effect of women stuck in marriages they don't want to be in because they don't have control over their money. One client cried tears of relief while signing up for an investment account. That woman told Sallie that her grandmother had been beaten by her grandfather every day of their marriage until the day she died, but couldn't afford to leave because she didn't have money. Opening her own account was an act of freeing herself from that cycle. So those 15 minutes? Well, let's just say they cascade and compound into financial power and personal strength.

There are encouraging signs that more women are dipping their toes in and investing in retirement accounts at younger ages.[34] One Fidelity study shows that on average women's portfolios do as well, or in some cases slightly better, than men's.[35] Still, only a third of women feel confident in their ability to make investment decisions and 56% of millennial women say it's fear that holds them back from investing. The findings show some women are still keeping too much money in cash, i.e. in a savings account, and may miss out on future growth.

This chapter will get you started on your investment journey. If you follow the steps covered here, by the end of this chapter you will understand how to actually begin investing.

I'm not going to go deep into the weeds here. Instead, I distill the often-complicated topic of investing into the basics—I give you enough guidance to get your feet wet. The goal is to take you from feeling paralyzed about where the heck to start with investing to literally putting your money into place in order to grow.

I know that feeling of paralysis well. I didn't feel confident enough to invest, even when I was appearing on TV at CNN every day to talk about the stock market. But reporting about the movements of the stock market is much easier than taking the plunge into it with your own money. The fear that stops most of us from investing is understandable: What if we lose our hard-earned money? So we leave that money in a safe bank account earning 2%–3% (if we're lucky). And you know what, if you're saving money, that's great because it means you're not living paycheck to paycheck.

But saving isn't enough—because of inflation. If you had $100,000 saved up in 2020, it would have an estimated equivalent value of $79,383 in 2023. Even though you saved money, that money has become a lot less valuable in terms of purchasing power. Inflation makes all goods and services more expensive, which in turn means money loses its value.

If you want your money to grow, you have to invest it. Investing means your money doesn't just sit there gathering dust, it goes to work in the stock market and grows at a rate that beats inflation, giving you *real* savings over time. When you have a large enough portfolio of investments, you can live off the income those investments generate. But you will never be able to do that with cash.

You might think that investing is too risky. Well it *does* carry risk, and that's why you must diversify your investments. If you diversify, you're likely to outweigh any losses with many more small wins. And with enough small wins, your money will grow over your lifetime.

One big caveat

If you've got an overwhelming pile of debt, let's back up a sec. I know I just blabbed on and on about the benefits of investing, but now I'm going to backtrack a bit—at least for some of you. Here's the thing: Not everybody should invest at this moment. You heard that right. Raise your hand if your credit card has such a merry-go-round of revolving debt that you're paying thousands of dollars in interest each month? If your hand is up, I'm talking to you. When the ship is sinking, you've got to first take care of the water that's coming in before you address the future. You first need to work on paying off some of that high-interest debt. Particularly with credit card rates at 25% and higher, you're just not going to see the stock market go up fast enough to make up for what it's costing you in credit cards.

Now raise your hand if you have a ton of credit card debt plus you don't have an emergency fund. If you're holding your hand high, you shouldn't invest at this moment either. Instead, focus on paying down the debt while you're building your emergency fund. You should have at least a month or two of money for necessities saved up before you jump into investing, because emergency savings is also your buffer against future credit card debt. If you don't have a really solid foundation, and every extra dollar goes toward the credit card bills, the next time the car's on the fritz or you have a medical bill you will load up the credit card and the cycle starts again.

Alright, here we go. Let's do this. Let's open an account together.

1. CHOOSE WHO YOU WANT TO MANAGE YOUR INVESTMENTS

Someone or something needs to manage your investment portfolio. There are several options available, so find the one you're most comfortable with.

A human professional

If you want a human to help you manage your portfolio, first decide how much help you want. There are different approaches: active management, passive management, or a combo of both.

With an actively managed fund, a fund manager tries to outperform or beat a particular benchmark for stocks, bonds, and other securities—like the S&P 500, the broadest measure of the stock market. Sounds like a no-brainer, right, because who wouldn't want their portfolio to kick ass so much that it does better than the average of 10% that the S&P 500 makes every year? But it may not be all that. Fees are usually higher for an actively managed account, and there's no guarantee the manager—through their frequent buying and selling—will in fact generate a return that beats 10%. But with an active fund manager you get an actual human who builds your portfolio the way you want, and you get that personal connection.

Passive portfolio management is a long-term strategy that you can do yourself. You buy a preset group of investments that mirror an index, again like the S&P 500. With this strategy, there's no stock-picking, but you can buy index funds of entire asset classes not just consisting of stocks but of bonds, commodities, real estate, and more. Passive investing also comes at a low cost because you're not paying a high-priced professional to do it. If you buy and hold, you can earn close to what the market's return is.

If you do go with a human, make sure it's someone who is licensed to manage your money! That includes relevant degrees, certifications, and/or membership of professional organizations. Ask upfront how they're paid. Again, their expertise will not come for free. Some get an hourly rate, others get a percentage of what your portfolio brings in each year. Even if you choose this route, you still need to have a good understanding about investing. Don't just tell the professional, 'Take the wheel with my money' and then you just go disappear. So even if you go with this option, keep reading here so you're in the know!

Robo-advisor

A robo-advisor is a digital platform that automates the process of investing with minimal human supervision. Lots of online brokers offer automated investing, including Fidelity and Vanguard, so you can sign up on their websites. With a robo-advisor, you can choose a taxable brokerage account or a tax-advantaged individual retirement account (IRA). With the help of a questionnaire you fill out, the software that runs the robo-advisor designs an investment allocation based on your finances, your financial goals and your risk tolerance.

Most robo-advisors charge about 0.25% to 0.50% of your account balance or a fixed monthly subscription fee or annual flat fee instead. On an investment balance of $10,000, a 0.25% robo-advisor fee would charge you $25 a year.

Self-managed

This is the DIY option where you will select your own funds, stocks, and investments. Most online discount brokerages offer zero-commission stock trading.

Once you've chosen a manager, it's time to set up an online brokerage account. And it will only take you 15 minutes!

2. PICK A COMPANY WITH AN ONLINE PLATFORM

Choose an online broker, or brokerage company, which is a fancy way of saying choose a company that has an online trading platform. It will be the place where your investments 'live'—similar to how you do online banking. Whether you go with a licensed professional, a robo-advisor, or you DIY, your platform to invest should be online so you can monitor what's happening.

A human professional will still use an online platform and will help you design a stock and fund portfolio.

If you're going DIY, an online brokerage allows you to buy stock and many other investments. Choose among Ellevest, Fidelity, Charles Schwab, Merrill Edge, and Vanguard, just to name a few. There are many out there, so how to choose? Look for brokerages that have an easy to navigate interface and app, zero commissions for transactions, low fees, and no minimum investment requirements to start investing. Many also offer educational resources and research at no additional cost which are super helpful as you navigate your way through.

3. OPEN AN INVESTMENT ACCOUNT

Go to the company's website. You will probably see a tab that says 'get started' or 'open your account.' You will then be asked if you want to open either a Roth IRA, a Traditional IRA, or a Brokerage Account. Think of these as bags that will hold your money for the long term. You could put your money in a regular brokerage account and buy stocks and funds there, but that kind of account won't help you minimize taxes that you pay on your investments. Instead, the better option is to put your money inside a tax-advantaged account, or a retirement account, like a Roth IRA, Traditional IRA, or SEP IRA. Retirement accounts are the best way to start because they offer you tax deductions, tax-deferred, or tax-free growth on what your money earns. I mean, who doesn't want to pay less in taxes, either now or down the road?

Once you've chosen the kind of long-term account you want to put your money in, you'll need to fill out your personal information, like your name, Social Security number, contact information, and so on.

Link your bank account to the new company and transfer the money you want to invest into your new account. When your money lands into the account, keep in mind this is just a savings account—a holding place for your cash before you actually go buy something to put inside your retirement bag. This savings or holding account may also be called your 'core position.'

Try to put the cash in a holding account that earns interest and doesn't charge you a fee. There could be times your uninvested money sits for a minute before you put it to work, so it may as well earn something. But ultimately the goal here is that you will be moving the money out of that holding account and into your bag of investments.

Some background on the bags to choose from

For IRAs there are some similarities. Your earnings aren't taxed while they're in the accounts, which can help your investments grow. There are limits to how much you can contribute each year and you can only contribute income that you've earned to an IRA. But beyond that, the main difference between a Roth IRA and a Traditional IRA is the way they are taxed.

Roth IRA

If you're embarking on the beginning of your career, you may want to start with a Roth. You pay the tax bill upfront and you don't owe anything on the back end. So with this type of retirement account, you don't get a tax deduction at the time when you make a contribution. It doesn't lower how much you will have to pay in taxes off your income, but here's the good part: When you retire and take the money out, that pile of money is tax-free. So if a 25-year-old contributes $5,000 each year until she retires and makes an average annual return of 8% on her investment, she'll have over $1.6m saved by the time she retires at 67. And all that money is hers! She won't have to give the Internal Revenue Service a cent of it if she waits until retirement to withdraw the earnings.

The thinking is, when you're young and most likely in a lower tax bracket, you don't need the tax break that the Traditional IRA gives. At age 59 and a half, you can withdraw both contributions and earnings without a 10% penalty on the withdrawal amount, if your Roth IRA has been open at least five years. But be aware that there are earned income limits for Roth IRAs. You aren't eligible to open or contribute to a Roth if you make too much money. The IRS publishes the income information on their website and the income limits change every year.

Other perks of Roth IRAs

You are allowed to take out contributions—not earnings—tax-free, penalty-free at any time for any reason, because you've already paid taxes on that money. Although I'm not a fan of this perk because it's best to leave your money in the account to grow instead of raiding your retirement account, it's nice to know there's a backdoor emergency fund.

Also, if you're younger than 59 and a half, the expenses you can withdraw your original contributions tax-and-penalty free for include:

- distributions of up to $10,000 to put towards the purchase of your first home
- qualified higher education expenses
- withdrawals made because you become totally and permanently disabled
- paying for health insurance premiums should you become unemployed

To withdraw earnings from your Roth without owing taxes or penalties you have to be at least 59 and a half years old and the account has to be five years old. Even if you're already old enough, you must have established and held the Roth for at least five tax years.

Roth IRA contributions and earnings

- Contributions are the money you deposit into an IRA.
- Earnings are your profits.

Both of the above grow tax-free in your account.

Traditional IRA

With a Traditional IRA your contributions are tax deductible during the years you make contributions, so you get a tax break now and owe taxes on the back end. When you retire and take the money out, you pay taxes at your income rate.

Why choose this option? A Traditional IRA could give you immediate tax benefits because, depending on your situation, those contributions generally lower your taxable earned income in the years you contribute. This is a better choice if you're earning more money because you can avoid income taxes at higher rates on your current income. It's a good choice if you're in a higher tax bracket now and if you think you will be in a lower tax bracket in the future, so that you will pay lower rates on future withdrawals. Unlike Roth IRAs, there are no income limits.

The perks for Traditional IRAs are more limited than with a Roth. You can use up to $10,000 from a Traditional IRA toward the purchase of your first home. You won't have to pay a 10% penalty on the withdrawal, but you'll owe taxes on that money. And if you take money out of your Traditional IRA for qualified college expenses, you won't pay a penalty, but you will pay taxes on the amount.

SEP IRA/SIMPLE IRA

SEP stands for Simplified Employee Pension. It's much like a Traditional IRA, and this bag is for self-employed people and small business owners. Your contributions are tax-deductible, and your investments grow tax-deferred until you retire. So if you are a business owner or you have freelance income, you can open a SEP IRA. A SIMPLE IRA stands for Savings Incentive Match Plan for Employees Individual Retirement Account. It also functions fairly similarly to a Traditional IRA, but it has a higher contribution limit and is typically for anyone who is self-employed with less than 100 employees.

Why a Traditional IRA?

Let's say an employee earns $75,000 gross income per year. The effective tax rate on that income is 24%.

The employee's tax liability for the year is therefore 0.24 x $75,000 = $18,000.

But if the employee contributes $15,000 toward a Traditional IRA plan, taxable income is taken off the top, so $75,0000–$15,000 = $60,000, and the employee's tax liability is now 0.24 x $60,000 = $14,400 instead of $18,000.

401(k)

If you're lucky enough that your employer offers this contribution plan plus gives you a match, TAKE IT, whatever the match is. 'Match' is a code word for 'free.' It's a guaranteed return on your investment. Plus, the other nice thing with this option is that a lot of the work is done for you—you've got guardrails where you say how much money comes out of your paycheck before taxes and you make your investment selections.

There are two basic types of 401(k)s: Traditional and Roth. If your employer offers both, you can contribute to one type or both types up to the contribution limit. Whichever you choose, the 401(k) with a match is a great way to build a retirement nest egg because the money you contribute automatically comes out of each paycheck and compounds with the help of the match.

Ideally, you want to invest in both a 401(k) with matching *and* your personal IRA. Not only does this help you diversify, or spread your money to numerous investments, both of these kinds of retirement accounts also give you the benefit of your money working to earn compound interest simultaneously—and that can create a serious boost to your retirement fund.

4. TIME TO FILL THE BAGS

You're not done yet. If you've chosen to put your money into a Roth or Traditional IRA, don't stop there. Placing your money inside one of those bags—inside your IRA account—IS NOT AN ACTUAL INVESTMENT. Your IRA bag may contain cash, but it's still empty of investments. It took me some time to realize this—I can't believe that the brokerage firm didn't at least flag this even in an email and say, 'Hey Alison, did you know that your money is just sitting there waiting?' That's why I'm screaming it from the rooftops now, so you don't let your money just sit, thinking it's already in an investment working for you. The whole point is you want your money to grow bigger inside your bag. How to do that? You have to put the money into an actual investment.

Alright, let's do it. Now it's really decision time.

But it ain't Hollywood

If you turn on the TV to the morning news, about a minute before the opening bell at the New York Stock Exchange, it's a little sweaty and a bit dramatic—you've got the countdown until the bell rings with traders—mostly men —running all over the place. It opens every day (except holidays), so why the drama? While at CNN, I reported from the middle of the trading floor at the NYSE and I can tell you that the most active parts of the day are during the opening and closing bells—the moments when TV news most often shows the trading floor.

Newsflash! The trick to building wealth is to keep things boring. Yep. Boring is best. Forget what you see on social media about stock-picking. You can get lucky doing that, and you can also get lucky going into a casino. But statistically you're not going to continue to win for long. So the best way to build wealth is to pick boring investments to put in your bags. Ideally you want to put the money to work in the most tax-efficient way with low fees. That basically means putting your money into 'funds.'

5. CHOOSE YOUR INVESTMENTS

Especially if you're an investing beginner, simpler is better. So let's keep it simple so you can get started with investing now. Once you grow your confidence, later you can branch out.

In deciding how to fill your retirement bags, diversification is key. That just means even if you're investing just $50, you should spread it broadly—mixing it among a variety of investments in your portfolio to try to reduce the likelihood that you lose money if any one investment tanks. You can do that with a variety of types of investments including stocks, bonds, and real estate, for example. You also want diversification *within* those investments. For our purposes here, because I just want to get your feet wet, I'm going to narrow things down and show you how to invest in a diversified way—in a variety of stocks and bonds. The idea is to buy shares of companies in different industries like healthcare, finance, technology, and energy. And, no, we are not going stock-picking. We are going fund-picking.

What is an investment fund? It's like a package of different investments in one basket. Or think of it as a box that has different kinds of chocolates inside. Funds take money from investors (you) which is then used to purchase a bunch of different stocks or bonds, so the investor ends up with a good variety. Investing in a fund allows you to make hundreds or even thousands of investments, so you don't have to buy everything individually or go stock- or bond-picking and it doesn't leave you with only one type of chocolate—I mean *investment*.

Let's focus on stocks (aka shares), which are small slices of ownership in an existing, functional business. We'll get to bonds later. When you buy stocks inside a fund, it doesn't have to get complicated. There are some basic types of funds to choose from: mutual funds, index funds, exchange-traded funds (ETFs), and target-date funds. All funds offer ways to instantly diversify your investments in stocks, because each fund already holds a bundle of stocks across a variety of industries. So buying a share in the fund really buys you a bunch of stocks. You can look up the fund to see what companies or stocks are in it, just by searching the name of the fund.

Mutual funds

A mutual fund is a collection of investments, usually stocks or bonds but sometimes both, that is owned by many different investors. If you buy shares in the mutual fund, your purchase will be processed at the end of the trading day at whatever the purchase price is at that time. A mutual fund's fees can run pretty high, which is because they are actively managed by investing professionals. Actively managed funds are those where the fund's manager chooses what to buy and sell in an attempt to 'beat the market,' i.e. to achieve better than average returns on the investments. If you don't have much money to start investing, one drawback to mutual funds (in addition to the higher fees), is they often have minimum initial purchase requirements of $1,000 or more.

A mutual fund's performance is measured against a 'benchmark' index, which brings us on to...

Index funds

An index fund is like a mutual fund on autopilot. In fact index funds are the mainstay of passive investing. Instead of paying for someone to beat the performance of the market, it simply tracks a market 'index.' For example, the S&P 500 is a market index. It holds 500 of the biggest companies in the U.S., so if you buy a share of an S&P 500 index fund it would perform just like the actual S&P 500 Index is performing. That one share in the fund that you bought would mean you've actually bought a tiny piece of 500 companies—that's great diversification! Because there isn't an active human managing the fund for you, you're charged a very low fee to have shares in the fund. While you can place an order for shares of index funds whenever you wish, the actual purchase happens only once a day, after the market closes—just like a mutual fund.

Exchange-traded funds

Better known as ETFs, this subset of index funds also holds many individual investments that are bundled together. So they offer instant diversification. ETFs are almost always index funds. They also tend to have low fees. One of the differences between ETFs and mutual/index funds is that ETFs trade throughout the day, much like an individual stock—so you can buy them at any time during the trading day at the current stock price.

Target-date funds

These are mutual funds or ETFs that are actively managed and take into account your target retirement date. If you have a company retirement plan, like a 401(k), it's probably a target-date fund. Whether you want to retire in 2030, 2040, or beyond, the target-date fund adjusts its strategy accordingly. It's like a GPS. The fund adapts your portfolio over time to match your changing needs. When you're young and have plenty of time ahead, it might invest more aggressively. But as your retirement date gets closer, it becomes more cautious and gradually shifts to more stable and conservative investments.

With the fund doing much of the heavy lifting for you, you can almost put the thing on autopilot. But be aware that some target-date funds come with higher fees than the funds within them. Also the earnings in the fund aren't guaranteed, just because there's an 'end date' put on the fund. If the target date happens to be on a down year for the market, your investment will also likely be lower. And one more thing: As you get closer to your target retirement date, more of your money is moved from stocks to bonds. But, with many women living more than 20 years after they retire, they may need extra growth in stocks during that time. One solution is to buy a target-date fund that matures five or ten years later than you actually want to retire. This later-dated fund will have a higher allocation to stocks, potentially giving you more growth.

What the heck is an index?

An index is a collection of a group of securities (aka investments) such as stocks. When you hear TV reporters like me talk about the movement of 'the Dow,' we are talking about how well a specific benchmark index, like the Dow Jones Industrial Average, is performing. So an index fund tracks a particular benchmark index like:

- **The S&P 500:** An index that's made up of the 500 biggest U.S. public companies.

- **The Dow Jones Industrial Average:** Comprises the 30 biggest U.S. companies.

- **The Nasdaq:** The Nasdaq Composite encompasses more than 2,500 technology-related firms in the U.S.

How to choose among a ton of funds

Let's do a little homework to figure out what will go inside your retirement bag. Especially if you're new to investing, most financial advisors prefer that you invest in funds instead of picking individual stocks. I mean, sure, a stock could rise in meteoric fashion. But the odds that any individual stock will make you rich are pretty slim.

For this exercise of actually getting you invested in the market, we're going to buy shares in an index fund because fees for them are often low cost and there's no minimum amount of shares that you're required to buy. You could literally just buy one share and that's okay—baby steps! I'm also assuming (and hoping) you already have a 401(k) set up with your employer, so you hopefully already have a target-date fund.

Both index funds and ETFs offer a consistent performance that cover your bases and win in the long run. The S&P 500—which is often seen as the best measure of how well the stock market is performing overall—has posted an average annual return of 8%–10% since 1928, so indexes tend to rise over time.[36]

The differences between index funds and ETFs are small. Many index funds are available in ETF form, so you can buy and sell throughout the day at rock-bottom fees. But just because you can buy and sell, avoid the temptation to day trade, or buying and selling the same stocks in the same day. It's not in your best interest—it's estimated that 95% of day traders ultimately lose money.[37]

Index funds also come in a variety of flavors. And there are literally thousands of indexes to invest in. For example, there are total stock market funds, where you invest in the entire U.S. stock market. There are funds where you can invest in the top 500 U.S. companies. There are funds which are composed of a bundle of companies that are either small, medium, or large-sized companies. Global funds are a good place to invest if you're looking to spread your money across a wide range of companies, industries, and countries. You could invest in funds that track an industry like technology or energy, where the collection of stocks is a variety of companies in just that particular industry. These index funds are less diversified than what you'd find in the broadest market index funds because they're focused on one industry or sector, but still are more diversified than if you were to buy individual stocks within those industries.

Choosing which index fund or funds to invest in can be overwhelming, but there are ways to narrow the field by doing a little research into the sectors or countries that interest you the most. Any index fund will have performed about as well as the market it is tracking, so as an investor in index funds you're looking for consistency rather than high performance. If you were to choose actively managed funds, on the other hand, you'll be looking for those with a long-term track record, particularly those that have been in business for decades. Look at the returns of those funds—how have they performed over the years when compared to their benchmarks?

Some things to look for when choosing an index fund

- Inception of the index fund: Is it new or has it been around a while? If it's been around, you can research performance.

- Type of fund. Is it aggressive or conservative? What's your risk tolerance?

- What is the fund's overall return? What does its three- or five-year run look like?

- Go back to the worst performing years of the stock market. How did the fund do then? It's easier to make money in a strong market. It's harder to preserve gains in a down market. Look at how the fund did in a bad year and then see if it was able to bounce back.

- Know the fees charged and compare them. Look for the expense ratio (see the next box).

- You can (and should) buy shares of more than one index fund. Different brokerages have their own funds and are identified by different ticker symbols. Ticker symbols are a bunch of letters that are essentially the 'name' of the fund. But if you buy different funds, find ones that have different holdings—make sure that each fund has different stocks than the other. Otherwise you're duplicating investments and not truly diversifying. To check if there's overlap, go to etfrc.com and type the ticker symbol of the fund you currently have in the box, along with the name of the fund you're looking to buy. It's alright to have some overlap, but you don't want too much of the same, because that wouldn't be diversifying.

- If you're located in European Union countries, you can look for the Key Investor Information Document, or KIID, which is a two-page fact-style document that can help you as an investor understand the key risks of the fund in order to make a more informed investment decision.

Additional costs with index funds, mutual funds, and ETFs

Why are there fees? Because someone has to get paid to do all the hard lifting putting those funds together. To find out how much these investments cost, look online for what's called the 'expense ratio' for the named fund. It's a fee you will pay out of your gains or on top of your losses, and the fund should tell you what the fee is. Here's an example of how fees work:

Fee: 0.1%. You make 9% on an investment. The fee comes out of the gains, so you will actually make 8.9 %. Or if you lose 4% on an investment, the fee is added to your losses, so you lose 4.1%. A good guiding principle is to not invest in a fund with an expense ratio higher than 1%. Instead find one with the fee falling between 0.05 and 0.20% for passive funds that simply mirror an index like the S&P 500. With these fees, you won't get a bill. The fee will be automatically deducted from your returns.

---

6. LET'S PLACE A TRADE

Now you know what you want to invest in, make a note of the index fund's name and ticker symbol and how much one share costs. Go to the online interface of the brokerage company where your account is.

Now you're going to buy that investment and literally put it inside your IRA account. Here are the steps:

1. Go to the tab that says 'Trade.'

2. Choose a trade type from a drop-down box. The list will show all the types of investments you can buy and sell. It will list some advanced options. Just focus on what's right for you—for now that's either index funds or ETFs.

3. Select an account to trade in—select your IRA.

4. Choose your investment. This is where you write in the letters or ticker symbol of the investment you want.

5. Select an action—buy or sell. This is another way to say you are trading. Buying refers to the investments you will be trading into your account. Selling refers to the investments you are trading out of your account. You will be buying.

6. Pick a quantity—either shares or dollars. If you have enough money in your holding account to cover the amount of shares you want to buy, write in the specific number of shares. For instance, if you have $1,000 to invest in an index fund, and the fund you're considering is selling for $100 a share, you'd be able to purchase ten shares.

7. Confirm the trade. Congratulations! You've officially invested in the stock market. And you did it on your own! Your money now has the potential to grow. You'll want to visit your investments every quarter, especially to see the growth. It's also very affirming!

Dollar cost averaging

Dollar cost averaging is a fancy way of saying you're going to invest small amounts of money regularly regardless of the price of the investment. It's a good way to develop a disciplined investing habit, be more efficient in how you invest, and potentially lower your stress level—as well as your costs. Dollar cost averaging is why you should automate your contributions. Consistently putting money into your investments over a period of time, regardless of whether prices are low or high, smooths out your average purchase price.

How much to invest

Fractional shares

Many stocks worth buying also come with big price tags. Even one share of some of the best performing ETFs and index funds are hundreds of dollars each. But if you don't have enough money to buy even one share, you're not shut out.

Something that I don't think is explained enough is the fact that you don't need to have a lot of money to actually make a purchase of a stock or an index fund. Just because the index fund says it costs $387 per share, doesn't mean you have to spend all of that money for one share. You can buy a piece of it.

You don't have to wait until you have thousands or even hundreds of dollars to invest. You can invest immediately—I mean with as little as $1. Or if you have $5 and put it into an index fund, you can invest in hundreds of stocks all at once.

You'd be buying fractional shares. I'm talking about literally a fraction of a share. You're buying a portion or a slice of a stock, index fund, or ETF. This way of buying stock lets you get into the market right away, and you can begin to benefit from compounding returns sooner. It's also helpful if you want to invest a set dollar amount in a stock or index fund every month—let's say $100—rather than to buy a specific number of shares, where the amount could fluctuate. Over time, those fractional purchases will add up to full shares of stock.

Fractional share buyers beware: Not every stock is available for fractional investing and not all brokerage platforms sell fractional shares. And if they do, they don't always make it obvious how to actually buy a fractional share. That's what I'm for, follow these steps:

1. Go to the tab that says 'Trade.'

2. Choose a trade type from a drop-down box. The list will show all the types of investments you can buy and sell. It will list some advanced options. Just focus on what's right for you, so maybe index funds or ETFs.

3. Select an account to trade in—select your IRA.

4. Choose your investment. This is where you write in the letters or ticker symbol of the investment you want.

5. Select an action—buy.

6. You may not see the words 'buy fractional shares.' So if you have less money than what it costs to buy a whole share, fill in the box next to 'dollars' and put in the amount you want to spend. The program will do the math for you and figure out how much of a slice your money will buy, based on what the share price is.

7. Confirm the trade. Congratulations! You've officially invested in the stock market, even with just fractions of shares.

See? You don't need to wait to start investing. Over time, those fractional purchases will add up to full shares.

Dividends

Speaking of slices of shares, there are also investments that give dividends: Money that's paid regularly to investors who own the stock or fund. It's almost like your investment is a money tree. Every few months to a year, this incredible tree grows extra shiny golden coins on its branches. These coins are called dividends, and they are like little gifts that companies give to their shareholders. Individual stocks aren't the only investments that pay dividends. Certain ETFs and index funds pay out a dividend, too. You can also buy into dividend ETFs that contain only dividend-bearing companies—their stocks—that pay out those gold coins monthly or at some other interval. Keep in mind that not all companies pay dividends. Many companies retain and reinvest their earnings to promote growth, while it's generally the more mature companies that offer dividend payouts. A 'growth' company usually grows faster than its counterparts in terms of sales and profits.

When you set up your brokerage account, you'll be asked whether you want the money reinvested in the stock that gave you the dividend in the first place. Reinvesting means the dividend money automatically goes toward buying more shares. You could also choose to not reinvest the dividend and then the money would be held in a money market or savings account. Many investors like to use dividend income to cover living expenses in retirement. Or you could use the cash balance to purchase another investment, if you already have a large position in a stock or fund and you don't want to buy more of the same security.

Especially if you're a long-term investor—which you should be!— the key is to resist temptation to take the money and instead reinvest the dividend. The power of reinvestment is pretty magical. Here's how that works. You are able to check a box on your investment platform that says 'reinvest.' So that money is automatically used to buy more shares of the company that gave you those dividend 'coins.' It's like giving your money tree some fertilizer to make it grow taller and stronger. Because as you keep reinvesting your dividends, your magical money tree grows bigger, thanks to compounding interest (which we'll cover shortly). Dividends are a way of earning passive income because you get paid just for being a long-term investor.

A couple of things to be aware of though.

Even if you reinvest dividends, they still count as taxable income. So don't be stunned come tax time. But dividends are taxed at lower rates than ordinary income. Additionally, companies can reduce or suspend their dividend payments at any time, which can impact the fund's performance.

If you're an investor outside the U.S., once you've selected which investment fund you'd like to buy, you have the option to choose either the income or accumulation version of the fund. An income unit will distribute any interest or dividend income from the fund directly to you. As a result, you may receive income from your investment at regular intervals. An accumulation unit is designed to offer you growth in the fund, so any income will be reinvested automatically, raising the value of your investment.

Invest often

Investing anything is better than not investing at all. The more you invest, and the earlier you contribute, the faster you'll get to a bigger retirement fund. What's the ideal amount?

Try to invest 20% of every paycheck. But it's okay if you can't. Work your way there over time. You can't afford not to start. Make investing a habit. The automation piece of this is so important. We can be really good at spending and not so much at saving. If you automate your contributions into your IRA, you're more likely to consistently invest.

One basic tenet of investing is that you want to take more risk when you're younger—meaning your overall investments should be more weighted toward stocks. As you grow older you put more of that overall investment pie into more conservative investments, like bonds. A good rule of thumb is that the percentage of stocks you should invest in is 100 minus your age, which the rest going into bonds. So if you're 30 years old, you want 70% in stocks. If you're 40, you want 60% in stocks.

Bonds

Bonds are an investment product where you agree to lend your money to a government or a company at an agreed interest rate for a specific amount of time so they can use that money towards new projects, acquisitions, or supplementing revenue from taxes. And what do you—the investor—get in return? The government or company agrees to pay you interest for that specific amount of time in addition to you getting the original value of the bond back.

Yes, you need bonds. Why? So you can balance and diversify your portfolio, or your collection of investments. Bonds—also called 'fixed income'—are like playing defense, so when the shit hits the fan in the market, bonds are a way you can protect the downside of your portfolio, especially as you approach retirement. Bonds do come with a different sort of risk. These investments generally offer low yields and the amount of money you put into them may not be large enough to generate enough income from interest or dividends. They're the ultimate in boring, but remember—investing is supposed to be boring. You can buy bonds through your online brokerage account or directly from the U.S. government.

How to earn money with bonds

- Buy and hold the bond until it matures, and then collect the principal and interest. Maturity is the date when the bond holder (company or government) returns the money to you that you lent them (principal) plus interest.

- If the bond price goes up from where you purchased it, another strategy is to sell it early and make a profit.

Can the borrower pay its bonds?

Remember how you received grades in school? Bonds are also graded—given a rating—so you can better understand the investment's financial standing. Bonds earn their grades from ratings agencies: Standard & Poor's, Moody's and Fitch. They estimate creditworthiness and assign credit ratings to companies and governments and the bonds they issue. The higher the rating— AAA or 'triple A' is the highest and it goes down from there—the greater the likelihood the company will honor its obligations.

Kinds of bonds

Before you dip your toe in, you'll want to do your homework especially about the types of bonds to invest in and the tax advantages that make the most sense for your financial goals. Here are a few:

- **Corporate bonds:** You can also figure out how safe a company-issued bond is by looking at how much interest a company pays relative to its income. Not to get into the weeds here, but start with the company's most recent annual operating income and interest expense. You can find it on a company's income statement. It's in their '10-K' filing which you can find on the company's website or on the U.S. Securities and Exchange Commission's website in the 'Edgar Database.'

- **Zero-coupon bonds**: These don't pay interest and are sold at a reduced price compared to their face value. A profit is made when the bond is held to maturity. Treasury or T-bills are examples of a zero-coupon bond.

- **Government bonds**: U.S government bonds are also called Treasury Bonds or T-bills, and are considered the world's safest and rated AAA. As a result, government bonds do not usually offer higher interest rates because of the low risk of default.

- **Municipal bonds**: Bonds issued by cities, states, and municipalities have been safe historically. But they're not a slam dunk. You can investigate these bonds more on the 'Electronic Municipal Market Access (EMMA)' website, which provides a bond's official prospectus, an issuer's audited financial statements, and ongoing financial disclosures, including payment delinquencies and defaults. Check out the credit rating too. Income from municipal bonds is generally tax-free at the federal level and sometimes at the state level, if you purchase them in the state where you live.

I know, your head is spinning

At this point, you're like, 'Alright Alison, which bonds are the best to get into?' The type of bonds that might be right for you depends on several factors, including your risk tolerance, tax situation, and time horizon, as well as when you need income from these bonds.

To be honest, diversifying a bond portfolio can be a stretch because bonds typically are sold in $1,000 increments, so it can take beaucoup bucks to build a diversified portfolio. Instead, it may be easier to buy bond funds. Bond index funds in the flavors already covered—much like stock index funds—can give you instant diversification to the bond types you want and you can mix and match bond funds even if you can't invest a large amount at once. And just like with stocks—or any investment for that matter—broadening your exposure gives you the benefit of lowering your risk because all your eggs aren't in one basket.

Investing doesn't have to be complicated

- Understand what you're putting your money into
- Pick index fund(s)
- Pick bond fund(s)

Rinse and repeat—contribute every month until you reach your goal.

WTF is compounding?

Compounding happens when the proceeds or earnings of an investment—from capital gains or interest—are reinvested over and over to generate additional returns. That causes the original investment to get bigger and bigger at a faster rate over time. The growth happens because the investment will generate earnings from both its initial principal and the accumulated earnings and interest from prior years. Over time, you'll earn interest on ever-larger account balances.

Compounding is the main reason that you should aim to invest early and often. It's a way to accumulate more money over time, just by staying invested in the stock or bond market.

Think of it in reverse. If you have credit card debt at a high interest rate—over time that builds and builds and winds up costing you a lot of money. The same can happen with your investments, where they grow exponentially and make you money.

Compounding is like a superpower for your money. It's like a snowball rolling down a hill, getting bigger and bigger as it picks up more snow. Except the snow is dollar dollar bills y'all.

That's why it's know as 'the magic of compound interest.' And it's why, if your investments earn dividends, you should harness that power of compounding by reinvesting those dividends instead of withdrawing them into cash.

The same idea goes for investing in general. Because of compounding, even modest contributions to an investment account can evolve into a substantial sum over time.

Let's play a game. Well, it's more of a question. Would you rather have a million dollars today or a penny doubled every day for 31 days?

Trick question? Maybe. If you're like, 'Well I think I should be choosing a penny, but I'm not sure why,' you picked the right answer, even though a million sounds great.

Drum roll please!

A penny doubled every day for 31 days gives you about $10.7m.

THE POWER OF EXPONENTIAL GROWTH

Day 1	$0.01	Day 11	$10.24	Day 21	$10,485.76
Day 2	$0.02	Day 12	$20.48	Day 22	$20,971.52
Day 3	$0.04	Day 13	$40.96	Day 23	$41,943.04
Day 4	$0.08	Day 14	$81.92	Day 24	$83,886.08
Day 5	$0.16	Day 15	$163.84	Day 25	$167,772.16
Day 6	$0.32	Day 16	$327.68	Day 26	$335,544.32
Day 7	$0.64	Day 17	$655.36	Day 27	$671,088.64
Day 8	$1.28	Day 18	$1,310.72	Day 28	$1,342,177.28
Day 9	$2.56	Day 19	$2,621.44	Day 29	$2,684,354.56
Day 10	$5.12	Day 20	$5,242.88	Day 30	$5,368,709.12
Total after doubling the penny every day for 31 days:				Day 31	$10,737,418.24

I guess it's no wonder (pun intended) Albert Einstein famously referred to compound interest as the eighth wonder of the world.

That's why it's so important to start investing early and often, giving yourself as many years as possible to build wealth.

The magic of compound interest

Let's say you're 30 years old and you start putting money into an index fund that tracks the biggest market index, the S&P 500.

- You contribute $400 a month.

- You invest for 30 years.

- You earn 8% interest on your investments (the historical 30-year return on the S&P is actually 10%).

By the time you're 60 years old, the $144,000 you actually invested has turned into more than half a million dollars. That's what compound interest can do for your nest egg!

Wait, then is it too late?

No, it's never too late to accumulate wealth. And don't beat yourself up! If you're 40 or even 50 years old and you haven't started to invest, this is a place where women's longevity helps us. We're living longer—50 or 60 doesn't seem as old as it used to. Of course, your investment strategy will be much different than a 20-year-old's. But even at 60 years old, many women will live another 25 to 30 years, so that's time right there to continue investing and allowing money to grow. Roth IRAs may be attractive to older investors because they don't require that you take money out of your account at any particular age. Start by increasing your contributions in your 401(k) and your Roth IRA. If you haven't already, balance your investment basket with bond funds too, to decrease your overall risk.

Start now. Start today.

If you're 40 you still have at least 25 years to have compounding work for you.

Investing $600 a month for 25 years will get you to $708,000 by 65 years old. That's more than the average 65-year-old has saved for retirement.[38]

A little goes a long way

As you contribute more money into your investments, over time you will grow more confident in investing. Remember, women are better at it than men. The trick is putting your money to work. And I think if you look hard enough, you can find some extra cash. Even $5. Don't laugh. Think $5 won't make a dent? Think again. Challenge yourself to invest what you pay for your cup of coffee every workday per month (20 workdays per month). That small daily expense adds up to $100 a month, and if invested it will compound annually. With an 8% return, in ten years that coffee money will add up to $18,500. In 20 years it will be worth $56,400. In 30 years—$150,000. If you invest more, those amounts will be higher. I'm not saying don't drink coffee. I'm just saying why not make it yourself? Or don't buy it every. Single. Day. You may realize it's easier to 'find' an extra $100 per month to invest than you originally thought.

Frugality alone won't build wealth. So much of our wealth building depends on women bringing in higher incomes. That's where the power of negotiation comes in. In the next chapter, I'll show you how to make it work for you.

NEKIA HACKWORTH JONES, DIRECTOR OF THE ATLANTA REGIONAL OFFICE, U.S. SECURITIES AND EXCHANGE COMMISSION *

In her own words

The reasons that women are reticent to invest, based on my own experience, align with some of the research and studies that have been done. The big three would be lack of knowledge, lack of money (and often perceptions of a lack of money), and risk aversion.

When it comes to lack of knowledge, some women believe that they just don't know enough. They don't feel confident in understanding things like investment jargon. And then some women don't feel that they have a good resource, person, or organization that can help educate them in a credible way. If you look at the Certified Financial Planning Board's website, there are around 96,000 Certified Financial Planners™ in 2023, but only 23% of them are women. And if you take it one step deeper, less than 2% are black. If you're a woman and you're thinking about who you can go to for help or who you may feel comfortable learning from, the process of finding a trusted resource may feel daunting.

The actual lack of money can be an issue because, if you don't have enough income, then you can't get to the point

---

* The views expressed are made in Nekia's official capacity as the Atlanta Regional Director, but do not necessarily reflect the views of the commission, the commissioners, or other staff.

where you're able to save and, by extension, you can't get to the point where you're able to invest. Even when people have enough income to invest, they don't believe that they do. Specifically, women might think that they need a certain minimum income to be able to put money into some type of investment. But even investing small amounts can yield great dividends. I must admit that this is not even something I did for myself over the years. Studies have shown that, if a person invested $30 into the S&P 500 every month for the past ten years, the investor would have around $6,000 in their bank account, with no more than half of that amount being from their own investment. Now, I know that for many women and, even more specifically, women of color, finding an extra $30 a month is a heavy lift. For others, this may mean eliminating or cutting back on some 'favorite things' or small indulgences (lattes!). Even just micro savings can yield big dividends, literally and figuratively.

The final investing challenge is risk aversion and a fear of losing money. There are different levels of risk. There's also risk of lost opportunity, things you could have invested in. But new investors, including women and women of color, don't understand that almost all things come with risk. It's just about having the right basket of investments to diversify that risk.

This has aligned with my own personal experience. My first investment was a stock gift that I received from a scholarship when I was 16 years old. But guess what? After two business degrees and a law degree, my next financial investment was eight years later when I was 24 years old. Even with the requisite level of knowledge, even with some income and some savings, I still didn't invest because of fear. So, if somebody like me was paralyzed by fear, can you imagine what it's like for others who have little to no investing knowledge or experience?

Being raised in a working class family, I had the belief, although wrong, that I had to be at a certain level or have a five- to six-figure income to take on what I thought was the 'luxury' of investing. And that's just not the case. To have a comfortable retirement, you must invest to get there. As a student and then a new professional, I viewed investing as something that really wasn't within my reach and I was waiting for that magical moment when I got my first 'big' job or "big" promotion. Now I can admit that, back then, I was afraid. I was afraid to lose the money that I worked so hard to earn and to save. The biggest lessons I learned are that it is important to shake off the paralysis, do the research using reputable sources (like investor.gov for basics and brokercheck.finra.org to research financial advisors and brokers), and use that knowledge to make that very first investment. After the first one, investing becomes easier with time and experience.

ELIZABETH HERSCH
CERTIFIED FINANCIAL PLANNER™

In her own words

There are exceptions, but I think what is typical is there's a specialization of labor in the household. No matter what age from millennials to baby boomers. If the wife is in a creative role or a doctor or teacher and the husband is in finance or law, she'll farm out the balance sheet management and investing to the husband. And frankly it's often the woman who will come to me, to seek out financial planning, because she's not sure if he's got everything right, but she doesn't know how to fix it or understand it. The husband will usually say I know exactly what I'm doing, I don't need help. And then we'll get into it. And I will show him and he will learn that he's made some dumb decisions.

I just had a couple in my office. They just got married—29 years old. She's a physical therapist, he's got an MBA. So he thinks he knows everything. And she said to me, point blank-he's investing in these crazy FinTech platforms. And the new wife said, "I let him do all of it. I don't understand it. I don't want to understand it. He's really smart. He knows what he's doing and he likes doing it. So I trust him."

Then there's the Wharton MBA and she was telling me how embarrassed she is that she doesn't know much about how her husband (who is a private equity guy) was handling their wealth. I yelled at her and she said to me, "I know I should push him on this but I just can't seem to do it and I'm so embarrassed." Sheesh... here's a woman who has been in the C-suite of some of the largest companies in the world with people listening to everything she says and she can't muster the confidence to insist that her husband discuss how their money is invested? There is NO excuse and I wonder what would/could help her feel empowered to have the conversations she really should be having. In her case, she's pretty literate financially but there's some weird dynamic thing creating a roadblock...

Why are so many women in the dark or hesitant to get involved when it comes to investing? Maybe because there's no right answer, there's no clear path when it comes to investing. Maybe there's an insecurity about making a bad decision or a wrong decision.

To the women reading this: You don't know what tomorrow brings. Get involved now, whether you're married or not.

You shouldn't abdicate your responsibility over your financial health.

KARINA B, VENTURE CAPITALIST

A cautionary tale

As a venture capitalist, 53-year-old single mother of two Karina raises money for other companies so they can grow, but she didn't help herself. She's highly successful in her position, launching and working with companies and helping them raise millions of dollars in investment capital.

Looking at her, driving a BMW, always dressed to the nines, you'd think she had her financial future locked up. Not even close. Karina didn't even know what an IRA is until recently, and her accountant never advised her to set up a retirement plan. She doesn't have any retirement accounts, has about $100,000 in savings and rents her home. She has never budgeted and doesn't know even the basics about personal finance. She admits that she is terrified about money and always has put her head in the sand.

Not helping matters, she had a difficult and expensive divorce and now has a deadbeat ex-husband who never fulfilled their settlement agreement. She was too embarrassed and ashamed to ever ask for help, so she muddled through financially. Now at 53 years old she is trying to figure out how she is going to be okay financially going forward.

Here's her story, in her own words:

One of the ironies here is, do you know how many people call me and want to meet with me for advice about growing their companies? And by the way, I'm really good at it. But when it comes to myself, obviously I'm horrible. It's the whole 'cobbler's children have no shoes.'

I was investing in companies and obviously not investing in myself. I just thought, 'Okay, our fund will do well and I'll have money at that point.' And that's not going to be the case because of the fact that the market is so terrible right now. One of our companies is even folding. I have a ton of regrets. So what do I do now? I feel like it's useless. Once I got behind, I felt like it was useless to start planning for retirement. So I just go ahead doing what I'm doing because I'm never going to be able to make a dent. Which is stupid, backward thinking. But I kept thinking, I'm so late to the game, how could starting now at my age possibly help me? I'm so behind, why would I even do this? I was told three years ago to set up a retirement account. But I ignored the advice. I also know I should cut back on spending, but nothing has stopped me from doing that. I make good money, I've just not put my money to work.

If I could roll all of this back, I would in a second. But since I can't, I just keep making the same stupid mistakes. It's like being on the same treadmill. I wish I could understand why. I don't know if it's fear. I don't know if it's embarrassment. Perhaps I'm just hopelessly optimistic, expecting everything to turn out for the best somehow!

CHELY WRIGHT, SINGER, SONGWRITER, AUTHOR, ADVOCATE, BUSINESS EXECUTIVE

In her own words

Concepts, conversations, language, and systems around investing are very male. I think these systems are meant to intimidate and exclude women. If it seems finance, personal wealth, and wealth management feel unapproachable, even to the most well-educated, highest paid, most confident women, I think it's by design. The patriarchy thrives as a result of these inequitable systems. And by the way, I am not a lesbian who hates men. I quite love men and have some really important relationships with men that enrich my life. But, a Latin doctrine of law, *res ipsa loquitur*, which means 'the thing speaks for itself' says it best. Given marriage was historically rooted in land ownership and property, it's no surprise girls and women still struggle to find their power when it comes to money. These are old and ingrained systems that are upheld by the patriarchy, and they're meant to leave women out.

They're meant to leave women with fewer choices than men. So many women I know are at the top of their game in their sector, their field, but they're still intimidated by money—how to demand it for their work and how to invest it for their futures.

Since the early 1990s, I have worked directly with a number of brokers as I'm active in choosing a lot of my own stocks and funds. I really enjoy it. All of the brokers I've dealt with have been men. I cannot tell you how many times over the years a broker has said something like, 'Oh wow, it's so unusual to have a woman investing in that kind of stock.' I recall one guy who said, "That's not really a stock that most women are interested in." I asked him what stocks women are most interested in? He told me women are most interested in consumer brands like clothing, body care, and make-up. Ugh. I pushed back to say how sexist that is. He said he didn't mean it in a sexist way, but it's just the truth.

(The stock Chely is referring to is Caterpillar, a global conglomerate that manufactures construction, mining, and other engineering equipment.)

Full disclosure about this chapter—this wasn't meant to be a deep dive into investing. What I hoped to accomplish here is to walk a beginning investor through the steps of how to set up an investment account within minutes and make an actual trade. I wanted to make you feel confident and not intimidated by it. So I took you through some baby steps to start investing and some of the fundamentals of investing. The idea is to not stop here. If you can, you should be investing regularly, even in small increments. When you're ready to go from dipping your toe in the water to taking the plunge, here are some other books you may want to check out:

- *How I Invest My Money* edited by Joshua Brown and Brian Portnoy.

- *Just Keep Buying* by Nick Maggiulli.

- *The Behavioral Investor* by Daniel Crosby.

- *The Psychology of Money* by Morgan Housel.

- *The Simple Path to Wealth* and *Pathfinders* by JL Collins.

- *The World's Simplest Guide to the Stock Market* by Edward W. Ryan.

CHAPTER 10: NEGOTIATE LIKE A MAN: WHAT WOULD HE SAY?

"The most common way people give up their power is by thinking they don't have any."

Alice Walker

I T'S REMARKABLE. IN the 30 years after *Shark Tank*'s Barbara Corcoran founded the Corcoran Group, a real estate brokerage in New York City, she says not one female manager or support staffer ever asked her for a raise. Not one. And 90% of the managers and staffers in her company were women! WTF, right? That was from the 1970s through 2001. You might think things would improve in the early 21st century, but they didn't really. In 2020, a Randstad survey showed a whopping 60% of women had never negotiated with an employer over pay.[39]

Maybe, just maybe, the trend is improving. Separate research from 2022 suggests that 70% of employed women *have* tried to negotiate their pay.[40] Of those women, almost 60% said their negotiations were successful. Not to be a Debbie downer, but this also means around 30% of women are *still* accepting their salary without negotiating. That's still bad news, because every woman— every woman!—should be negotiating her salary.

WHY THE F*CK AREN'T WE ASKING?

Part of it may be that many women don't know the best way to approach salary negotiation, because women often face judgments that men don't when they ask for more. Sheryl Sandberg tells me that negotiating often doesn't work as well for women as it does for men, because of cultural expectations. Think about it. Why do we call girls 'bossy'? Women can be perceived as too pushy and selfish, while men can aggressively negotiate without fear of repercussions.

In negotiating for increased salary during the application process for a new job, one common fear is that the employer could rescind the job offer. Or by negotiating for a pay raise in a current job, there is a very real fear, backed by research, that negotiating may not lead to gains but instead, may come at the cost of being disliked.[41] The research shows that "Relative to men who ask for more, women are penalized financially, are considered less hirable and less likable, and are less likely to be promoted. Men, on the other hand, can typically negotiate without worrying about backlash—and are four times [as] likely to do so—because bold, assertive behavior is consistent with traditional masculine gender norms." As if that's not enough to hold us back from rocking the boat by asking for more money, other reasons we don't negotiate and just accept the salary we're offered include:[42]

- not feeling equipped for the conversation

- inexperience

- lack of confidence

But, if you don't ask, you don't get.

It really, really matters if you just throw away the opportunity of negotiating your salary—especially when you're going for a new position. At that new company, all future raises you get will be based on your starting salary. The long-term difference between employees who negotiate a starting salary and those who do not is staggering. The research on this finds that over the course of a 45-year career, the non-negotiating worker stands to lose between $650,000 and $1m relative to the negotiator.[43] That's not just from lost earnings, but also from the loss of compounding interest over the years that you don't invest any of those earnings.

Another reason to negotiate is that women who avoid negotiating for a higher salary when offered a new job inadvertently contribute to the issue of the gender pay gap—the difference between what women make and what men make. Women who work full time, year-round earn just under 84 cents for every dollar men earn for doing the same job. That's 16% less! It means women each year earn a median annual income that's $10,000 less than men.[44] That money can be lifechanging. If you invest $10,000 at an 8% return (remember that the average return of the stock market is 8%–10%) every year for 40 years? You get $2.8m. That's money you're missing out on because of the gender wage gap.

For Black and Latina women it's even worse. Compared to men, they're getting 67c and 57c on the dollar, respectively.

The pay gap is not about a single paycheck. The pay gap also widens the wealth gap—the void between the overall money that women and men own or accumulate. Single white women own 92c on the dollar compared to single men. And shockingly, single Black women own less than 8c on the dollar compared to white men.[45]

A lack of negotiation leading to lower salaries isn't the only thing perpetuating the gender pay gap. There are bigger reasons:

- Discrimination from gender bias at both a conscious and unconscious level. We've got what it takes: A Harvard Business Review study found women rank more highly than men in 17 out of the top 19 leadership qualities. But women are consistently overlooked by employers, who still tend to view men as being more competent.[46]

- Women are being short-changed in performance bonuses. What really burns about this is that men are receiving up to 35% more in their bonuses than women, even when they both receive the same performance rating.[47]

- Men and women tend to work in different industries, with female-dominated industries like childcare, social work, teaching, and nursing attracting lower wages. Why isn't anyone questioning why these female-dominated industries are attracting lower wages in the first place? Here's what's crazy: Research shows that when women take over a male-dominated field, the pay drops—for the very same jobs that more men were doing before. A striking example of this happened in the field of parks and recreation. Wages dropped by 57 percentage points as the field went from predominantly men to women workers. But even when women join men in the same field, the pay gap remains. Female physicians, for instance, earn 71% of what male physicians earn, and female lawyers earn 82%.[48]

- Women take more time out of work to raise a family. When they drop out of the labor force for some time, women often do not have the same continuity of work experience as their male counterparts, which contributes to lower wages.[49]

- When women return to work after having a child, they often face what's known as the 'motherhood penalty.' Most workplaces don't offer much flexibility for mothers, who are often forced to take on lower-paying and less demanding jobs.

Despite these 'reasons,' the persistent gender pay gap is perplexing because women are better educated than men. For decades, women have been graduating from college at higher rates than men. But diplomas aren't translating to dollars. The pay gap remains, even at higher education levels. It's more evidence of women being undervalued.

GO FOR IT: NEGOTIATE

Here's the irony of it all: Negotiation is actually a thing that most women are super good at. We are natural negotiators. We already have the skills! We just need to learn how to use them and reimagine the whole idea of negotiating. So, I've done the work for you. I interviewed a few negotiation experts to gain insights into the tools women need and the steps they should take to ace the negotiation process.

The big issue for women is that we often see the perceived negotiation as conflict. And when women think of conflict, they think someone has to win and someone has to lose—that it's this testosterone-driven, competitive, male activity that's dirty or sneaky and we wish we didn't have to engage in. But what if I told you that if you flip the paradigm of how you think about negotiation, so as to not think of it as a conflict or a confrontation but instead as a conversation, you would have a much better chance at success with it?

That's because negotiation *is* really just that—a conversation with a goal in mind, and most women innately have the skills that are needed to do really well in a conversation. This is because we can empathize and understand what the other side's situation is, we have intuition to decode all the non-verbal messages coming at us, and our listening skills are typically amazing. We also have more oxytocin than men, so we tend to be more cooperative. When exhibited by employees, these traits are linked with an increase in long-term value for companies.[50] They also make women highly effective problem-solvers. In fact, research by Laura Kray at the University of California, Berkeley, and Jessica Kennedy at Vanderbilt University, shows that women excel at generating goodwill through problem-solving.[51] The researchers found women possess unique advantages as negotiators, including greater cooperativeness and stronger ethics. But often those strengths are overlooked or severely undervalued.

WHAT TO DO BEFORE THE NEGOTIATION

Now that we know we've got the innate skills, how can women best leverage them? This is where strategy comes in. If you're starting a new job, your salary negotiation strategy will be different than if you're already working somewhere and want to get a raise. But whether you're negotiating salary for a new position or you're trying to get a raise at the job you've had for five years, it's all about preparation, asking strategic questions, and playing the long game.

Prepare, prepare, prepare!

You have to put time and effort into the preparation phase. Meggie Palmer, who runs classes on how to negotiate as part of her work to close the gender pay gap, says five of her clients were able to get an extra $100,000 plus because they went the extra mile with the prep. I know, it's not sexy or exciting. But preparation is power. She feels it's the most important step because researching who you're interviewing with (whether for a new job or to get a raise at your current job) helps you to know where the other party is coming from, so you can structure your request and conversation in a way that will speak to what they want. Whether you're a prospective or existing employee, these are some of the questions you should answer and keep in mind as you prep:

- What is the company's market?
- How many employees do they have?
- What's the size of the company? Is it a Fortune 100 company? (How you negotiate and what you ask for in terms of salary is very different than negotiating with a mom-and-pop company.)
- What do employment websites like Glassdoor say about salaries for the position under discussion?
- What is the culture like within the organization?
- What is the latest news about the company?

Practice ahead of time. This is key! The more mental gymnastics you can do before you get into that room or into that Zoom, the better the outcome. You are going to feel much calmer because you've already run this through in your head or practiced with someone. Any preparation in a role play sense is helpful, even if you feel a little bit of an idiot doing it. But our brains are funny things. Even though it's role play, your brain is subconsciously processing what you're saying.

Let's say tomorrow you will be trying to get an extra $5,000 to $10,000 a year for your raise. Sometimes saying that number can feel like an out-of-body experience. So you want to get used to saying it. Say it out loud in the shower. I want you to tell your friends that it's the number you're asking for. Get comfortable saying that number out loud, because for a lot of us, the first time we say the number or the salary or even the title that we want is in that negotiation.

Once we've trained ourselves to say that number in a natural way and it just rolls off the tongue, it will be perceived more positively by whoever we're negotiating with. Instead of mumbling, 'Oh, you know, um, I was thinking like, how would you think about 25 grand? I don't know.' you'll say, 'Hey listen, given my value and the impact that I've contributed to the company this year, I'd love to talk about an extra $25,000 in my salary going forward.' See the difference? It's a very different conversation in terms of the tone of voice and how you are perceived. Because for better or worse, perception is really important.

Similarly, body language, words, and tone all matter when you're trying to get a better result. Shifting your language to be non-threatening and to be open is really powerful. It's the same with body language. Body language can be powerful, too. That's where the preparation of actually roleplaying is so helpful. And you can even do this with your cell phone. You can just set your phone up to record you in a wide shot talking to the phone as though you're having a practice negotiation. Then watch the video back with the sound off. What you'll notice is your body language. You might be fidgeting or touching your hair a lot. Being aware of those non-verbal cues is very important as well.

Hot Tip#1

Google the company's news on the day you have your interview/ negotiation. What if the company had mass layoffs yesterday? Or what if their CEO is on the front page of the paper for all of the wrong reasons today? You'd be surprised at how often and coincidentally this happens. In the past, I've interviewed with a company (that will remain nameless) on the same day that they announced there would be layoffs on the way. You want to make sure you have that information so you have some context about how you may have to tailor your discussions.

The idea is to check the temperature of the company you're dealing with. It's important to keep up-to-the-minute information in the back of your mind during the meeting. It helps you to read the room. If the company announced that they're doing well, maybe ask for a figure toward the top of the salary range you were going to negotiate for. That's versus an announcement about layoffs—after which you'd want to be sensitive to where the company is business-wise and what compensation they're likely to offer you at that moment. But even bad news, like layoffs, can mean a good opportunity for you.

Hot Tip #2

Whether you're interviewing for a new job or trying to get a raise in your current job, having an organized 'brag book' of your collected accomplishments can help you sell yourself. This is the proof that you deserve a raise or a particular salary. If you find that throughout your job you just scribbled things on index cards or on your phone notes app and it's all over the place, may I suggest a way to keep this stuff in an organized fashion? Of course, there's an app for that—and it's free! PepTalkHer is like an online brag book that makes it easy to keep track of your wins at work and also lets you upload screenshots of glowing emails you've received over the years. Keeping all of your achievements in one place is helpful not just for negotiations but for performance or pay reviews, too.

Hot Tip #3

If you're in the interview stage of getting a new job, companies are much more willing to be transparent with external candidates than with current employees. Companies are often required by law to share pay ranges on job postings, but the same isn't true for internal pay ranges. Those external pay ranges are absolutely a useful source of information for internal employees to benchmark their own pay.

Hot Tip #4

The best time to negotiate your salary is during the offer stage. Many companies—especially large, highly structured corporations—limit the percentage an employee's compensation can be raised by during a calendar year.

Some bosses are financially incentivized to pay their team less. Let's say they have a million-dollar budget for payroll. If they hire ten people at $100,000 each, that's the million dollars spent. But some companies will incentivize them to pay everyone $90,000 and come in at $900,000 total, for which the boss will get a percentage of that $100,000 as a bonus. So if they are incentivized to pay you less, the way to get a pay raise is either have another offer from another company, or be open to non-monetary benefits.

PREP CHECKLIST

- Who is the individual you'll be negotiating with? You'll want to go to their LinkedIn, but also check out their social media like Instagram and X. Do they like dogs? Which Netflix series are they always talking about on social media? The more information you gather, the more you can get below the surface of the individual person and the better you will be able to connect with them. And the better relationship you have with someone, the better the outcome of the negotiation. Because people like to do business with people they like. It's not necessarily fair or reasonable, but that's the reality. If you can form that connection early on in the negotiation, you'll have a lot more power and you're going to be able to get a better outcome.

- If you know the person you're negotiating with, think about what levers the person responds to and how you can steer the conversation. If they're data driven, they'll respond to the fact that you improved the website's SEO by 13% year on year and that it's contributed an extra $75,000 in sales (or whatever metric is used in your particular industry). Communicating your achievements in the conversation is essential to giving color to your value. If you're a nurse, have you reduced the waiting time in the waiting room? If you're an executive assistant, have you negotiated with vendors about how to get stationery at a discounted rate? You should think about what things are important to your current or potential boss, and what makes *them* look good to *their* boss. The case you make has to make it very easy for them to see how saying yes to you is going to make them look good in terms of the hierarchy up the chain as well.

- Know your 'wish,' 'want,' and 'walk' figures. You should have three numbers in mind before you go into any negotiation, whether it's with your current employer or potential employer. The wish number is a crazy high number. A salary or raise that leaves you thinking, 'I cannot believe someone's going to pay me this much!' (also known as your fuck off number). Hell yeah! The walk number, at the other extreme, is low enough that you're going to begin looking for another job. It's that low-ball number that screams 'you're not valued' and indicates that your boss isn't even going to try to entice you to stay at the company. The want number is somewhere in the middle. It doesn't have to be smack bang in the middle, but it's a number that will make you stoked to get out of bed and work super hard. It feels fair and reasonable, and you know you're being valued for your time and expertise.

- Have those figures in mind before you walk in. Barbara Corcoran told me, "If you leave it up to the boss to dream up the number, you won't get as much as you want. The boss always has a lower number in their head. Always. I always do. I'm always startled when someone asks me for a $20,000 raise when I was going to give her $5,000. That puts me in the position of needing to come back with less. But compromising on a raise always gets you more than you would have gotten if you hadn't named a price. I think you must name a price that you think would be reasonable. And a little bit above that."

- If your organization isn't transparent about salary ranges, research comparable roles on Glassdoor, Salary.com or Payscale. Informational interviews are also helpful. Let's say you wanted to break into public relations to help market clients' products. Reach out to ten people on LinkedIn and just say to them, "I'm really excited to pivot into public relations. I'd love to chat for five minutes to get an understanding of your job and what it's like working at your company."

- Have a contingency plan. If you can't secure your target salary, decide what you would want to get instead. Think about what things you value. Do you want a different title? More vacation days? Do you want to split your time in the office and working from home? How about a commuting stipend? Or paying for parking, committing to business class travel, or a stipend to contribute towards higher education? Childcare, meals provided at work, or gym memberships are other benefits companies may offer. Your boss may be more flexible with things like this, because all of that money comes out of a different line item than salary.

NOW IT'S TIME TO PLAY LET'S MAKE A DEAL

Everyone should have a conversation every single year about their salary. If you have good leadership, this chat will automatically come up. If you have bad leadership, and you don't ask for the discussion, they're probably not going to offer it to you. That said, how successful you are in getting a raise that does more than just keep up with inflation really depends on your performance. And even if you're crushing it at work, it's not a given you will be handed a raise.

'What have you done for me lately?' is the kind of thinking that's going through your boss' mind when you ask for a big raise. It's often not enough to remind them that you won a deal or that you've been at the company a long time. When she ran the Corcoran Group, Barbara Corcoran would offer raises only to employees who had taken on more responsibility than they were hired for: 'I'm not going to pay you more just because you've been here six months and you're doing the same shit. I want to pay you more if you've taken on more responsibility and you can show me evidence.'

The principle is similar when asking for a more senior title or more responsibility at the company. What data points do you have to prove and back up your argument as to why you should be promoted? Want to be vice-president of your unit? Well, why? Tenure isn't enough. Have you brought in new clients? Cultivated new revenue? What's your evidence? And if you have evidence, maybe the pitch is 'I've specifically hired an extra three people, saving us $120,000 in recruiting costs. You will see from these pieces of feedback from internal teams that I work well with the group, and that my behavior and my processes are exemplary. It's clear that my skills and impact match up to the company's key performance indicators for the VP title. For that reason, I would love to be considered for the VP position.' Your argument is much stronger if you've got meat on the bone to prove why you should get the role.

This is also why it's so super important to log and keep track of your metrics and your wins regularly—like every single week. So that way, when it comes the time for reviews, promotions, or raises, you have a whole catalog you can look back on to demonstrate everything you've accomplished. It helps you defeat imposter syndrome because you see your achievements for what they are. The PepTalkHer app makes it really easy to pop that information in really quickly because who remembers these things themselves? I mean I genuinely don't remember what I had for dinner three nights ago, let alone what happened at work last December or March.

How to set up the meeting

You should never just walk into your boss' office for this kind of conversation. Make an appointment via email a week out. Say something like, 'I'd like to go over my job with you and see how I'm doing, would you have time next week?' Career Coach and Influencer Sam DeMase says that you should be transparent about the discussion, letting your boss know that it will be about your compensation. Say something like, 'I would love to discuss my impact, my compensation and my future at this company.'

Have an opening line

Whether you're interviewing for a position with a new company or with your current boss for a salary raise, a great way to start is with gratitude. Something like, 'Thank you so much for the opportunity. I'm excited about the possibility of joining this team.' Spend a minute saying how much you enjoy working for that individual, whether it's true or not, and how much you adore the company.

Before we get to 'the ask,' though, think about this: Don't focus on your desire for more money right out of the gate. Instead, focus on your value to the company and quantify it by talking about your achievements in depth. DeMase says when you're asking for a higher title that offers more money, you'll get a better result if you don't make it just about you. How can you make your request such that it's benefitting the organization? For instance, let's say I was a sales leader and I was going in to ask for more money, I'd say something like, 'Here are my metrics, and I'm really proud of the work that I've done building a cohesive team, and I know I've got their support to step into this next level. It would be such a privilege to continue leading them with the style that I've developed. For this organization, this role will really mean that I feel committed to staying with this team for at least the next five years because I'm incentivized to continue building this team. So this title would really help me cement my role here for the long term.' Notice it's not just about why I want this extra money, it's also about why this is actually great for the organization.

Sam DeMase suggests you should write out the data and examples of your wins, noting them in a couple of strong bullets. Better yet, expressing your achievements visually—for example, using a PowerPoint presentation—can be very impactful. List any ways that you're working outside or beyond the scope of your job description and make sure that you cover them all in the meeting.

'The ask'

Now you put these elements—gratitude, your accomplishments, and how the organization will benefit—together into 'the ask.' You can do this however you feel comfortable. But be clear and transparent. Here are some example phrases you can work from.

For a new job:

'Given my unique experience, the value that I'm bringing to this role, the impact I plan to make right out of the gate, I'm looking for a salary of $X. Can we make it happen?'

'I'm obviously really excited about this organization, really believe in your mission, and am super happy to be having this conversation. I've always been well compensated for my expertise. And so I'd love to hear from you what you've budgeted for this role?'

'You've given me a lot to think about. Can you talk me through what you are thinking budget-wise? Then I'll give it some thought and come straight back with you.'

If they say they want you to give them a number, you could say:

'My rate depends on the hours and what I'm doing. Let's talk about what range you had in mind.'

Or give them a range:

'My rate varies from $500 to $2,000 a day, depending on the work. Just just let me know where you fall and let's figure something out together.'

For a raise at your current job:

'You and I have been working together a long time. I love my job and I want to stay here. Inflation is going bananas right now. I've achieved A, B, and C, and this has been an impressive year. I've had positive feedback from X, Y, and Z divisions. I want to make something work and I also need to make sure that I'm not going backwards financially.'

Or:

'I love being a part of this team. Thank you for your leadership. I've learned a lot and I love working here. I do want to talk about compensation, and I want to advocate for what I'm worth. How much room do you have to move? I know that we can come to an agreement here that's mutually beneficial.'

Corcoran suggests not asking for an answer on the spot. She says it's like cornering a cat. "They're going to come out scratching." Instead say, 'Can you give it some thought and can I meet with you in about a week?'

While it's probably the smartest move to make, it could also work against you because the boss has a chance to come up with reasons why they *can't* give you a raise. So make sure you're using that time to come up with your own counter-arguments.

Ultimately, you have to read the situation and decide what the best strategy is.

If you get a 'no'

In a negotiation, 'yes' lives in the land of 'no.' It can even lead toward yes if you respond to it by asking the right strategic, open-ended questions. You might even learn the 'why' behind the no. So, if you don't initially get the answer you want, you could say:

'Look, I'm disappointed, but I'd love to understand more behind that reasoning. Tell me what you need from me over the next six months to make sure that it's an easy yes when I re-visit this with you. Tell me what I could have done better because I really value your feedback.'

Or:

'I'd love to learn the good, the bad, and the ugly so that I can grow and improve going forward. What do you need to see from me in the next 90 days so that your perception changes?'

Or:

'Listen, I'm really disappointed. Can you tell me more about that decision?'

Or:

'I hear you that the budget is capped, but based on my unique experience and the value that I'm bringing to this role, I'd like to ask that we meet in the middle at X dollars. Can we make that happen?'

By keeping the conversation going, and by not just accepting a no and walking out of the boss' office to cry at your desk, you're steering the relationship. Even if there's a rejection, if you steer the relationship properly, you can actually steer that rejection in a new direction. 'No' doesn't have to mean 'no forever.' The idea is to continue to foster a good relationship with your boss.

This is also where you could enter the next phase of negotiation for non-monetary benefits. Aren't you glad you thought about this stuff already during your preparation? So, the dialogue could go something like this:

'I'd love to have a conversation about non-monetary benefits. You offer 15 days of paid vacation. Would you consider 20?'

Or:

'Could we have a creative conversation about how we could move the needle? What about working from the office three days a week and working the other two at home. Is that possible?'

Or:

'I have to commute in on the Amtrak. Would you consider a $500 a month travel stipend?'

Can't get what you want, but you can get what you need?

By asking strategic, open-ended questions, the answers you get could also tell you whether you're wasting your time at a place, spinning your wheels at a company where you thought you could move ahead and you really cannot. And I know, that's so devastating. I've been there. You work your butt off for years, even winning accolades from your colleagues, and you're passed over for a promotion. It's heartbreaking. And you know what? You're allowed to sit with that and you're allowed to be upset and disappointed, and you're allowed to steer your career in a better direction going forward. You get to decide what's next. You *can* stay there where you feel overlooked and undervalued. That's a choice you might have to make. You have bills to pay. I get it. You can also make a choice to keep taking the paycheck and look for something better. Or if you so vehemently disagree with the answers you get, you can just put your notice in and walk away.

If you can, have a plan B

We can't always have a plan B for a second opportunity waiting in the wings. But having that leverage, even if you keep it quiet, will make you a stronger negotiator. Because that clear plan B can be your parachute if your current situation isn't working for you and you get an unwavering 'no.' Whether it's a side hustle, a passive income stream or a savings buffer, having a plan B means you can ask for what you're worth and not be worried about what happens if you get a no or you're subject to the unspoken 'backlash penalty'—the negative repercussions suffered by women who behave assertively. The reality is, it is harder for women to succeed in a negotiation because of the unconscious bias of many decision-makers (including other women). However, you can still ask for big numbers and big things in a way that makes it easy to continue the conversation.

Roadblocks can be a blessing

Sometimes hitting a roadblock during a negotiation is a blessing, because you can make a decision to pivot or use the moment to get more information to play the long game. It's why asking questions is so important. Your boss might tell you there's a hiring freeze and 10% of the staff are going to get laid off next month. So your raise is never going to happen. All of a sudden, you've got this inside info you wouldn't have had if you didn't ask the question. Their information can give you insight into where their heads are at. You could also say to your boss, 'What would you need for me to make it easy for you to give me a promotion?' If you're in sales, they may say you need to bring in three more clients and then you can have a conversation. Or you could ask if your boss is open to revisiting the salary conversation in three to six months after you've had time to make progress in certain areas.

If you think about it for a minute, it's not like there are a bunch of unknowns in negotiating. There are really only three outcomes to any negotiation. They're going to say yes, no, or maybe. That's it. You can brainstorm and plan out your responses to each outcome, especially the 'no' or 'maybe.' What would you say in each scenario? How can you continue the relationship in the long term? Especially if you're interviewing with people in your industry, with people you respect, these are relationships you don't want to screw over. So even if you turn down an offer because they can't pay you enough, or because you take a better offer, you can still do it in a way that preserves the relationship. This negotiation is a reflection of you, in terms of how you handle it, regardless of what they say.

You have more power than you think

It's easy to forget that you have power in this situation, too! Because if you choose to leave, your boss has to hire. Granted this power doesn't exist in every industry, but in many industries there is a recruiting cost that comes with losing one employee unexpectedly and then having to fill their role. Almost every corporate employer in America is paying a recruiter to hire people, and recruiters are expensive. Their fee can often be 15% to 30% of the salary of a new hire they introduced! So if you're making $100,000, the recruiting fee would be anywhere from $15,000 to $30,000. If you're an executive on six or seven figures, that recruiting fee is huge. So if you don't leave and your employer can retain you, it's cheaper for them. I mean it's even cheaper for them to send you to Bermuda to meet the team than it is to lose you. It could take three months to hire, three months to onboard someone and then all of a sudden they've lost six months of productivity.

There's also a gap in institutional knowledge that opens up when an employee leaves. That affects other employees, too, sometimes piling more work on their shoulders to fill the void.

So don't forget that your boss actually needs you, and so you do have power. We're not charity cases. They hired you because you're doing a job that's making the company money, keeping the company efficient, making clients money, whatever the case may be, so you're adding value to the business. Remember what that value is.

The power of silence

When you're negotiating, there's a power in silence. So after you state your business case, you've articulated your achievements, and you've asked for a specific number, there's usually a pause in the conversation while the boss is considering what you just said. Many times, we're tempted, especially as women, to fill the silence and say something like, 'If you can't do that, I'd be happy to take X.' Or, 'If you can't do that, you know, we'll just figure it out later.' Never do that. It undermines what you just said. It lets them know that they don't have to meet you where you're at, that you are too flexible. So just let the silence happen. It puts the ball firmly in their court and they have to respond to what you're asking for. So never undermine what you've just said by taking it back or sugarcoating it.

Red flag phrases: What not to say (and what to say instead) in a salary negotiation for a new job

Don't say: 'That's great, I accept.'

Instead say: 'Thank you so much for the offer. Can you email me all the details so I can review and get back to you?'

Don't say: 'I currently make $X so I was hoping for at least that.'

Instead say: 'Based on my unique experience, achievements and current market rates—I'm looking at roles that pay $X. Is that within your range?'

Don't say: 'That salary is too low given the cost of living in my area.'

Instead say: 'Given my role, my related achievements, and the fact that I plan to make a similar impact here right away, can we get my salary closer to $X?'

Red flag questions: What not to ask (and what to ask instead)

Don't ask: 'Can I work from home?'

Instead ask: 'Given the recent widespread shifts to remote work, what does flexible work look like at this organization?'

Don't ask: 'Why did you have layoffs last year?'

Instead ask: 'Considering last year's layoffs, what are your thoughts on the company's outlook currently?'

Don't ask: 'Who are your main competitors?'

Instead ask: 'What brands do you look to for thought leadership and inspiration?'

Don't ask: 'What exactly does this job entail?'

Instead ask: 'What are the top goals you'd like to see someone accomplish in this role in the first six months?'

IF YOU FIND OUT YOU'RE MAKING LESS THAN HE IS...

If you discover that a male colleague is making more money than you for doing the same exact job, don't freak out. I know it can be emotional, but don't. Then look at the whole situation. Are your titles the same? What about geography, how is the cost of living? Do you both have the same number of years of experience? Could there be other factors at play? Let's say you've run through it, and you're certain you deserve more. Then it's time for a little online research. What does fair market pay look like for your job title, for your geography, for your years of experience, and the role that you currently have? So when you go into your boss' office, it's not about saying so-and-so makes more than me, naming the person in the other cubicle or comparing yourself to others, it's going in and using the power of the data points.

You might say something like this to your boss: 'I've done some research online into what fair pay looks like, and I wanted to talk with you about my current salary. I see fair pay is in the range of $60,000 to $80,000 for this role and I'm currently making $55,000. Can we talk about that? Especially based on my last performance review, where I got an excellent rating.'

It pays to job hop

It may pay to switch jobs. Recent stats from the Federal Reserve Bank of Atlanta show people who stayed at their jobs increased their wages by about 5.4% per year. Those who changed jobs got a raise of 6.1%. per year.[52]

NEGOTIATING TAKEAWAYS

Of all the skills to learn in your career, being a good negotiator has the biggest potential to pay off—literally. It does take some practice and confidence, but you have to try. Remember recruiters or your current employer are usually trying to fill a role at the lowest possible rate or keep your salary low for the benefit of the company. But this job is your livelihood—your life—so squeeze as much juice out of it as you can get. If you don't advocate for yourself, who will?

Different cultures, different strategies

People from different cultures negotiate differently. Americans prefer a linear, one-issue-at a time approach. The

French prefer a more holistic approach, and will move back and forth on issues that other negotiators may have believed were long settled. While the latter approach may appear confusing or chaotic to some, the multi-issue or package approach to negotiating enables women to be viewed as less competitive or aggressive. When there is one issue, the negotiation is more likely to be seen as adversarial: to win or to lose. However, when multiple issues are considered, women can be more collaborative and problem-solving: 'If I give you this, then you can give me that.' This will help them to be seen in a more positive way.[53]

NEKIA HACKWORTH JONES, DIRECTOR OF THE ATLANTA REGIONAL OFFICE, U.S. SECURITIES AND EXCHANGE COMMISSION *

In her own words

The black community has a spending power of approximately $1.6 trillion. But, based on my experiences, I think there are some reasons that money does not stay in the community in a way that allows us to build wealth. Some of those reasons are individualized, but others are systemic. For example, black women are often reluctant to invest because of a lack

---

* The views expressed are made in Nekia's official capacity as the Atlanta Regional Director, but do not necessarily reflect the views of the commission, the commissioners, or other staff.

of knowledge, their own perceptions of not having enough money to invest, and in the lack of additional funds that give them opportunities to save and invest. I've seen it in my own life. It is easy to say, 'just save more' or 'just spend less.' That could be the answer for some people and some households, but we must acknowledge that there are these larger gaps and challenges.

Studies have shown that, despite attempts to close the earnings gap, women continue to earn less than men on average. This means that, from a financial perspective, women are often starting off behind our male counterparts. And the disparities widen for women of color. I have experienced this disparity first-hand at various points in my own career. In my career, which has spanned 20 years, I've had a couple of experiences (not with my current employer) where white male colleagues were being paid more than me. There was one point in my career where, in my view, all of my colleagues were equal in education and experience. But I quickly learned I was being paid thousands of dollars less. I literally had no idea why. And if I was experiencing that, given my level of knowledge and background, I can't imagine what other people are going through. While women can certainly educate ourselves and exercise discipline to get better financial outcomes, realistically, we are not always dealing with an even playing field. The first step to solving this systemic and complex issue is acknowledging that the disparity is not some historical phenomenon that has no contemporary relevance. The earnings gap still exists—and persists.

JESSICA ALBA, ACTRESS AND FOUNDER OF THE HONEST COMPANY

In her own words

I've had many conversations with women in professional settings. A lot of them have noticed a big difference between men and women and their professional development trajectory. Women are often 'unofficially' already doing the job that they wish to be promoted into for long periods of time before they are acknowledged or officially move into that position. Whereas men, I would say 90% of the time in the discussions I participated in, were promoted based off perceived potential.

I think it also has to do with bias and with negotiation skills. The most inspiring leaders today are kind and likable along with being honest and strategic. When I'm feeling undermined and overlooked in comparison to a male colleague, it makes my blood boil and I find myself getting into brass tacks execution mode, rather than the kind and likable inspiring version of myself. When I'm negotiating or advocating for something in business or life and I get resistance, it feels like a hammer to the head. I often need to check myself and not take it so personally. I have to look outside myself and see the true context of the situation so I can have a reasonable understanding and response.

Tact is tremendously important and a skill I have seen the most effective people in business use. Ironically, the skills I leaned on to get me here are not the ones that will help me get to where I'm going. I have had to unlearn my rogue warrior mentality. My tendency is to go all iron fist, but the velvet glove is the magic of how to level up.

Here are some tips that could be helpful when negotiating a promotion or next step in your career:

Step 1: Compassion and understanding are important—see the full picture of what you are stepping into and be realistic with what's achievable.

Step 2: Have a set goal for yourself and know what's non-negotiable for you. Clarity is everything.

Step 3: Have (or find) mentors and advocates that can advise you and support your career trajectory and help you achieve your goals.

Now that we've learned how to get what we want from others, let's learn how to give what we want to the people we love. Estate planning is up next.

CHAPTER 11: YOU BET YOUR ASS-ETS YOU NEED AN ESTATE PLAN

"There's nothing fun about stuff like estate planning, getting mammograms, or talking to a guy about long-term disability insurance, but do it anyway. Trust me, the stress of not having done the above is prematurely aging."

Jen Lancaster, author

DON'T THINK YOU need an estate plan? Think again. If you're an adult you should create a plan, full stop. Oh, you say your bank account barely has enough to cover your bills and you don't have kids? Get back here, this includes you too.

Don't let the phrase 'estate plan' make you think it's just for the ultra-wealthy or the elderly. It's for everybody who has *stuff*. Everything from furniture to a checking and savings account to a million-dollar house. It's basically a plan that you put in place before you die, concerning all the stuff you have.

But many of us don't make an estate plan. We're too busy. It can get complicated. We procrastinate. Who wants to make decisions about what happens after we die? Recent surveys show only 34% of Americans have an estate plan.[54] A big chunk of women—72%—are without an estate plan, compared to 59% of men.[55]

That's a problem, because on average women live longer than men. It should be a priority not just to make sure her loved ones are taken care of when she's gone, but to also protect herself. Getting this stuff in order now means your loved ones are more likely to avoid a mess of big family fights and drawn out and costly court proceedings. If that's not enough, let this be your motivator: By being proactive, you can avoid having the government take a big chunk of your estate through a giant tax bill that's slapped on your loved ones.

HOW TO START THE ESTATE PLANNING PROCESS

The main thing to realize about estate planning is that it's all about paperwork and documents—having the right documents in place to convey your decisions about your future and about where your stuff goes. I like to put the documents into two broad buckets:

- Documents you need in place if you become sick
- Documents you need to have prepared before you die

Ways to make your estate plan

There are lots of ways to start the estate planning process. To create documents—whether it's a health directive, power of attorney, a will, or a trust—you don't need an attorney, but having one may help you avoid common mistakes. Still, you can DIY online if you have a simple estate. Go online to services including Trust and Will, Freewill and Legal Zoom to create legit estate documents. These online services walk you step by step through exactly what you need to do in order to get in there and create your estate plan.

DOCUMENTS YOU NEED IN PLACE IF YOU BECOME SICK

An advance health directive (AHCD)

Every adult needs a basic plan in place in case they become so sick and can't communicate their medical wishes. If you don't do anything else suggested in this chapter, at least create this.

It comes in four parts:

1. Living will

2. Medical durable power of attorney

3. Financial power of attorney

4. HIPAA document

Living will

In a living will, if you become incapacitated and can't communicate your medical wishes, this part of an estate plan will do the talking for you. Here you can give your preferences concerning medication, treatment options, surgical procedures, end-of-life-care, and organ donation. This takes the burden off your loved ones and provides them with peace of mind knowing they're carrying out your wishes. By clarifying exactly what treatments you want and don't want, you're removing a lot of the guesswork. Your loved ones can opt out of costly treatments that go against your wishes, such as long-term life support.

Medical durable power of attorney

A medical durable power of attorney, also called a health agent or health proxy, is a document that states who you chose to make healthcare decisions for you if you're unable to. That person would step in to make decisions if you were in a coma or unconscious.

Financial power of attorney

With a financial power of attorney you give someone the legal authority to handle financial transactions for you if you are incapacitated. These include paying bills, making bank deposits, and managing your real estate property.

Now, you may want to keep 'em separated. I mean you could throw the healthcare and finance matters into one power of attorney document, but each document is very personal. Healthcare documents have little details you don't want shared with your financial broker and you probably don't want to share all of the details of your finances with health care professionals.

HIPAA document

Finally, a HIPAA, or Health Insurance Portability and Accountability Act form should be part of the medical-related documents. HIPAA creates standards for healthcare and privacy. The part that affects your estate plan is the privacy part. Through a HIPAA form, you can give authorization saying it's okay for your private medical information to be released to specific people in your life.

DOCUMENTS YOU NEED TO HAVE PREPARED BEFORE YOU DIE

If you want to go further than just creating an advance health care directive, the next thing to think about is: What do I have now that I would need to let someone else take care of, or have, if I die. Things like:

- a car

- a house

- an apartment
- money in the bank/investments
- airline miles
- credit card points
- jewelry
- sentimental items like collections or recipes.

To make sure all of these valuables end up in the right hands after you die, you're going to need to create a will.

Creating a will

Everyone needs a will, especially if they're not going to do anything else. Someone with 20c in their bank account needs a will just as much as someone with millions of dollars. It basically tells everyone how you want your assets distributed when you die. It also covers several more crucial points:

Executor

A will is where you name your executor—the person you select to be in charge of handling your estate when you die. This should be someone you trust completely, and you should ask if they'd be up for the task. Your executor will oversee distributing your property, filing tax returns, and processing claims from creditors. You'll also list a backup person if the person you named as the first executor dies before you do.

I know, this is really uplifting stuff.

Guardianship

This is the best place to spell out who should be the guardians for your children. If you don't have a will when you die, the court system will take over and decide for you. And here, you have to account for almost every possibility. Like what happens if the people you've named to care for your children are unable to do that? Or they die before you? So you're going to name your second choice, third choice, and your fourth choice for this role, knowing it's incredibly unlikely they will need to step in. But just in case.

Furbaby guardianship

Have a cat, dog, frog, or guinea pig? The most straightforward way to make sure your pet is taken care of after you die is to name a new owner for your pet in your will. You can also choose to leave part of your estate to be used for your pet's care, as well as written care instructions for your pet's new owner to refer to.

Assets

You specify where and how your assets or personal property go to your heirs. This includes any building, structure, or home that you own at the time of your passing.

Digital legacy

Calling all zillennials. Into social media? In your estate plan, you can address your digital legacy. Yes, this is a thing. In fact, a staggering 74% of millennials in a recent survey appointed their executor to handle their online affairs and social media accounts after they die. What happens to their actual digital communications matters, too. Millennials are 29% more likely than older generations to want their emails, direct messages, and texts kept private from their family and are more than twice as likely to want their social media preserved or memorialized when they're gone.

Digital assets

If you've invested in digital assets like NFTs and cryptocurrencies, these need to be in your estate planning documents too, because they have real value! Too may people forget to add in their crypto assets to their will. If no one knows you have them, where they are, what wallet they are on, or how to access the accounts, then they could be lost forever.

Frozen eggs, sperm, or embryos

Yes, fertility planning is an estate planning matter. What happens to your frozen eggs, embryos, or sperm if something were to happen to you? If you're considering or have already frozen any of your genetic material, take time to think about what should happen to these biological assets if you were to pass away. Since there isn't much federal guidance regarding frozen genetic material, outcomes vary from state to state, or even between courts within the same state. That uncertainty surrounding rulings and outcomes means that estate planning is even more necessary for this area. Using an estate plan, you get to make important decisions regarding your personal fertility. For example, you could create your own definition of when a posthumously conceived individual would be considered legally entitled to an inheritance, whether from your estate or estates of other family members, like your parents. The number of possible ripple effects from freezing genetic material can be overwhelming, especially if you leave the decisions up to the courts. By putting this issue into your estate plan, you can make as many specific provisions as possible to address and circumvent a number of 'what if' scenarios.

Final arrangements instructions

A big part of your estate planning is specifying funeral arrangements and your wishes for your remains. These are part of the final arrangements you can make for what you want to happen directly after you pass away. The more direction you can give your loved ones, the better, so they'll be able to grieve while trusting they're honoring you the exact way you want. A letter of last instruction can be as specific or as basic as you want. Here are some things you may want to consider:

- How do you want your remains handled—burial or cremation?

- Which mortuary would you like to use?

- What casket, urn, or other container would you like your remains placed in?

- Do you want your remains present at your service or ceremony?

- What other information can you give about the type of ceremony you'd like to have?

- Where should your remains be scattered or stored?

- What headstone or marker would you like?

- Where can your executor find your cemetery deed (if you have one)?

Don't leave your final arrangements only in your will, though. That's because a will may not always be immediately accessible. There are some decisions—like if you want a specific mortuary used, or if you want cremation versus a casket burial—that would need to be made fairly soon after your passing. If your will isn't immediately located, it could be a problem in terms of executing your final wishes.

It would be better to back up the will by writing a letter to your closest relatives and have that on hand for them.

DARIA, DOCTOR

A cautionary tale

Daria is an example of how, even in the worst of times, being involved is so important when your spouse dies unexpectedly.

My husband took his own life. He hanged himself in our basement. He struggled with mental health issues his whole life. But I still didn't expect it, didn't know it was coming.

I paid for the household expenses like utilities and the kids' stuff. He paid for the big-ticket items and invested the money. I knew where everything was but didn't take an active role in investing or growing our money. This was just his area of expertise more than mine. But he would fill me in. So I knew the big picture of how much we have but not the very specifics. I had logins and passwords.

I think that money has always been something I'm just not terribly interested in. With him gone, I've had to get more interest in it. I think there's sort of a dread for me when, even now, I have to tackle some of the things I have to do. And I'll do any other stupid thing around the house to put it off even another hour or two. It's just something that gives me a pit in my stomach.

Maybe I don't feel as confident about my knowledge or my skills. I hate looking at this stuff. He was heavily invested in stocks, and I've not even looked at that to make changes. I think it's just a lack of knowledge, a lack of information, that gives me the most dread. And the other part of it is I don't want to mess anything up. He wanted to provide well for his family, and I think he set us up for that.

DO I NEED A TRUST?

If you have a simple estate, a will is probably enough. But you don't have to be super rich to need a trust. If you own a home and have over $100,000 in assets, you should go the extra mile and set up a trust.

A trust is a second type of written document that's used in estate planning. In a trust, you can put all the information you'd spell out in a will, including who gets what, when and how much. But the trust goes much further. It's used to help manage your money and distribute it after death. Unlike a will, it also allows beneficiaries to avoid paying taxes on the appreciation of assets like a home.

Why would you set up a trust? There are a few main reasons. For starters, it allows a very manageable transition of your assets if you die or if you become incapacitated. If something were to happen, your 'trustee'—the person you are trusting to disperse the assets in the trust according to your wishes—would come in and manage those assets according to the instructions.

Also, if there's just a will, the whole process of transferring assets to a beneficiary has to go through a costly and often drawn-out court process known as probate, which takes six months to a year or more and will cost 5% or more of the value of your estate. So a will does those very important tasks of designating guardians for your kids and pets and specific funeral instructions, but if you have to move property or assets from one person to another, it gets complicated and costly if the transfer of it all is stated just in the will.

So in the situation of creating a trust, you give the assets to the trustee and say 'Hey trustee, hold these assets for the benefit of my beneficiaries.' In this way you're not giving directly to the beneficiaries, you're retitling assets and putting each one in a beneficiary's name.

If you have your assets controlled by a trust, you can avoid those court proceedings entirely. Because a trust is like a box. Anything that's within your box, inside your trust, can bypass probate.

So why don't more people set up trusts? Because when you're alive, you still have to put your assets inside the box. And that takes a minute to create. It can also get pretty complex. But the burden of putting all the financial stuff inside a trust now is worth having, since it means your beneficiaries avoid the burden of court costs and headaches later.

Types of trusts for estate planning

Trusts come in two types: revocable and irrevocable.

Revocable trust

This is the most common option. With a revocable trust, you as the trust owner are the trustee during your lifetime. Also referred to as a living trust, you can amend it at any time and you can terminate it completely during your lifetime. You can change who becomes the trustee after you die, and you can change the beneficiaries. It's very flexible. With a revokable trust you can keep all your options available to you. You can put assets in, you can take assets out.

While you're alive a revocable trust has no effect whatsoever on your taxes. You file your taxes as you always have under your social security number. As the grantor of the trust, in the eyes of the

IRS, the trust is treated as an extension of yourself. So any income generated by the trust is still taxable to you personally.

There are some disadvantages to revocable trusts. While you're alive, as its trustee you still own and have control over the assets in the trust, even though assets are being put in another person's name should you die. Because the assets are still yours while you're alive, this type of trust will not protect them against creditors and lawsuits. Also, when the owner of a revocable trust dies, beneficiaries of the trust typically pay taxes on the distributions they receive from the trust's income. Beneficiaries are not subject to taxes on distributions from the trust's principal, however (the original sum of money that was placed into the trust).

Irrevocable trust

An irrevocable trust can be very difficult to change or terminate after it's been executed. And the grantor may not be able to access their assets, even if a life event makes it necessary. So you have to assume that any assets you put in there are going to be there until you die. Assets that you put in there are no longer in your name, they're in the name of the trust, so when you die they are not in your estate, which is good for tax purposes in some situations. Why get an irrevocable trust instead of a revocable? One reason people get irrevocable trusts is asset protection. Because the assets you put in there are no longer in your name, they're protected from lawsuits, creditors, and ex-spouses.

So you forfeit ownership of any assets in the trust and the trustee takes control of those assets. Another reason for an irrevocable trust? Those assets won't be subject to an estate tax for the beneficiary.

If the trust is a guarantor trust, the creator of the trust covers the income tax of trust assets, and the beneficiary will not owe income taxes on distributions. If the trust is not a guarantor trust, the trust pays income taxes on its assets while they are in the trust, and the beneficiary will owe income taxes on distributions.[56]

More about those other protections

A trust isn't only used after you die. It can go into effect if you're incapacitated or unable to make decisions. It allows your family members to use your money and assets to provide the care you require. If you only have a will, that money for your care would not be accessed, because a will is only triggered when you die. But when you create a living trust, you will name one or several people with whom you will entrust all of your affairs, if you should become incapacitated. These people can make decisions for you when you are not in a mental state capable of making important decisions.

If you're incapacitated only temporarily, the trustee will gain control over your affairs during that time, and when you recover the control returns to you. So you don't have to worry about what someone else may be doing with your assets. Essentially, the trust allows people to step in and take care of you financially. You can try to accomplish this through a financial power of attorney, but those need to be updated every three years. Who remembers to do that? So the trust checks off a lot of boxes.

How do I create a revocable trust?

It's not advisable for anyone to attempt to create an irrevocable trust online. An attorney should create an irrevocable trust because there is too much at stake. It is for practical purposes permanent and would take court action to change it. The flexible nature of a revocable trust means nothing is written in stone (although at death it becomes irrevocable). So if you're creating your trust online, make sure it's revocable.

1. Decide who will inherit the assets in your trust. You will also need contingent or alternate beneficiaries.

2. Choose who will be your 'successor trustee' who will distribute the assets in your trust.

3. Choose someone to manage property for youngsters. If children or young adults inherit assets, you should choose an adult to manage whatever they get. To give that person authority over the child's property, you can make that person a property guardian, a property custodian under a law called the Uniform Transfers to Minors Act (UTMA), or a trustee.

4. Prepare the trust document either through a lawyer or an online service like LegalZoom.com, TrustandWill.com, or Freewill.com

5. Sign the trust document and get your signature notarized. It's very important to sign the document in front of a notary public so it is valid.

6. To make the trust effective, now you must move legally titled assets to the trust.

How to pack or fund the 'trust box'

Technically, your trust is a legal document and you can go to a lawyer or an online service to create it. I've described the trust as a box, and it's one that you have to pack while you're alive in order to make it valid. This step is essential because until you 'fund' the trust with your stuff, it's worthless to you. Your trust holds your assets.

Assets that can be put in a trust include:

- Real estate
- Insurance policies

- Bank accounts
- Non-retirement investment accounts like brokerage accounts
- Securities like stocks and bonds
- Cryptocurrency
- Collectibles, art, and other personal property
- Safe deposit boxes

When you set up a living trust, you transfer assets from your name to the name of your trust, which you control. So it could go from 'Alison and Tony Smith, husband and wife' to 'Alison and Tony Smith, trustees under trust dated month/day/year.' So you're basically moving assets to the box and putting a label on the box that sounds a little different.

When you transfer assets into a living trust, legally you don't own those things because they now belong to your trust. But you do not lose control of those assets. You keep full control. As the trustee of your trust, you can do anything you could do before—buy and sell assets, change, or even cancel your trust. That's why it's called a revocable living trust. You even file the same tax returns. Nothing changes but the names on the titles.

Example: How does putting a house in a trust work?

Let's walk through an asset to bring this concept to life!

Let's put your house in a revocable living trust, since for most people this is the most significant asset they have. Ultimately, you'll be legally changing the title of your home from your name to the name of your trust. You'll also name your beneficiaries and a successor trustee who'll take over when you die.

12 steps to DIY move your house into a revocable living trust

1. First make sure you've set up a trust.

2. Find the deed of your home when you bought it. You should have one with all the documents you got at the closing of your home. It's probably called a warranty deed.

3. To move your home into the trust, you'll need to fill out a new deed. You can typically find state-specific deed forms online, or you can have your attorney complete this process for you. They may be called quit claim deeds or grant deeds. All deeds basically need the same information.

4. Notice how your name is used on your original deed and use the same name on the quit claim deed you're about to fill out. Your name is the 'grantor' and the 'grantee' is the name of the trust.

5. Then on the quit claim deed and in the place where the new owner's name is to be used, put the name of your trust exactly as it is stated in your trust document. So I would be transferring it from 'Alison Kosik' to 'Alison Kosik as trustee of the Alison Kosik living trust, a revocable living trust.'

6. After the paragraph where the names are, there will be a large place on the form to insert the legal description of the property. Look at your current deed and copy the legal description from your current deed to the new deed verbatim.

7. Once you've done that, go over it word for word and make sure you've got it right.

8. Then take your deed to a notary and sign it and date it in front of them. Have them notarize the document.

9. Take the document to your local county office where land

records are kept. You'll most likely have to pay some kind of fee, but it shouldn't be too much.

10. In most places, the clerk will take your original deed, make a copy of it, and file that in the records before giving you back the original.

11. Once that deed is filed, your home will be in your trust! Your new deed will officially show that you've transferred ownership of your home to the trust (which is still you, while you're alive).

12. Contact your homeowner's insurance company next and tell them what you've done, because they will probably want to put your trust as an additional insured item on your policy.

When you die, your successor trustee will be responsible for following the instructions of the trust and distributing the asset to your beneficiaries.

Takeaways

It is possible to refinance your home if it's in a living trust, but there may be some steps you need to go through. First, check the language of your trust to make sure that it contemplates refinancing of property that is held in the trust. Next, check with your mortgage company before you do anything. Some mortgage companies will allow you to refinance a home that is in a trust, other mortgage companies will want you to take the home out of the trust, put it back in your individual name, refinance the home, then place it back in the trust. So there may be a few extra steps, but it's worth it to have the trust.

Or, if you're considering refinancing your mortgage, do it before you begin the process of putting your home in a trust.

Having your home in a trust doesn't prevent you from selling your home. Even if your home is in a trust, you can still sell it at any time. And any income you receive from the property will simply be reported on your personal tax returns. Nothing changes but the name on the title.

And contrary to popular belief, even if your home has a mortgage, you can put it into a trust. A bank cannot require you to pay off a loan just because you want to put your home into a trust.

By putting your house into a trust, the person who gets the house is shielded from paying capital gains taxes. Those are the taxes on the profit from the sale of the home.

This is why you should never let your parents just gift you their house. For example, if your parents bought a house for $300,000 and it's now worth $800,000, if they transfer it to you, you would be responsible for paying capital gains taxes on the $500,000 when you sell it. Putting the house in a revocable living trust and naming you as the beneficiary would be the better way to go. That way you can inherit the house, without paying any taxes *and* avoid probate court.

Keep your kids off the deed

If you put your kids' names on the deed to your home, it could cost you way more than you realize. They will own part of your home. You can't sell it without their permission. They can sell their ownership.

Your home will be subject to their creditors, their lawsuits, their bankruptcies, their ex-spouses, plus, when you die and they sell it, they will need to pay capital gains taxes.

Why a will by itself may not be the best

Having a will by itself may not be enough, which is why you would also want a trust. A will is not a bad tool. It will get you to where you want to be—ultimately getting your assets distributed to the beneficiaries that you want them to go to. But there are three issues if you have only a will.

Cost

To be legally enforceable, every will has to go through the probate process. But in the end, the court fees will end up costing more than a trust. Between lawyer fees, court fees, appraiser fees, and everything else, it's going to end up costing in the ballpark of 3% to 8% of the total value of the assets being probated. Let's say it's 5%. So for a $500,000 estate that's $25,000 which has to be paid. If it's a million-dollar estate, you're talking about $50,000. Creating a trust will cost you much less down the road than winging it with a will only. You don't have to go through a court process to distribute a trust.

The time factor

Probate in most states takes a long time—at least six to nine months. And that's without any complications. If anybody objects to the will, then all bets are off—a year to a year and a half is not uncommon. The administration and distribution of a trust should happen much faster than that.

LACK OF PRIVACY

Once you submit a will for probate, anybody can go online and find out what's in it. Ultimately, anybody can find out everything that's in the estate, what it's worth, and who is going to get it. For some people the privacy issue won't make a difference. But for those who care about it, it's important to have your eyes wide open about this.

COMMON ESTATE PLANNING MISTAKES

Certifying documents incorrectly

It's incredibly important that you follow the technically precise instructions for signing an estate plan. Signing the estate plan is the act that turns it from a piece of paper into a legally valid document, and you need to be sure that you sign it properly. So for a will, for example, two witnesses have to be in the room with you to watch you sign it, and then the two witnesses need to sign it and you may have to have it notarized.

Failing to identify beneficiaries

Who is the beneficiary on your checking account? Savings account? Brokerage account? Life insurance policy? Your Roth or Traditional IRA? Your 401(k)? That's what I thought. You either don't know at all or aren't completely sure. If you don't know who *all* of these beneficiaries are, you need to find out now. And make sure the beneficiaries are not minor children. Minors can't receive money. Beneficiaries who are designated on financial accounts and insurance policies supersede what you've put on your will and your trust. For example, say you list your husband as the primary beneficiary on your retirement plan at work, but then you get divorced and marry someone else. If you forgot to take your first husband off the account and he is listed as the account beneficiary, your ex will receive those assets at your death, even if your will or trust say otherwise.

The lesson here? Because beneficiaries named on your retirement and brokerage accounts prevail every time, no matter what you say in your will or trust, make sure your beneficiary designations are up to date in all of your financial accounts and match what is in your will and trust. This is so important! A trust is not a one-and-done situation. A good tip to remember is if you get married, divorced, have a child, or experience another significant life event, you need to re-check your beneficiaries each time.

Make sure you know who your beneficiaries are—now.

Adding retirement assets into trusts

While you *can* transfer ownership of your retirement accounts into your trust, estate planning experts would put up a big red stop sign. This includes individual retirement accounts (IRAs), 401(k) accounts, and 403(b) accounts. When you transfer a retirement asset to a trust, the transaction may be treated as if you've cashed out of the account. This can trigger a taxable event on these accounts, which can lessen their overall value. And if you're not yet at the age where you can withdraw funds from your retirement account, you may have to pay a penalty for withdrawing early.

The better option is to designate a primary beneficiary of your retirement account. The beneficiary of your account is the person that you've chosen to inherit your account after your death. You can even specify a percentage and split the amounts between beneficiaries—for example, 50% to each of two children.

If you have a trust, name the trust as the secondary beneficiary. In your trust, you can include more instructions for dispersion of these funds.

By naming beneficiaries on your investment accounts, you will avoid a situation where your loved ones can't get money out of your accounts after you pass. Here's the thing: You have to name a beneficiary in *each* investment account you have. So the brokerage accounts, the IRAs, and the 401(k)s. Once you log into your account, there should be a tab to put this information into each account.

Making children joint owners of your bank accounts

You should never add your adult children as joint owners of your bank accounts. It's just not a good idea. While this can be well intentioned, and a gesture of love and trust, there are some major issues. A joint account holder can access the account and withdraw all of the funds. Life happens. Even when a child can be trusted completely, the account is subject to your child's creditors, or, if there's a sudden lawsuit or divorce, that money can be fair game for other people in a settlement. All of this means your account could be at risk of being cleaned out. There's also the issue of gift taxes. You can gift away up to $18,000 a year, but above that you have to file a gift tax return, which means you could be responsible for paying a tax rate of 18% to 40% on the money.

I know what you're thinking: If your bank accounts are only in your name, what happens to that money when you die?

If you were to die having bank accounts in your name and your name only, the bank is going to freeze those accounts and no one in your family will be able to get into them. Your heirs would not be able to access those accounts until they get a court order allowing them to.

The lock on those accounts could happen almost immediately, especially since banks find out about deaths in any number of ways. But the most common is that the funeral home will notify the Social Security Administration, who will immediately notify any banks that come up under the deceased's Social Security number.

However, most banks allow you to designate someone to be paid any money that is in your accounts upon your death. But if that person dies before you do and you forget to name anyone else, the money would still be subject to a probate court.

An even better way to avoid frozen accounts is to create a living trust and to put your bank accounts in the name of the trust.

With your checking account, it's important to leave the account in your own name and make the trust the primary beneficiary of the account. Turn your savings account into a trust account. Depending on how the bank wants to do it, the account may first be closed and a trust account created under the trust's name. By doing this, any money in the trust account would be immediately available to the successor trustee when you die. Any money in the checking account would be transferred by the bank to the trust account. Keep in mind that a death certificate would be required first, which will take some time to obtain.

You may not realize it, but by naming your bank accounts this way, you are funding your trust, and instead of your loved ones suddenly needing to chase down cash to pay bills and funeral expenses when you die, you are taking the pressure off of them. All of that money will flow right into the trust you created.

Telling nobody that your estate plan exists

Don't be secretive about it. What's the point of going through all the trouble of making an estate plan if no one knows it exists? Store your original documents somewhere safe, like a fireproof safe in your house. If you've named an executor or a guardian, tell them where the documents can be found. That alone, just sharing that you have the estate plan and where it's located, will solve 95% of any problems with your assets finding their way to your beneficiaries.

Setting it and forgetting it

You'll likely need to revisit your trust or will every couple of years. Life changes—if you have kids, when you acquire new property, or if one of your trustees or guardians dies—things like that. You wouldn't have to start from scratch on the document. In many cases you just have to amend it. Just make sure your estate plan evolves as your life does.

JIAN CHONG, MOTHER OF TWO

A cautionary tale

Jian's husband was diagnosed with colon cancer about two years before he died, but had no estate planning documents, despite having that two-year runway. He also didn't have enough life insurance. Besides her story being a cautionary tale of the importance of having a will and trust, and getting your beneficiaries correct on your investment accounts, it is also a warning about the importance for women to keep a toehold in their career, even if they don't work full time. It's going to be really difficult for her to re-enter the workforce. This is why your spouse needs more life insurance if you are not working full time.

Here's her story in her own words:

With no will in place, he took a sudden turn for the worse. On the Thursday it was very hard for him to talk. I called the estate planners to let them know that he wasn't going to make it much longer. So they rushed it. They got me all the paperwork to get signed and we reviewed it on Friday. They were going to come to the house on Monday to get it signed and notarized and everything ready to go. But he passed on Sunday. He died with no will. We had thought we had weeks, and it turned out to be days.

For some reason my husband and I procrastinated on this. We always knew we had to do it. But neither one of us took the next step. We both researched lawyers in the area, we got recommendations, we did all of that. We just never did it, you know? And the only thing I did, a year before he died, was to ask him to please make sure I'm the beneficiary on all his accounts. He later told me it was done. So I thought that was at least something.

But I don't know what he thinks he did. When I went into his TD Ameritrade account to look at the retirement accounts, he had no beneficiary assigned to one of them. His brother was the beneficiary of the other two accounts. I do not get along with his brother. I've had to get a lawyer to take it to probate and I reached out to his brother to ask him to renounce the accounts, which I don't know if he will do.

It's so unfair that someone dies and then the spouse has to take on closing out their life and figuring out their children's life and their own life. I don't work and now I have to try to get a job, but I don't have time. He did not have enough life insurance. He got $1,000,000 and a ten-year term in 2016. I remember when he got it, he was so proud of himself because he got it. But you know, if he would've just consulted with me first, I would have told him $1,000,000 is not enough, we have two kids, and the term isn't long enough. But he was just so proud he did it.

INHERITANCE TAXES

The person who receives an inheritance pays the inheritance tax.

Unless you are a high net worth individual, for the most part you don't have to worry about inheritance taxes. Of course it depends on what state you live in. But only about 5% of people in the U.S. have to worry about federal and state inheritance taxes. An individual would have to receive about $13m before they're subject to federal inheritance taxes. The gift threshold is also high. You can give away $18,000 per year before it's considered a taxable gift.

A WORD ABOUT PASSWORDS

It's probably safe to say there's a password attached to just about every financial thing we do in our lives. It begs the question, how do you let someone else in on these passwords while we're alive, so they're in the know when we die? If you've set up a trust, one good option is to add a memorandum to it that states the location where all of your passwords are kept. Or it could say where the master password is located in order to gain access into your password manager app on your phone. You could also specify who is allowed to have access to that information. If you only have a will you probably do not want to include your passwords in there. As the will goes through the probate process, all of those passwords would become public information.

iPhone legacy contact

If you have an iPhone, it has a feature that allows you to designate someone who can access all of your data if you're no longer around. You may not want to give someone access to all of your data while you're alive, so there is a way you can name a person who can get to all of your data after you die.

You can access this feature by going into iPhone settings, then tap on your name, then tap on password and security. Then go all the way down the page and you will see legacy contact. Once you've designated someone as your legacy contact, an access key is generated. You then have the option of texting that key to the designated person or printing out the access key. After you die, that person can access your iPhone data by contacting Apple and giving them the access key that you've given them along with a death certificate. A legacy contact designation does not have to be permanent. You can change it at any time. You can revoke someone's access and give access to someone else. You can designate more than one person and they don't have to have an Apple device.

Even if no legacy contact is named in the phone, in most states Apple will accept a copy of a will or trust which names a digital executor, who can then gain access to the phone. You can also designate a legacy contact on your Facebook page so that person can have access to your account after you die. And be sure to include your wishes for all of your digital assets in your will or trust.

WHERE TO STORE YOUR ESTATE DOCUMENTS

The goal is to keep these documents safe and accessible. A safety deposit box that only you can access may not be the best place, because your family might need a court order to retrieve it. Although, if you do this, you could also authorize a designee to have access to your bank safe deposit box. A waterproof and fireproof box or safe in your house or an online document vault are good alternatives. Keeping your password information with your other estate documents is probably a good idea, too. Your attorney or someone you trust should keep signed copies in case the original documents are destroyed.

Top ten requested memorial songs for millennials

In your estate plan, you can include the songs you want played during your memorial service. Here are some of the most popular:

1. 'Somewhere Over the Rainbow,' Israel K's version

2. 'In My Life,' The Beatles

3. 'I was Here,' Beyoncé

4. 'How Great Thou Art,' Carrie Underwood

5. 'Three Little Birds,' Bob Marley

6. 'Another One Bites the Dust,' Queen

7. 'Dreams,' Fleetwood Mac

8. 'These Three Words,' Stevie Wonder

---

9. 'When I Get Where I'm Going,' Dolly Parton and Brad Paisley

10. 'Sweet Thing,' Van Morrison

Men and women in estate planning

"Our numbers show that the majority of people who take that first step to create an estate plan with Trust & Will are women. So we have more female visitors than men. However, there are more men than women who complete the purchase. There's the traditional notion of hey, the male should make these business decisions. The other thing we've seen is a shocking number of cases, where it's the wife in the relationship who will create the account under their husband's email address. And so they will list their husband as the first name. There's still a lot of inequality in the estate planning and the responsibilities in the decision-making."

Patrick Hicks, Trust & Will

The chief drawback to creating a trust is the initial cost. While it is true that attorneys generally charge more to draft a living trust than a will, the cost will likely be offset by other savings later, such as through the elimination of probate and legal fees, appraisals and associated costs.

"We made our estate plan and trust in 2012. I had them put in a 'floozy clause,' so that if I died and my husband ever remarried—which I am fully supportive of—she could never take from what my kids get. She would be entitled to zero and it all goes to the kids. And my husband or my brothers would manage it for my kids, who would be the beneficiaries of everything. My husband came up with that. He's like, do you want a floozy clause? And I said yes, I do."

Rebecca Minkoff, designer, fashion mogul, author, founder of the Female Founder Collective

If you take one piece of advice from this chapter, make your advance health directive at bare minimum. I know life gets in the way, but find the time to make a will or trust. After all of your hard work earning money to buy the things you cherish, you don't want to leave what happens to it up to chance. Make sure the wealth you've created can be passed to the people you want to have it. Making a will or a trust—and creating these documents correctly—ensures that lawyers or the government won't come in and throw a wrench in your plans once you're gone.

CONCLUSION—THAT'S A WRAP!

W E'VE COME TO the end of our journey. I've given you the tools to take control of your financial life. You've figured out how to cut your expenses and come up with a budget you can live with, done the work to assess whether you need life insurance and how much, gotten a grip on your investments, and much more.

Even if you do just some of the things in this book to gain more clarity and control in your financial life, that, my friend, would mean you're on your way to financial independence. Use this book as a resource and continue to revisit it over the course of your life.

The cautionary tales we've encountered may have been wake-up calls for you— telling you that now is the time and the time is now to become involved in the money stuff.

I hope the most important thing you've learned is to trust yourself—to have faith that you can take on new challenges and succeed. With patience and some hard work, you will gain knowledge—and knowledge leads to understanding and understanding leads to confidence.

There's no better feeling than going to sleep at night not worried about your money, because you decided to take charge.

NOTES

1 UBS, 'Own Your Worth 2021: Building Bridges, Breaking Barriers.'

2 UBS, 'Own Your Worth 2021: Building Bridges, Breaking Barriers.'

3 UBS, 'Own Your Worth 2022: Women On Purpose.'

4 UBS, 'Own Your Worth 2023: Tradition, Trust and Time.'

5 UBS, 'Own Your Worth 2019: Why Women Should Take Control of Their Wealth To Achieve Financial Well-Being.'

6 Libby Cameron, 'From Imposter Syndrome to Success, a Guide to Acing Assessment Centres,' FemaleInvest, March 15, 2024.

7 Fidelity, 'Money fit women study,' 2015.

8 Emily Guy Birken, 'Women Aren't Talking About Money – Here's Why,' Part-Time Money, May 25, 2021.

9 IDEO.org, 'Women and Money.'

10 UBS, 'Own Your Worth 2019: Why Women Should Take Control of Their Wealth To Achieve Financial Well-Being.'

11 World Bank Group, Missile East and North Africa Gender Innovation Lab (MNAGIL)

12 World Bank Group, 'Nearly 2.4 Billion Women Globally Don't Have Same Economic Rights as Men,' March 1, 2022.

13 FINRA, 'National Study by FINRA Foundation Finds U.S. Adults' Financial Capability Has Generally Grown Despite Pandemic Disruption,' July 18, 2022.

14 Chicago tribune, 'A spirited topic: Money and religion,' April 6, 2012.

15 Rachael Ede, '5 Ways My Catholic Religion Worked Against Me Building Wealth,' Business Insider, 2022.

16 Fidelity, '2021 Women and Investing Study.'

17 Stefon Walters, 'Study Shows: Women are investors than men', The Motley Fool, April 27, 2023.

18 Lyle Daly, 'Investing for Women, What you should know', The Motley Fool, February 20, 2024.

19 Dr. Brad Klontz, et al., 'The Sentimental Savings Study: Using Financial Psychology to Increase Savings,' FinancialPlanningAssociation.org, October 2019.

20 Census.gov, 'Equal Pay Day,' March 12, 2024.

21 Goldman Sachs, 'Navigating the Financial Vortex: Women and Retirement,' December 7, 2022.

22 Transamerica Center for Retirement Studies, '19 Facts about Women's Retirement Outlook,' November 18, 2019.

23 Gabrielle Olya, '39% of Women Have Less Than $100 In Savings,' GOBankingRates 2024 Survey, February 19, 2024.

24 Javier Simon, 'Nearly Half of Women Have Less Than $25,000 Saved For Retirement,' Gold IRA Guide/Money.com, November 18, 2021.

25 Varo Bank, '2023 Wealth Watch Insights Report,' November 6, 2023.

26 Jessica Lautz, 'Celebrating Single Women Home Buyers,' National Association of Realtors, January 24, 2024.

27 Kelly Shue and Paul Goldsmith-Pinkham, 'The Gender Gap in Housing Returns,' Yale Insights, February 25, 2020.

28 World Health Organization, 'Disability,' March 7, 2023.

29 Social Security Administration.

30 Census.gov, 'Equal Pay Day,' March 12, 2024.

31 American Association for Long-Term Care Insurance.

32 Alzheimer's Association.

33 Grace Enda and William G. Gale, 'How Does Gender Equality Affect Women in Retirement?' Brookings Institution, July 2020.

34 Dan Doonan and Kelly Kenneally, 'What Do Women Think of Retirement?' National Institute on Retirement Security, April 2024.

35 Fidelity Investments, 'New 10-Year Analysis Reveals Women Out-Performing Men,' October 8, 2021.

36 James Royal, Ph.D., et al., 'What is the Average Stock Market Return?' Nerdwallet, May 3, 2023.

37 Sam Swenson, CFA, CPA 'Day Trading Definition: Why It Differs From Investing,' TheMotleyFool.com.

38 Investor.gov U.S. Securities & Exchange Commission Calculator; FederalReserve.gov, Federal Reserve Survey of Consumer Finances Data SCF 2022.

39 Randstad, '2020 U.S. Compensation Insights Survey.'

40 '85% of Employed Women Believe They Deserve A Pay Raise; More Salary Transparency Can Help,' Glassdoor Economic Research, March 9, 2022.

41 Suzanne de Janasz and Beth Cabrera, 'How Women Can Get What They Want in a Negotiation,' *Harvard Business Review*, August 17, 2018.

42 Glassdoor, 'Why Women Don't Negotiate Their Salaries [But They Should],' May 1, 2023.

43 Suzanne de Janasz and Beth Cabrera, 'How Women Can Get What They Want in a Negotiation,' *Harvard Business Review*, August 17, 2018.

44 U.S. Dept of Labor, March 14, 2023.

45 Leanin.org.

46 Jack Zenger and Joseph Folkman, 'Women Score Higher Than Men In Most Leadership Skills,' *Harvard Business Review*, June 25, 2019.

47 Workplace Gender Equality Agency, 'Bonuses Drive Up Gender Gaps,' May 21, 2018.

48 Claire Cain Miller, 'As Women Take Over a Male-Dominated Field, The Pay Drops,' *New York Times*, March 18, 2016; TheStreet.com via Harvard economist Claudia Goldin, 'Why Full-time Working Women Earn $320,000 Over A Lifetime,' September 30, 2014.

49 Deborah Rho, 'What Causes the Wage Gap?' The Gender Policy Report, February 24, 2021.

50 Elizabeth Terris, Laura Beavin, et al., 'Endogenous Oxytocin Release Eliminates In-Group Bias in Monetary Transfers With Perspective-Taking,' *Frontiers in Behavioral Neuroscience*, March 4, 2018.

51 Laura Kray and Jessica Kennedy, 'Changing the Narrative: Women as Negotiators and Leaders,' September 5, 2017.

52 Federal Reserve Bank of Atlanta's Wage Growth Tracker, June 2023.

53 Suzanne de Janasz and Beth Cabrera, 'How Women Can Get What They Want in a Negotiation,' *Harvard Business Review*, August 17, 2018.

54 Caring.com, '2024 Wills Survey Finds That 40% of Americans Don't Think They Have Enough Assets to Create a Will,' July 30, 2024.

55 D.A. Davidson & Co., 'Survey Finds That Two-Thirds of Americans Do Not Have an Estate Plan,' October 2022.

56 Alyssa Zebrowsky, 'Irrevocable Trusts: What Beneficiaries Need to Know to Optimize Their Resources,' J.P.Morgan Private Bank, September 19, 2022.

ACKNOWLEDGMENTS

SPECIAL THANKS TO the following sources for their invaluable help in developing the content for the following chapters: Chapters 2 and 3: Tim Jordan, Certified Financial Coach; Chapter 5: Ted Rossman, Bankrate; Chapter 6: Mark Reyes, Certified Financial Planner; U.S. News & World Report; Investopedia; Bankrate.com, CFPB, McKinsey & Co., Rocket Mortgage, NerdWallet, Chapter 7: Phillip Reed, Automotive Expert; Marc Ellis, former car salesman and COO of Beachside Golf Cars; Michael Rumple, former car salesman and founder, Your Car Buying Advocate; Chapter 8: NerdWallet; Chapter 9: Barbara Ginty, Certified Financial Planner; Charles Schwab; Fidelity Investments; Chapter 10: Sam DeMase, career coach and influencer; Meggie Palmer/PepTalkHer; Barbara Corcoran; Glassdoor; Leanin.org; Marianne Eby, CEO Watershed Associates; Chapter 11: Pamela Maass, attorney; Jerry Taylor, Jerry Taylor Law; Patrick Hicks, Trust & Will.

I am so lucky to have such a supportive family. For their encouragement, feedback and willingness to lend an ear when I needed their advice during this multi-year project: Tony Mangurian—I love you for brainstorming with me and having the patience of a saint; Sydney Goltzman—for your energetic support and for drawing the art in this book; Ethan Goltzman—for putting up with me as I took over the kitchen table for years to write this book! To mom and dad—my tough-love childhood led me to now; to Ronnie Kosik, to Todd Kosik, and to Stacy and Jack Fried for supporting me to write this.

And to some of my really supportive friends—I am indebted to you for your support and for your writing advice: Jamie Gruttemeyer Symonds—you said I could do it and I believed you; Amanda and Billy Greene; Steven Sharp; Alice Ericsson and Bob Wagner; Steve Forrest; Laurie Frankel; Alisyn Camerota; Christine Romans; Dawn Miller; Alicia Shick; Jane von Mehren; Susan Gutfreund; Rochelle Weinstein; Ivy Diel; Courtney Friel; Betty Salinas, Phil Gurin, Margot Herrera.

ABOUT THE AUTHOR

ALISON KOSIK IS a journalist and freelance correspondent and anchor at ABC News. Prior to joining ABC, Alison was a business correspondent and anchor at CNN and CNN International. She is a CFEI: Certified Financial Education Instructor.

Alison has interviewed leading CEOs, investors, executives, international dignitaries, musicians, and sports figures. She has interviewed some of the biggest names in business, politics, and technology, from Warren Buffett to Hillary Clinton to Mark Cuban and Michael Saylor.

Alison covers the companies and business leaders who influence everyday life. She's also covered some of the hottest initial public offerings since the financial crisis, including Meta, X, and Alibaba.

She has also worked as a reporter at several local stations including WCBS in New York, WPEC in West Palm Beach, and KRIS in Corpus Christi.

She has two children and lives in the New York area with her partner.